Dedication

To Cheryl –
my favorite canoeing companion
and very best friend.

Boundary
-Waters-
Canoe Area

Volume 1: The Western Region

Robert Beymer

 WILDERNESS PRESS · BERKELEY, CA

The Boundary Waters Canoe Area Volume 1: Western Region

1st EDITION September 1978; 2nd EDITION March 1981;
3rd EDITION May 1985; 4th EDITION April 1988; 5th EDITION January 1994
6th EDITION June 2000
  2nd printing March 2002
  3rd printing April 2004
  4th printing March 2006

Front cover photo copyright © 2000 by Robert Beymer
Interior photos by Robert Beymer
Maps: Roger Butler (foldout map);
      Larry B. Van Dyke and Jaan Hitt (interior maps)
Book and cover design: Jaan Hitt

Library of Congress Card Number 00-025846
ISBN 0-89997-237-3
UPC 7-19609-97237-2

Manufactured in the United States of America

♻ Printed on recycled paper

Published by: **Wilderness Press**
             1200 5th Street
             Berkeley, CA 94710
             (800) 443-7227; FAX (510) 558-1696
             info@wildernesspress.com
             www.wildernesspress.com
Visit our website for a complete listing of books and for ordering information.

Cover photos: *(clockwise from top)* Lower Pauness Lake, Oyster Lake moonrise, Horse River
Frontispiece: Kawishiwi River

SAFETY NOTICE: Although Wilderness Press and the author have made every attempt to ensure that the information in this book is accurate at press time, they are not responsible for any loss, damage, injury, or inconvenience that may occur to anyone while using this book. You are responsible for your own safety and health while in the wilderness. The fact that a route is described in this book does not mean that it will be safe for you. Be aware that route conditions can change from day to day. Always check local conditions and know your own limitations.

Library of Congress Cataloging-in-Publication Data
Beymer, Robert.
    The Boundary Waters Canoe area / Robert Beymer. -- 6th ed.
      p. cm.
    Includes index.
    Contents: v. 1. The western region
    ISBN 0-89997-237-3 (alk. paper)
    1. Canoes and canoeing--Minnesota--Boundary Waters Canoe Area--Guidebooks. 2. Boundary Waters Canoe Area (Minn.)--Guidebooks. I. Title.
    GV7776.M62 B6815 2000
    917.76'7--dc21   00-025846

Boundary Waters Canoe Area Wilderness

VOLUME I: WESTERN REGION

Acknowledgments

A book like this could never have been written without the help and encouragement of many people. Foremost are those with whom I have paddled during the past thirty years. While I stepped off portage trails, paused to take notes, backtracked on lakes to seek a desired photograph, or paddled and portaged out of the way to investigate some unknown territory, the patience of my companions was (and still is) certainly appreciated.

Long before the idea for this book ever entered my head, my father, the Scoutmaster, introduced me to the joys of camping experiences while my mother, the English teacher, always encouraged me to write about those experiences. Throughout the years since the publication of my first book in 1978, U.S. Forest Service personnel were quite helpful in answering my questions and supplying statistical data included in this and previous editions.

When finding the time for research could have been a serious obstacle, my employers (formerly the Eddie Bauer company and most recently the State of Minnesota) granted me summer leave to explore the Wilderness. Canoes were loaned for research trips at no charge by the Eddie Bauer company, Lowe Industries, Piragis Northwoods Company and Hill's Canoe Outfitting. The W.A. Fisher Company supplied the maps used for most of my research, while Chuckwagon Foods supplied the trail food at a discounted price for many of my earlier trips. Most of all, I thank my wife of over 22 years for her steadfast support and encouragement—and for not divorcing me when I spent $200 on my first electric typewriter at a time early in our life together when funds were extremely tight!

Preface

This book was written for the peripatetic paddler — the canoeist who wants to explore the BWCA Wilderness. Base-campers and easy-going anglers, however, should also find a good deal of useful information herein to help them plan their trips.

I have been canoeing in the Boundary Waters for more than 30 years. My introduction occurred in 1967, along with 14 other members of my Explorer Post from Indianola, Iowa, and I've dipped my paddle in the cool, clear waters of "canoe country" every summer since then. While guiding BWCA canoe trips for Camp Northland from 1969 through 1977, I saw the need for a published trail guide. None existed at that time. My trail notes at Camp Northland became the foundation for this book.

The BWCAW, with over 200,000 visitors each year, is the most heavily used wilderness in the nation. With over a million pristine acres of lakes, rivers and forests within its borders, however, the Boundary Waters should be large enough to accommodate its visitors. In 1976, less than one-third of the available quotas were actually used. Unfortunately, however, over two-thirds of the visitors to the Wilderness used less than 14% of the designated entry points. The result was (and still is) congestion at some of the most popular entry points. My book was written to help you discover the entry points and routes that suit your desires and will result in the highest quality wilderness experience possible.

Since publication of my first book in 1978, nearly 70,000 copies of both volumes have been sold to inquisitive paddlers. During the past 21 years, I have received feedback from friends and strangers alike. At my work with camping stores in the Twin Cities and in Ely, as well as at speaking engagements throughout the upper Midwest, I had opportunities to personally meet many of my readers — a valuable experience that presents itself to few writers. Because of the feedback received, and because of continuing research conducted from my cur-

Lifting over a beaver dam on Ge-be-on-e-quet Creek

rent home near the Wilderness, there have been many changes made to these guidebooks in successive editions and printings. After 20 years in print and 5 revisions, it was time in 1998 to thoroughly update the books. So my wife, Cheryl, and I spent the entire summer of 1998 exploring the water routes—again—to ensure that the information contained in this book is accurate, informative and useful. That summer, we paddled 421 miles on 190 lakes and 20 rivers. We also hiked 191 miles on 250 portages and 4 hiking trails. Yes, it was tough work, but somebody's got to do it!

It may seem odd to the casual wilderness observer that frequent changes are necessary to update a guidebook like this one. "How can a wilderness change?" you might ask. Well, the BWCA Wilderness itself has changed very little over the past 20 years. Natural changes do occur, however, and readers need to know about them. Forest fires and windstorms occasionally alter the landscape. Beaver dams deteriorate and small lakes upstream literally dry up. Or new beaver dams are constructed, flooding portage trails.

More often, the changes that may significantly affect your visit are caused by decisions of Forest Service officials. During the past 30 years, I have witnessed many changes in the administration of the Boundary Waters. The ban against non-reusable food and beverage containers (cans and bottles) took effect in 1971. The visitor distribution (quota) system was started in 1976. Implementation of the BWCA Wilderness Act of 1978, which eliminated motorboats from most of the interior lakes, took effect on January 1, 1979. Since then, entry points have been eliminated, renamed, grouped together or separated for the purposes of quota restrictions. The use of trucks to transport motorboats from Lake Vermilion to Trout Lake and from Sucker Lake to Basswood Lake was banned by a court ruling in 1992, only to be reinstated by a congressional act in 1998. In 1995, a decision was made to restrict the number of people in a group to nine and the number of watercraft to four. Canoe rests on portage trails were also eliminated that year. These and many other changes did occur in the BWCA Wilderness.

Both my publisher and I want this guidebook to serve you, the paddler. We will continue to make changes in the future, reflecting new regulations, alterations to existing routes, and the wishes of our readers. I've tried to make this book interesting and useful. Above all, my goal has always been to impart accurate information. I believe that this attention to accuracy and to the concerns of our readers is why this book continues to be as popular today as it was when first published over 20 years ago.

This book was written for the canoe camper who is capable of taking care of himself or herself in a wilderness environment. It does not take you by the hand and lead you through the often-complicated mazes of lakes, streams and portages that characterize the BWCA Wilderness. It does not tell you when to turn right, when to veer left, or when and where to stop for lunch. You should already possess the understanding and the basic skills that are essential for a canoe trip into a wilderness, particularly the ability to guide yourself along the suggested routes without detailed directions. This book also does not include such topics as how to paddle a canoe, how to carry your gear across portages, how to shoot rapids, or how to pack your gear. Many good "how to" books have been written about canoeing and camping in the Boundary Waters. This guide is a "where to" book.

If you need information about canoeing or camping techniques, or about other things related to the BWCA Wilderness, I suggest you read several of the books listed below and pick out what is appropriate to your needs.

- ◆ Books about canoeing or camping techniques:
  American Canoe Association, *Introduction to Paddling: Canoeing Basics for Lakes and Rivers*. Menasha Ridge Press, 1996.
  Bell, Patricia J., *Roughing It Elegantly: A Practical Guide to Canoe Camping*. Eden Prairie, MN: Cat's Paw Press, 1994.
  Drabik, Harry, *Harry Drabik's Guide to Wilderness Canoeing*. Minneapolis: Nodin Press, 1987.
  Furtman, Michael, *Canoe Country Camping: Wilderness Skills for the Boundary Waters and Quetico*. Duluth: Pfeifer-Hamilton, 1992.

Jacobson, Cliff, three fine books from Merrilville, IN: ICS Books:

Boundary Waters: Canoe Camping With Style. 1995.

The Basic Essentials of Canoeing. 1997.

The Basic Essentials of Camping. 1988.

◆ Books about Boundary Waters wildlife:

Heinselman, Myron, *The Boundary Waters Wilderness Ecosystem.* The University of Minnesota Press: Minneapolis, MN, 1996. Stensaas, Mark, **two indispensable books** from Duluth: Pfeifer-Hamilton:

Canoe Country Flora: Plants and Trees of the North Woods and Boundary Waters. 1996.

Canoe Country Wildlife: A Field Guide to the Boundary Waters and Quetico. 1992.

◆ A book about environmental protection of the BWCAW:

Proescholdt, Kevin, Rip Rapson and Myron Heinselman, *Troubled Waters: The Fight for the Boundary Waters Canoe Area Wilderness.* St. Cloud, MN: North Star Press, 1995.

◆ To capture the mood of canoeing in the Boundary Waters:

Any of Sigurd F. Olson's vivid accounts (New York: Alfred A. Knopf), including:

Reflections from the North Country, 1976 (1997).

Listening Point, Random House, 1958 (1996).

The Singing Wilderness, Knopf, 1956 (1997).

Brandenburg, Jim, *Chased by the Light.* Minocqua, WI: Northword Press, 1998. Incredible photos with tantalizing text.

The Boundary Waters Journal, a fine magazine with exceptional photographs, published four times each year by the Boundary Waters Journal Publishing Co., 9396 Rocky Ledge Road, Ely, MN 55731.

◆ Books about other canoeing areas adjacent to the BWCA Wilderness:

Beymer, Robert, *A Paddler's Guide to Quetico Provincial Park.* Virginia, MN: W.A. Fisher Company, 1997.

Beymer, Robert, *Superior National Forest.* Seattle: The Mountaineers, 1989.

This book is a comprehensive guide, including all entry points that are used by canoeists in the western half of the Boundary Waters Canoe Area Wilderness, from Crane Lake to Isabella Lake. Volume II takes over where this leaves off, dealing with entry points in the eastern half of the BWCAW, from Hog Creek to North Fowl Lake.

SPECIAL NOTICE ABOUT WIND DAMAGE

On July 4, 1999, after this book was written but before it went to press, a massive summer storm raced through the BWCA Wilderness. Straight-line winds estimated at between 80 and 100 mph severely damaged about 350,000 acres of woodlands. Another 150,000 acres also suffered damage, though not as severe. Nearly half of the Boundary Waters was affected by the storm, including much of the north-central and eastern parts of the Wilderness from Basswood Lake to the Tip of the Arrowhead. The primary path of the storm was 10-to-12 miles wide and 35-to-40 miles long. It was estimated by the Minnesota DNR that 80% of the trees blew down or snapped in that area. Forest Service crews reported trees stacked 6-to-8 deep, with some piles rising as high as 15 feet above the ground. Of course, that made scores of portages and campsites unusable immediately following the storm.

Soon after the storm, Forest Service officials reported that 800 campsites, 80 miles of portages and over 130 miles of hiking trails in the BWCAW were impacted by the storm. Some of the worst damage occurred along lakes that I describe in my book as among the most scenic in the Wilderness — including Knife, Kekekabic and Little Saganaga lakes in the central BWCAW, and parts of the Tip of the Arrowhead region. Eyewitness reports from paddlers caught in the storm included such descriptions as "phenomenal," "terrifying" and "devastating." Some biologists suggest that the storm could have been the biggest of its kind in 1,000 years. Certainly nothing like it has occurred during the recorded history of northeastern Minnesota.

Immediately after the storm swept through the region, helicopters were permitted in the BWCAW to facilitate evacuation of about 20 injured campers and to help survey all campsites and portages in the Wilderness for other parties in distress. To expedite clean-up of the debris, the Forest Service authorized the use of chainsaws and other motorized equipment through December 31, 2000. These were unprecedented decisions necessitated by an unprecedented natural catastrophe. If you hear chainsaws operating in the Boundary Waters during the summer of 2000, don't be alarmed or perturbed. They are being used to make the Wilderness more accessible and safer for you and other visitors in the most heavily used wilderness area in America.

Some of the descriptions in this book may serve to remind you of what the area looked like before the storm rather than what it looks like now. All of the photos in this book were taken prior to the storm of July 4, 1999. Some of the scenes illustrated by these photos may not appear the same to you as they did when the photos were taken. So, what should you expect to see during your next visit to the BWCAW? In some parts of the Wilderness — the northwestern and south-central parts — you may not notice anything unusual. Even in the most affected parts of the Boundary Waters, the shorelines of the lakes were sometimes the least affected parts of the forest. So you may still see trees standing along the edges of the lakes on which you are paddling, while on higher ground between the lakes the devastation is nearly 100%. It may look like a massive timber clear-cut with the trees left on the ground to rot. The sight may bring tears to the eyes of visitors whose favorite destinations of the past have been altered nearly beyond recognition — and will remain so for decades. Some of the lake descriptions in this book may serve to remind you of what the area looked like before the storm, rather than what it looks like now.

For sure you can expect a ban on campfires in the affected parts of the Wilderness for several years. Five weeks after the storm, the Forest Service imposed campfire restrictions "in response to the heavy fuel buildup resulting from the storm." Only gas and propane stoves were allowed in the restricted areas. The sketch (right) shows the only two parts of the BWCAW that were *not* severely affected by the storm and thus not included in the 1999 fire ban.

Beyond the immediate and obvious changes in appearance of the woodlands, there are less obvious results that have already occurred

Wind damaged area

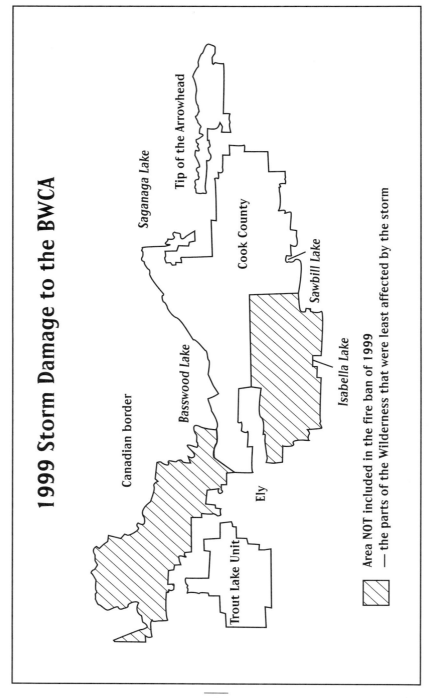

and long-term effects of the storm that can be predicted. Destroyed by the storm were many longtime nests of eagles and ospreys, as well as countless other birds that made their summer homes in the Boundary Waters. It's far too early to estimate other wildlife casualties of the storm. The long-term ecological effect may be similar to that of a massive forest fire. Indeed, fires ignited by lightning are likely to burn parts of the dead, downed forest. Roughly 80% of the forest covering half the Wilderness is now dead, and during a dry season this mangled pile of tinder could be virtually explosive for several years to come. The rest of the fallen forest will simply decay. Old forests will be replaced first by the lush new growth of small plants and shrubs and eventually by young forests. Animals like moose and deer, which thrive in open areas created by fires and clear-cuts, may proliferate — to the benefit of the wolf population. Other types of wildlife which benefit from older forests may now be absent from the storm-effected parts of the BWCAW. At this time, we can only speculate about the forthcoming changes to America's most popular wilderness.

A year after the storm, the Forest Service authorized prescribed burning of 75,000 acres of blown down forest. It began in the fall of 2001 and will continue for five to seven years at a rate of 5,000 to 20,000 acres per year. The primary goal of the project is to reduce the risk of wildfire that could put people at risk and threaten property adjacent to the Wilderness. The USFS declares that its objective "is to accomplish this goal while being sensitive to ecological and wilderness values."

Routes originating at the following 10 entry points in the Western Region of the Wilderness were most impacted by the storm:

1 — Trout Lake
4 — Crab Lake
6 — Slim Lake
7 — Big Lake
8 — Moose River South
9 — Little Indian Sioux River South
24 — Fall Lake
25 — Moose Lake
26 — Wood Lake
27 — Snowbank Lake

The singing wilderness has to do with
the calling of the loons, northern lights,
and the great silences of a land lying
northwest of Lake Superior.
It is concerned with the simple joys,
the timelessness and perspective found
in a way of life that is close to the past.
I have heard the singing in many places,
but I seem to hear it best in the wilderness
lake country of the Quetico-Superior,
where travel is still by pack and canoe
over the ancient trails of the Indians and Voyageurs.

— Sigurd F. Olson

1

Introduction to the BWCA Wilderness

THE BOUNDARY WATERS CANOE AREA WILDERNESS IS PARADISE FOR THE wilderness paddler. Stretching for nearly 200 miles along the Canadian border of northeastern Minnesota, this magnificent region offers more than 1,000 lakes, nearly 2,000 campsites, 160 miles of portage trails, and over 1,500 miles of canoe routes through some of the most beautiful country in the world. That's why over 200,000 people visit it each year and make it the most popular wilderness area in America. At over a million acres, it is the second largest unit of our National Wilderness Preservation system, containing the largest virgin forests remaining east of the Rocky Mountains.

History

The canoe routes on which you will paddle are the very same water trails used for hundreds of years by the Sioux and Chippewa Indians and by the French-Canadian Voyageurs. Jacques de Noyons, in about 1688, was probably the first white man to paddle through the lakes and streams that now compose the BWCAW. At that time, the Sioux may have still been the dominant Indians in the area. But by the time of the first fur traders in the 18th century, the Chippewa Indians had moved into the region from the east and had driven the Sioux farther

Voyageur welcomes tourists to Crane Lake

west onto the plains. From then to about 1800, French-Canadian Voyageurs paddled their birch-bark canoes from the hinterlands of northwestern Canada to the shores of Lake Superior, transporting furs from trappers toward the European markets.

The populations of fur-bearing animals that had once flourished in the region were nearly depleted by the mid-1800s. The trappers moved on to more promising areas and the colorful Voyageur era came to an end.

After years of boundary disputes between the British and Americans, the two governments signed the Webster-Ashburton Treaty in 1842. It established the international boundary along the "customary" route of the fur traders. The Americans had argued that the customary route of the Voyageurs was along the Kaministikwia and Maligne rivers to the north. The British had claimed that the St. Louis River, far to the south, should constitute the boundary. The existing boundary was a compromise.

During the latter half of the 19th century, settlers moved into the area, including farmers, loggers and miners. Mineral prospectors first sought gold along the border region, and a short-lived gold rush did attract considerable attention to the area. Far more important to north-eastern Minnesota, however, was the discovery of high-grade iron ore. Numerous mines sprung up at the present sites of Ely and Soudan and in the area southwest of those towns. After the railroad penetrated this part of the country, extensive logging and mining operations threat-ened to devastate the entire region.

The Superior National Forest was designated in 1909, and within it, in 1926, approximately one thousand acres were set aside as a prim-itive roadless area. This area was enlarged in the 1930s. In 1939 the wilderness area was re-designated as the Superior Roadless Primitive Area, establishing boundaries containing over one million acres. In 1958 the current name was adopted. The BWCA Wilderness Bill of 1978 established the current boundaries, containing 1,075,000 acres. It also prohibits logging, restricts mining operations and limits the use of motorboats to 24% of the total water area on just a few large perime-ter lakes. The BWCAW is administered by the United States Forest Service, Department of Agriculture.

Thanks to the efforts of conservationists throughout the years, this beautiful region looks just as wild and enticing to visitors today as it did when De Noyons first viewed it.

Wildlife

Perhaps nothing represents the Boundary Waters to its visitors better than the eerie wail of the common loon, the Minnesota State Bird. But many other birds are equally at home here, including the bald eagle, the herring gull, the great blue heron, the osprey, the Canadian jay and several varieties of hawks and owls. The tranquilizing song of a white-throated sparrow is as much a part of the wilderness experience as is the scolding chirp of a red squirrel. In the BWCAW you will also find the last substantial population of timber wolves in the "lower forty-eight," as well as large populations of moose, white-tailed deer, black bears, beavers and red fox. Other less visible mammals include otters, lynx, fishers, mink, muskrats, martens, weasels, coyotes and a variety of squirrels. The more quietly you travel through the Wilderness, the greater are your chances of seeing these and other forms of wildlife along the way.

One creature of particular interest to most visitors is the magnifi-cent moose. Where will you see moose? Just about anywhere! But they are most abundant in large open areas that have been cleared of dense forest. During the 1970s, there were two places in the Boundary Waters that contained two of the densest populations of moose in North

America. One was in the vicinity of the Isabella Lake, Hog Creek and Kawishiwi Lake entry points — the south-central part of the Wilderness — where recent logging operations had cleared the forest. Another area was between the Moose River North and Little Indian Sioux River North entry points — the vast region north of the Echo Trail that had been burned by the Little Indian Sioux Fire of 1971. Both of these regions still contain good populations of moose, but they are not nearly as dense now that the forests have grown back. So where are moose most likely to be seen today? Expect to see them in and near large areas where the forest recently burned. The Gabbro Lake Fire, the White Feather Fire, the South Temperance Fire, the Winchell Lake Fire and the Saganaga Corridor Fire all resulted in clearing substantial parts of the forest during the 1990s, creating habitat that is quite favorable to moose and other wildlife. As the forest in these areas grows back to maturity, the moose will move on to other regions that recently burned. It's a natural cycle that is essential to sustaining the population of these burly beasts.

While traveling throughout the BWCAW, always treat the wildlife with respect. Remember, you are a visitor in the Wilderness but the wildlife are residents. You can help the wildlife stay wild and healthy by not feeding the creatures and not interfering with their normal routines. Don't paddle close to loons or try to imitate their calls, which are used for communication. Should you find yourself near any nesting birds, observe them from a distance. Human disturbance at a nest site may lead to nest abandonment and loss of eggs.

The predominant game fishes are northern pike, walleyes, smallmouth bass and lake trout. Black crappies and bluegills are also plentiful in many of the lakes. Even rainbow and brook trout have been stocked in some lakes.

Contrary to the perception of most paddlers, water covers only about 12% of the BWCA Wilderness. A coniferous forest of jack pine, Norway pine, white pine, tamarack, black spruce, white spruce, balsam fir and white cedar covers most of this region. There are also extensive stands of deciduous trees, including paper birch and quaking aspens. Very few dry land areas in the BWCAW are not forested. Bogs occupy the rest of the region that is not covered by lakes or forests.

Bears

Black bears are common throughout the BWCAW. Although they are not considered to be dangerous and are usually quite shy around campers, they may be pests when searching for food — your food.

Over the years bears have learned that canoe campers always travel with food packs and (unfortunately) often leave food scraps and garbage lying around their campsites. Where people most frequently camp, bears are most frequently a problem. Actually bears are not the problem, people are! Where campsites are kept clean and food packs are suspended properly, bears are not a problem. Nor are the smaller creatures that might otherwise depend on humans for their daily sustenance (chipmunks, mice and the like).

Seeing a bear on a canoe trip should be a treat, not a tragedy. Nevertheless, an unpleasant encounter with a bear could bring an abrupt end to your canoe trip — regardless of who caused the problem! There are no hard-and-fast rules to ensure protection from a bear. Bear behavior differs under different conditions. The bears you may encounter while visiting the BWCAW are wild animals and they *could* be dangerous. Always remember that! With a few precautions, however, you should have no problems with these fascinating and beautiful creatures.

- Avoid camping on the most popular lakes where there are numerous, frequently occupied campsites located relatively close together. A small island located well away from the shoreline and away from other islands offers a *degree* of safety. But don't let an island campsite lull you into a false sense of security. Bears are very good swimmers.

- When you are away from your campsite (even just fishing nearby) and at night, always hang your food pack off the ground. It should be at least 10 feet above the ground and 6 feet away from tree trunks and large limbs. Bears are good climbers, so the food must be a safe distance away from the trunk and from any limbs large enough to support a bear's weight.

- Never store food in your tent. And if food was spilled on your clothes, leave your clothes outside your tent at night.

- Keep a clean campsite. Thoroughly burn or safely bury all food scraps and leftover grease, or seal your garbage in an airtight plastic bag and carry it with your food pack. Do not dispose of leftovers in the latrine. Bears will find them and destroy the latrine in the process.

- Never get between a mother bear and her cub(s). If you see a cub, its mother is probably nearby. Female bears are extremely protective of their young.

- If a bear does wander into your campsite, don't panic! They are usually frightened off by loud noises. Try yelling or banging some pots together. Don't charge the bear; it may become defensive.

- If a stubborn bear does not back off or acts strangely, move to another campsite. It is extremely rare for a black bear to attack a human being; but it did happen to two campers in separate incidents (same bear) during the summer of 1987. Neither camper was seriously injured and the bear was later killed by authorities.
- Don't lose any sleep worrying about the sounds you hear outside your tent at night. In general, the noisiest critters are also the smallest — mice among the worst! (Moose are exceptions to this general rule.) Bears are extremely quiet, often stealthy creatures that can wander through a campsite in the black of night without arousing any attention from its human occupants. If you hear rustling leaves at night, chances are good that it's not caused by a black bear. Rest assured!

Finally, don't let a fear of black bears detract from your enjoyment of the BWCA Wilderness. Use good common sense, observe the tips above, and you should have no problem with bears — or any other wild animal.

Climate

For the canoeist in northern Minnesota, spring, summer and fall are essentially crowded into a span of five months — May through September. The ice is usually (though not always) off the lakes by the first week of May, but the trees are not fully leafed out until at least the middle of the month. That period, when the water levels are high and before the biting insects invade the Boundary Waters, is an excellent time to explore the tiny creeks that may later be too low for navigation. Be prepared, however, for weather cold enough to produce snow. Early June is often a wet, cool and gloomy time of year, usually plagued by hordes of mosquitoes, sand flies and ticks. The fishing is best then. July and August normally offer the best weather for campers and the worst for anglers (too warm for some fish species). As the summer progresses, the water levels of some shallow streams may become too low for navigating a loaded canoe, eliminating some excellent route possibilities. From late August through September, after the first frost, biting insects have nearly disappeared. This is a wonderful time to explore the Wilderness. But you must be prepared for extended periods of cool and rainy weather, or even snow. After September, contact local authorities for weather updates. It is not unusual for the lakes to ice over in October, and snow may accumulate on the ground. On the other hand, that month may also be mild and dry, with crisp nights that are ideal for sleeping.

Temperatures and rainfall vary, of course, throughout the BWCAW. The following statistics, recorded in International Falls, represent approximations for the western region of the Boundary Waters.

	May	June	July	Aug.	Sept.
Ave. temperature	51	60	66	63	53
Ave. low each day	38	48	53	51	41
Ave. high each day	63	72	78	76	64
Ave. precipitation	2.6"	3.9"	3.5"	3.6"	2.9"

Because of its close proximity to Lake Superior, the eastern part of the BWCA Wilderness sometimes exhibits extremely variable weather. While the lakes in the far-eastern region may be blanketed with a cool, misty fog from Lake Superior, nearby lakes to the northwest may be enjoying warm sunshine, thanks to the subtle yet significant effects of both Lake Superior and the Laurentian Divide. Consequently, no weather data from any one reporting station can accurately represent all of the Boundary Waters.

Geology

The rocks in this area are mostly Precambrian rocks covered by a thin veneer of glacial deposits. For approximately two billion years, during the Precambrian era, vast changes were generated by a large amount of diverse geologic activity that reshaped the landscape many times. Following long periods of erosion and igneous intrusions, the great ice sheets of the Pleistocene Epoch began to form nearly two million years ago. Ice scoured the Precambrian bedrock, gouging out the softer rocks and leaving behind irregular blankets of glacial debris. This created the topography that we see today.

The BWCA Wilderness contains some of the oldest exposed rock in the world, estimated to be as old as 2.7 billion years. It is part of the vast region known as the Canadian Shield, which underlies almost two million square miles of eastern Canada and the Lake Superior region of the United States. In Minnesota this belt of ancient exposed rock extends west from the area of Saganaga Lake on the international border through Ely and International Falls to the northwestern part of the state, where the old rocks disappear beneath younger sedimentary deposits. Included in this expanse of ancient rocks are the metavolcanic Ely Greenstone formation, the metasedimentary Knife Lake Group and great granitic batholiths like the Vermilion and the Saganaga batholiths.

7

A mountain-building period began about 2.6 billion years ago, during which the rocks became metamorphosed and strongly deformed, and the granites were intruded from below into the older rocks. The rocks that had been formed or altered deep within the earth's crust became exposed at the surface and were then subjected to erosion.

The geologic events that may have been the most economically significant to the state of Minnesota began with the encroachment of a broad arm of the ocean upon the eroded terrain. Inland seas covered what we now call the North Woods. Layers of sedimentary rocks were deposited at the bottom of that enormous sea. Called the Animikie Group, these rocks lie in a belt extending westward along the border lakes from Lake Superior to just south of Saganaga Lake, and then reappearing in the Mesabi Range south of the BWCAW. The Animikie rocks include the Pokegama quartzite, the Biwabik iron formation and a sequence of shales and sandstones. Flint, too, is found in abundance in the vicinity of Gunflint Lake. Rich deposits of iron ore are scattered throughout northeastern Minnesota, upon which mining communities sprung up in the early 20th Century. Iron ore became the economic basis for many communities in northeastern Minnesota and it is still one of the most important industries for the state of Minnesota. The iron ore is so concentrated in some places that it will cause a compass needle to be deflected from magnetic north. Magnetic Lake, in fact, received its name because of just such a phenomenon.

Around 1.7 to 1.6 billion years ago, another period of mountain building occurred when the sedimentary rocks and other existing rocks were folded, faulted, metamorphosed and intruded by granitic magmas. Later an outpouring of lava in and around the area now occupied by Lake Superior created the major rock of the North Shore. After this volcanic activity subsided, stream erosion and deposition again became the dominant processes in the area.

The inland seas had long since disappeared and new mountains had risen on the continent when the great ice sheet of the Ice Age advanced from the north and began to cover northeastern Minnesota. It was the ice sheet that turned this mineral-rich region into the world's best canoe country. During four major periods of glaciation, the glaciers altered the landscape considerably. These periods began almost two million years ago. The last glacial advance and recession (the Wisconsin Glaciation) lasted from about 100,000 to 10,000 years ago. Evidence of the Ice Age is everywhere in the Boundary Waters today. Parallel grooves called striations are visible on many rock ledges that were scoured by the ice. Glacial debris from small pebbles to huge boulders is widespread. Here and there, you will see the large boulders, called erratics, that were left "stranded" when the glaciers melted.

Perhaps the greatest distinction of the border lakes area is the presence of exposed bedrock. This region is unlike the rest of the state, which is almost completely covered by glacial deposits. This domination of exposed bedrock in the Boundary Waters resulted in distinctive patterns of lakes and ridges, which reflect the underlying rock structures. In the eastern third of the region the lakes form a distinctive linear pattern. Long, narrow lakes give the terrain a notable east-west "grain." These lakes are set in two major types of rock formations. The lakes on the Duluth Gabbro formation, which is exposed over an area from Duluth north and east to the Canadian border, developed their particular pattern because alternating bands of less resistant rock and more resistant rock are oriented east-west. Erosion removed more of the less resistant rock, creating lake basins. In the area where the Rove Lake formation is exposed — along the international border from Gunflint Lake to Pigeon Point (the very tip of the Arrowhead) — the east-west linear pattern has a different cause. In this area intervening ridges separate the lakes. These ridges are the exposed edges of south-sloping layers of dark igneous rock that was intruded into sedimentary rocks after they were deposited. The north-facing slopes of the ridges are very steep and form escarpments 200-500 feet high. Huge piles of talus blocks cover the lower parts of many escarpments, the result of erosion by the advancing glaciers as they passed transversely over the ridges.

The lakes set in the Knife Lake group of rocks show a similar linear pattern, but the trend is northeast-to-southwest. In the rocks associated with the Ely Greenstone formation, the pattern is less regular and the depressions in the bedrock are not as deep. Thus shallower lakes are found there.

In the area underlain by the Saganaga Granite the story is a little different. Here the shapes of the lakes are dictated by cracks in the Precambrian rock. As the cracks were made wider by erosion, they became linear depressions that lakes could occupy. Many of the lakes lie in collections of linear depressions oriented in more than one direction, so that the lakes have zigzag shapes. An overhead view of the area reveals many jagged lakes interconnected by linear channels. Saganaga Lake itself is a good example.

Because of the glaciation of the Ice Age and the characteristic Precambrian rock of northeastern Minnesota, the Boundary Waters Canoe Area, with all of its interconnected lakes and streams, is one of the most extraordinary recreational wilderness areas in the world.

Fires

Under a Forest Service policy implemented in 1987, lightning-caused fires in the BWCA Wilderness are allowed to burn without suppression if the fires fall within certain prescribed limits. Those limiting considerations include location, risks to property and public safety, and weather factors. Natural fires that are not within prescribed limits and all human-caused fires are suppressed.

For centuries, large areas of the Wilderness burned from lightning-caused fires, which reduced fuel accumulations and created diverse wildlife habitats. The USFS fire policy is intended to partly restore fire to its natural role in the Wilderness, whenever it can occur within the limits of safety. The Forest Service informs the public about ongoing fires. Notices are posted at canoe landings, and field crews notify paddlers within the Wilderness about threatening blazes.

You may encounter natural fires in the BWCA Wilderness. Forest Service personnel may not be present at the fire site, although all fires are under some form of surveillance. If you choose to observe the fire, do so from a safe distance, and consider the following tips:

- ◆ Fires normally move in the same direction as the wind. Find a safe location away from the fire's path.
- ◆ Be careful while visiting a recently burned area. Ashes may remain hot for days, and there is always a danger of falling snags and tree limbs.
- ◆ Do not attempt to extinguish a prescribed fire. A natural fire is part of the Wilderness. It results in ecological changes that are consistent with Wilderness management.
- ◆ Fires may smolder and burn very slowly for days or even weeks without much increase in size. Then weather changes can cause dramatic and dangerous increases in fire size. Respect all fires as potentially dangerous.

Although wilderness fires result in positive benefits to the forest, fire can also be devastating. YOU HAVE A RESPONSIBILITY to prevent human-caused fires. The long-standing Smokey Bear message of fire prevention is still valid. Please be careful!

Safety

Risk is an integral part of a wilderness expedition. Risks associated with isolation, tough physical challenges, adverse weather conditions and lack of rapid communications are inherent in a visit to the BWCAW. At

Walking Thomas Creek

all times exercise caution, use common sense, and consider the following tips:

- ◆ Do not take chances to save time.
- ◆ Always wear a life preserver, even if you can swim. It is a law in Minnesota to have one wearable U.S. Coast Guard-approved personal flotation device (life jacket) readily accessible to each person in a canoe.
- ◆ Do not attempt canoe travel during a lightning storm or when there are large waves.

- ◆ Never stand in a canoe; keep your weight low and centered.
- ◆ If you should capsize, stay with the canoe; it won't sink.
- ◆ Use the portages. Do not run rapids unless you are confident you can do it safely, and only after you have scouted them. Remember that water levels change considerably during the summer months. Rapids that may have been perfectly safe to run during your last trip in August could be a dangerous, raging torrent during your next trip in June (or vice versa). Canoeing mishaps occur every summer in the Boundary Waters. Some result in drowning. Many result in damaged canoes. Most result in spoiled trips.
- ◆ Carry a good first-aid kit and know how to use it. See to it that *every* member of your group knows CPR. Be alert for hypothermia, especially when any member of your group becomes wet.
- ◆ If a *serious* accident occurs, send one canoe for help immediately. Or use a heavy smoke signal to attract a Forest Service patrol plane. If you have a cellular phone with you, use it to get help *only* if an accident is life threatening! (Note: having a bear in your campsite is *not* a sufficient reason to summon assistance!) Evacuation by plane or other motorized vehicle is approved only when there are no other options available and a person needs the immediate services of a doctor. The local county sheriff authorizes all emergency searches, rescues and evacuations. *If an evacuation is necessary, you will be billed for the cost.*
- ◆ Boil or treat water before drinking. Even then, if algae are visible, don't drink the water. Although lake water may look pure, drinking it without first filtering, boiling or chemically treating it may cause illness. When using a filter or chemicals, be certain that they are designed to remove or kill *Giardia lamblia*, in particular—a nasty parasite that can cause a harsh intestinal illness.
- ◆ Before setting out on your trip, be sure that someone—Forest Service official, outfitter or friend—knows your itinerary and when you expect to return, with instructions to contact authorities if you are overdue. The Forest Service has no way of knowing when (or if) you exit the BWCAW.

Visiting a Wilderness

A wilderness, in contrast with those areas where man and his own works dominate the landscape, is hereby recognized as an area where the earth and its community of life are untrammeled by man, where man himself is a visitor who does not remain.

Using this definition, Congress passed the Wilderness Act of 1964 and created the National Wilderness Preservation System. Included as the only water-based wilderness, and the largest wilderness in the lower 48 states, the Boundary Waters is also the most heavily used wilderness in America. Many of the 200,000 annual visitors are not familiar with minimum-impact camping techniques and the need to protect the fragile wilderness from damage. Litter strewn along portages and left in fire grates; birch trees stripped of bark; red and white pines with carved initials; and fire-blackened areas resulting from campfires left burning are just some of the signs of abuse seen far too often in the BWCA Wilderness. Other problems caused by the large number of visitors may be less permanent but still inappropriate in a wilderness setting. Large, noisy groups shouting across a lake or singing boisterously around a campfire, and bright-colored equipment easily seen from across a lake detract from the feeling of quiet and solitude that wilderness visitors seek.

Wilderness areas are managed to protect and maintain the environment in its natural state for our enjoyment and for the enjoyment of generations to come. The responsibility for protecting these areas lies not only with professional managers, however. As a visitor, you and your group also share in this responsibility. You must realize that your place within the wilderness is not as a conqueror, but as a wise keeper and a good steward of this land and water. By ensuring a quality wilderness experience for yourself and others, you will be preserving the area for generations to come.

Regulations and Recommendations

In General...

- ◆ Travel permits must be obtained before entering the BWCAW and must be in your possession while in the Wilderness. This applies to overnight use as well as daytime visits.
- ◆ Party size is limited to 9 people, with a limit of 4 canoes per party. This applies to daytime travel as well as to campsite occupancy. Not only must two groups of 9 people each camp separately, they must also paddle separately.
- ◆ Airplanes must not fly at an altitude below 4,000 feet while passing over the Boundary Waters.
- ◆ Unauthorized use of metal detectors is strictly forbidden.
- ◆ The use of firearms, while not illegal, is discouraged. There is no need for them in the Wilderness.
- ◆ All federal, state and local laws must be obeyed. (Prior to your

trip, call the Minnesota Department of Natural Resources for boating and fishing regulations: toll-free (888) 646-6367 or local (651) 296-6157.

◆ Though dogs are not banned from the Wilderness, they are better off at home. Many dogs become barkers, even if they never bark at home, and barking is a disturbance to other campers. Other dogs may charge wild animals, including bears. They are also susceptible to attacks by timber wolves. If you choose to bring your dog, it must be kept on a leash at landings and on portages.

While traveling...

◆ Motorized travel and mechanical portaging are permitted only on certain specified routes. Use of any other motorized or mechanical equipment of any type is not permitted within the Wilderness.

◆ Watercraft, motors, mechanical devices or equipment not used in connection with the current visit may not be stored on or moored to National Forest land and left unattended.

◆ If a portage is crowded, patiently wait on the water—away from the landing—for your turn. There should never be more than 9 people or 4 canoes together, even if they are not traveling in the same group.

◆ Unload, move and reload as quickly as possible on portages. Don't stop for lunch or prolonged rest breaks where you might interfere with others along the trail.

◆ Avoid dragging your canoe at portage landings and across the trails. Not only does it damage your canoe, but the noise may also be heard a great distance away.

While camping...

◆ Camping is permitted only at Forest Service campsites that have steel fire grates and box latrines, and within certain designated Primitive Management Areas.

◆ Camping is limited to a maximum of 14 consecutive days at one campsite.

◆ Open campfires are permitted only within constructed fireplaces at developed campsites, or as specifically approved on the BWCAW travel permit.

◆ Use dead, downed wood for campfires. The best place to look is back from the shore, away from campsites. Usually the driest wood is found on fallen trees that are leaning against other windfalls and not lying directly on the ground. The best firewood comes from dead, dry jack pine, white pine, spruce, tamarack, white cedar, aspen and ash. Paper birch is usually poor fire-

Campsite near Lower Basswood Falls

wood when found lying on the ground, because it rots quickly. Red pine and balsam fir also make poor firewood. Do not cut live trees! Green wood from any tree burns very poorly, if at all. Damage to live trees (cutting, carving or peeling off the bark) is not only unsightly, but it also causes irreparable damage to the forest. It's also illegal. Carry some fire ribbon or other starting material to ignite fires in wet weather.

◆ Fires must be drowned with water and be dead out before you leave a campsite—even if you just go fishing for awhile. Pour water over the fire while stirring the ashes. Then, if you feel any warmth in the ashes with your bare hand, douse the ashes again.

◆ Non-burnable, disposable food and beverage containers (cans and bottles) are not permitted. Containers of fuel, insect repellent, medicine, and personal toiletry items, however, are permitted.

◆ It is unlawful to cut live trees, shrubs or boughs, or to use moss or boughs for a bed. Digging trenches around tents, tarps or anywhere else is also not permitted. Trenching and using pine boughs for mattresses (once accepted practices but now illegal) inflict harm to the environment.

◆ Cord should be used instead of nails or wire.

◆ Demonstrate common courtesies. Leave clean campsites for those who follow. Preserve and respect the peace and solitude of the Wilderness. Sound carries far across open water—especially on a quiet evening. Keep noise to a minimum and you'll improve the quality of the wilderness experience for yourself and for others. You will also greatly improve your chance of seeing wildlife.

◆ Use Wilderness latrines. If no latrine is available, bury human waste in 6 to 8 inches of soil at least 150 feet from the shores of lakes and streams.

◆ Keep soap, dishwater and grease away from lakes and streams. Take your dishes and hot water back away from the lake to wash them. Rinse them well and dump all the soapy water at least 150 feet from the lake. Use biodegradable soap instead of detergents. Likewise, when you feel the urge to wash yourself, jump in the lake to get wet. Then soap up and rinse off at least 150 feet from the shore.

◆ Use the bottom of a canoe for a table, rather than constructing one from native materials.

◆ If your tent or tarp is bright-colored, set it up as far from the shore as possible, so that it cannot be seen by other campers across the lake.

◆ **Leave no trace!** That's the general rule for camping in any wilderness. When leaving a campsite, leave no trace of your presence there. Regarding leftovers, eat them, burn them or pack them out. If you burn them, do so in a *hot* fire. If you must bury leftovers or fish entrails, paddle along the shore away from campsites, go into the woods at least 150 feet from the water and bury them in 6 to 8 inches of soil. After a fire is dead out, sift through the ashes for twist ties, foil and other debris not completely burned. Pack them in your litterbag, along with any cigarette filters and other trash, and carry them out. Add to that any litter found on portages and at canoe landings. *Always leave an area cleaner than you found it.*

The Use of Modern Technology

To most people, the allure of a wilderness canoe trip is the opportunity to live simply and to travel much as the Voyageurs did over 200 years ago. While it is not illegal to take and use cellular phones, transistor radios or GPS devices, they really have no legitimate place in a wilderness setting.

Of course, some might argue that lightweight Kevlar canoes, ultralight nylon tents and camp stoves also do not belong in a wilderness. Perhaps they are right. Each of us must draw a line somewhere. Some folks need three trips across each portage to carry all their gear from lake to lake. Others can do it in just one trip. Most need two trips. Obviously, people have different requirements for comfort in the woods. Those of us with weak backs *need* lightweight canoes and other gear. Many use camp stoves not for their convenience but to mitigate the effect of their visit on the natural environment.

For some people, it is extremely hard to escape for a week in the wilderness, leaving all contact with their jobs and families, and with civilization in general. To not lose touch, however, is to deprive you of a truly unique experience that can only be found in a wilderness setting. While physically challenging, nothing is more mentally relaxing and emotionally recharging than *totally* escaping for several days from the evening news, the stock market reports, the family bills, the rush-hour traffic and the multitude of decisions that everyone makes during a daily routine. Listening to news reports on your radio or calling work from your cellular phone robs you of that experience. Indeed, even using your watch during a canoe trip should not be necessary. This is a time to enjoy the "natural rhythms." The sun will be your alarm clock. Your stomach will tell you when to eat. The sun will also tell you when it's time to make camp. When tired, you will sleep. Your only concerns should be basic—food, shelter and clothing. Since you will be carrying all three in your canoe, your only practical concerns are the weather (which dictates your clothing requirements) and finding a campsite at which to construct your shelter. (For some, catching fish may be another serious concern, if they brought no other food with them.)

Using a GPS (Global Positioning System) device, which is fascinating and remarkably accurate, deprives you of the traditional challenge of using a map and a compass to find your way. There is no disgrace to getting temporarily lost in the BWCA Wilderness. It happens to nearly everyone at one time or another. It surely must have happened to the Voyageurs, back when maps were mere approximations of the landscape. Accept the challenge. Leave modern technology at home and learn to explore the BWCA Wilderness much like the Voyageurs once did.

Primitive Management Areas

For small groups of visitors who desire a more primitive and secluded wilderness experience, there are 12 designated areas in the BWCAW that are managed like Quetico Provincial Park on the Canadian side of the border. PMAs occupy 124,000 acres of the least used parts of the Wilderness.

PMA access requires more effort and skill than do most parts of the BWCAW. The Forest Service does not maintain portage trails and campsites. Most lakes within the PMA must be reached by traveling cross-country or bushwhacking. To minimize damage to the environment, it is suggested that party size not exceed six people. Visitors may camp at any suitable location. Shallow latrines may be dug at sites that do not have box latrines, and campfires are permitted where there are no fire grates, as long as special care is paid to ensure that there are no environmental scars remaining after use. Camp stoves, however, are strongly recommended instead of open fires.

To enhance the opportunities for solitude, access to these areas is very limited. After obtaining a travel permit for the desired BWCAW entry point, you must also get special authorization from one of the USFS ranger stations where permits are picked up. Each PMA is divided into zones where only one group per night is allowed to camp. (There is no restriction on day-use activities by other groups, however.)

Reservations are not taken for the PMA visits. Authorizations are available only on a first-come-first-served basis. For more information about the specific locations of these remote areas, as well as the unique regulations that govern them, contact the Superior National Forest headquarters in Duluth or one of the USFS district offices listed in Chapter 2.

Provisions of the BWCA Wilderness Act

In the fall of 1978 Congress enacted legislation that drastically altered the regulations governing the Boundary Waters Canoe Area. The Wilderness may not *appear* any different now than it did before 1979, but it may *sound* different in places.

Before January 1, 1979, the BWCA was administered in accordance with the 1964 Wilderness Act. Logging was allowed in parts of the Wilderness and motorboats were permitted on 60% of the water surface area.

The BWCA Wilderness Act of 1978 added 20 small areas totaling 45,000 acres to the existing BWCA, and it established the current boundaries to include 1,075,000 acres. It also prohibited all logging, closed most of the interior motor routes, and restricted motorboats to 24% of the water surface area after 1999—mostly large perimeter lakes served directly by access roads or mechanical portages. A few lakes have no horsepower limits, but most are limited to either 10 or 25 horsepower, as follows:

- No horsepower limits: Little Vermilion Lake, Loon River, Loon Lake, the southwestern end of Lac La Croix to Wilkins Bay, and on portions of lakes that lie partially outside the BWCAW (Fall, Moose, Snowbank, Sea Gull, Clearwater and East Bearskin lakes).
- 25 horsepower limits: Trout Lake, Fall Lake, Moose Lake, Newfound Lake, Sucker Lake, Newton Lake, South Farm Lake, East Bearskin Lake, Snowbank Lake, Saganaga Lake east of American Point, and Basswood Lake (except that part lying northwest of Washington Island and north of Jackfish Bay to the Basswood River).
- 10 horsepower limits: Sea Gull Lake east of Three mile Island, Clearwater Lake, North Fowl Lake, South Fowl Lake, and the Island River east of Forest Route 377.

Mining is also restricted and the Secretary of Agriculture has the authority to acquire mineral rights in the Wilderness and along three road corridors in a 222,000-acre Mining Protection Area. No other federal land controls are involved in the MPA.

Quotas were established for the daytime use of motorboats on the lakes where they are allowed. Resorts, cabin owners and their guests are exempt on their own lakes. Camping from motorboats is allowed for visitors with overnight camping permits. Towboats in excess of 25 horsepower are not permitted in the Wilderness.

Snowmobiles are prohibited in the BWCAW except for permanent use of the Crane Lake to Little Vermilion Lake winter portage to Canada and the Saganaga Lake winter route to Canada. The Secretary of Agriculture, however, is allowed to permit grooming by snowmobile of a limited number of cross-country ski trails near existing resorts.

Old and deteriorating dams within the Wilderness may be maintained only to protect wilderness values or public safety.

The federal government is given authority to enforce the motorboat and snowmobile regulations on state water. No other federal jurisdiction over state waters is asserted. The state is allowed to impose more stringent regulations.

Paddling Along the Canadian Border

Several of the BWCA Wilderness routes described in this book follow parts of the international boundary between the United States and Canada. It is important for visitors to respect Canadian property. While the Webster-Ashburton Treaty of 1842 permits use of the border lakes and their connecting portages by the citizens of both countries, it does not permit Americans to fish in Canadian waters without first securing an Ontario fishing license. Nor does it allow Americans to camp, picnic or even set foot on Canadian soil (except at portages connecting border lakes) without first being authorized by Canada Customs to enter the country. Furthermore, since Quetico Provincial Park borders much of the BWCAW on the north, you must also have authorization from the Ontario Ministry of Natural Resources to enter the Park after first clearing Customs. Don't stray out of the United States. Illegal entry into Canada is a serious matter.

A True Wilderness?

There are those purists who would not classify the BWCAW as a true wilderness. In one sense, they are right. Portage trails are regularly cleared of fallen trees and clogging brush. Regulations dictate that you must camp only on Forest Service campsites equipped with unmovable fire grates and box latrines. There are obvious signs all around you that other people have camped at the very same spot many, many times before.

There are also those who declare that one must paddle for weeks before feeling a true sense of "wilderness." Regarding the BWCAW, I must disagree. "Wilderness" is as much a state of mind as a physical condition. Seldom are more than one or two long portages necessary for visitors to feel a true sense of wilderness around them. The disquieting drone of motors fades into the past, and one enters a world of only natural sensations. Depending on your point of entry, it could take a day, or maybe two, to find your wilderness. On the other hand, it may be waiting only minutes from your launching site, scarcely more than a stone's throw from the road's end. Wherever you start, a magnificent wilderness it not far away in the Boundary Waters Canoe Area.

Wilderness involves emotions. A wilderness experience is an emotional experience. If a person cannot sense deep emotion while camped on the shores of some placid wilderness lake, hearing the cry of a loon, he will never understand the pleas of those who would save the Boundary Waters Canoe Area.

— Charles Ericksen

Portage between Hustler and Oyster lakes

An organization that has worked diligently for years to protect and preserve the BWCA Wilderness is the **Friends of
the Boundary Waters Wilderness**, 1313 Fifth Street SE,
Suite 329, Minneapolis, MN 55414-4504. **Northeastern
Minnesotans for Wilderness** is a regional grassroots
organization that formed in the 1990s to represent people
who believe that wilderness is good public policy and is
worth defending: PO Box 625, Ely, MN 55731.

|2

How to Plan a Wilderness Canoe Trip

Pre-Trip Planning

A SAFE, ENJOYABLE WILDERNESS EXPERIENCE STARTS AT HOME WITH careful planning. First, ask yourself and all members of your group if you really want a trip into the Wilderness—a place where you will find no running water, prepared shelters, predictable weather or easy travel. There are no signs to direct the way. You must know how to build a fire, administer first aid, read a map and use a compass. In an area that is unfamiliar and sometimes downright hostile, you must rely on your own resourcefulness for your comfort and perhaps for survival. You must be your own doctor, guide and entertainer—prepared for accidents, extended periods of rain, and obstacles such as large waves whipped up by strong winds.

Keep your group size small. Few campsites have tent pads for more than two or three tents. Some are barely large enough for one tent. If your group is large, plan to split up and travel separately. Better yet, plan completely different routes. You'll have more pictures and experiences to share when you get home. A small group has much less impact on the Wilderness and on other visitors. You will also have better opportunities to observe wildlife along the way.

Vacationing with a group of people is always challenging, because of variations in skills, interests and physical strengths. Get your group together ahead of time to plan the trip. Talk about what *each* person is looking for and expects on the trip. Decide as a group where and when to go, what equipment to take and what to eat. By considering these things ahead of time, the entire group will get a better idea of what to expect from the trip. There will be fewer surprises later to dampen spirits. Consider the positive aspects of a BWCAW canoe trip—sun-drenched afternoons on sky-blue lakes, gentle breezes, magnificent orange sunsets, fish striking at every cast, and a refreshing swim in a cool lake at day's end. Then consider the dreaded conditions that plague many canoe trips—hordes of hungry flying insects, fish with no appetite at all, long and muddy portage trails, prolonged periods of cold rain, and gale-force winds that make canoe travel extremely difficult or impossible. Both trip scenarios are possible—indeed likely—at one time or another. Hope for the best, but be psychologically and physically prepared for the worst.

When planning your route, make sure you are not overly ambitious. Consider all members of the group, and plan to travel at the speed of the least experienced or weakest paddler. It's a good idea to plan a layover day for every three or four days of travel. You'll have more time to fish or relax. If you encounter rough weather, you won't have to worry about taking unnecessary chances just to stay on schedule.

Plan to make camp early enough in the day to assure finding an available campsite. Most wilderness visitors are there for solitude... quiet...to seek respite from the hustle and bustle of day-to-day urban living. Each person wants the sensation of being the first and only person in an area. To accomplish this objective, consider campsites that are off the main travel routes and in back bays. They are used less often and offer a better opportunity for privacy. Firewood is usually more plentiful without having to search as hard for it. You will also have a better chance of avoiding "problem bears" where few others camp.

Respect for other Wilderness visitors starts before you ever leave home. The first portage is no place to learn how to get a canoe up on your shoulders. Practice picking up a canoe and other canoeing skills before you start your trip. Know who is responsible for each pack, each canoe and each piece of miscellaneous equipment *before* setting foot on a portage trail. Accountability reduces the possibility of leaving something behind. It also reduces the amount of time needed on each portage, thus alleviating possible congestion on some of the trails.

Equipment, Clothing and Food

Equipment: When selecting equipment for your trip, choose environmentally "natural" colored tents, packs and clothing to help you travel and camp inconspicuously. Bright colors contribute to a crowded feeling. Carry a small stove and fuel to use when dry wood is hard to find. Stoves heat more cleanly, quickly and evenly than campfires. Axes and hatchets are not necessary (although a small hatchet is useful in an emergency to prepare dry wood for burning). There is plenty of suitable firewood that can easily be broken or cut with a small camp saw. See that at least one person in each canoe carries a map and a compass and knows how to use both. Kept in a plastic case and tied to the canoe, the map is readily available for quick and frequent reference. Line your packs with large heavy plastic bags to keep all the contents dry. And, by all means, practice packing before you leave home. Remember that everything you pack will have to be carried on portages—by you.

Clothes: Clothing needs may vary somewhat from season to season, but always plan for extremes. Layering is the most efficient method to stay warm and dry. Lightweight cotton is comfortable in warm weather, while wool provides warmth on chilly days and at night, even when it's wet. Polypropylene and other synthetic garments that wick moisture away from your body are excellent choices for any temperature. Good raingear is essential, and it can also serve as a windbreaker on cool, windy days. Bring two pairs of footwear—boots or sturdy shoes for traveling and sneakers or moccasins for walking around the camp-

Lunch break on Hula Lake

site. Wearing the latter at campsites is not only kind to your feet; it also causes less soil compaction damage to the campsite. Aqua Socks are also a good idea to wear while swimming, to protect your feet from sharp rocks. A pair of pants with zip-off legs is quite practical in the BWCA Wilderness, where temperatures may vary considerably from early morning to mid-afternoon.

Food: Since cans and bottles are not allowed in the Boundary Waters, some foods will have to be repacked in plastic bags or in other plastic, reusable containers. If possible, pack each meal's food together in a plastic bag to make meal preparation easier. Also line your food pack with a large and durable plastic liner to protect the contents from moisture. When sealed tightly at night, this may also help to contain the food's aroma from attracting animals. If you plan to catch fish, *don't ever count on fish* for your primary sustenance. Fish are good supplements to your diet, but if you depend on them, you are likely to be hungry.

If you don't have access to all the right stuff in your home town, you can find all the gear and clothing you'll ever need for a BWCAW canoe trip in the *Boundary Waters Catalog*, published by the Piragis Northwoods Company, 105 North Central Avenue, Ely, MN 55731. Call (800) 223-6565 or (218) 365-6745. Or access the catalog by Internet at http://www.piragis.com/catalog.

Choosing a Wilderness Route

Any group entering the BWCA Wilderness must have in its possession a travel permit, granting permission to enter through one of the 71 designated entry points. Thirty-six of those entry points are located in the western half of the Boundary Waters. Of those, 27 canoeing entry points are described in this book:

1 Trout Lake	26 Wood Lake
4 Crab Lake	27 Snowbank Lake
6 Slim Lake	29 North Kawishiwi River
7 Big Lake	30 Lake One
8 Moose River South	31 Farm Lake
9 Little Indian Sioux River South	32 South Kawishiwi River
12 Little Vermilion Lake	33 Little Gabbro Lake
14 Little Indian Sioux River North	34 Island River
16 Moose River North	35 Isabella Lake
19 Stuart River	67 Bog Lake
20 Angleworm Lake	75 Little Isabella River
23 Mudro Lake	77 South Hegman Lake

24 Fall Lake   84 Snake River
25 Moose Lake

Hikers use 9 other entry points (see Appendix V):
3 Pine Lake Trail
10 Norway Trail   21 Angleworm Trail
11 Blandin Trail   74 Snowbank & Kekekabic Trail
13 Herriman Lakes Trail   76 Big Moose Lake Trail
15 Sioux-Hustler Trail   86 Pow Wow Trail

Thirty-four entry points are found in the eastern half of the BWCAW, including 28 canoeing entry points that are described in Volume II. One entry point (71) is for paddlers who enter the Boundary Waters from Canada.

Planning a route while resting near Slim Lake

The entry points included in this guide are grouped according to accessibility. Chapter 3 includes 6 entry points that are accessible from and located *south* of the Echo Trail. Chapter 4 includes 7 entry points that are accessible from and located *north* of the Echo Trail. Seven entry points accessible from the Fernberg Road are described in Chapter 5, while the remaining 7 entry points are accessible from State Highway 1 southeast of Ely.

Using statistical data and personal observations by the author, each entry point is briefly discussed. Statistics are from the summer of 1997, the most current data available when this book was written.

- ◆ **Seasonal Permits:** The number of overnight travel permits issued to groups using the entry point in 1997, including all modes of transportation.
- ◆ **Popularity Rank:** The relative popularity of the entry point, compared with all other BWCAW entry points (a total of 70 in 1997).
- ◆ **Daily Quota:** the maximum number of overnight travel permits that can be issued each day to groups using the entry point (as of 1999).

Further discussion includes the entry point's location, how to get there, public campgrounds nearby, amount of motorized use (if any) through the entry point, and other comments of interest to canoeists.

Following the discussion of an entry point are suggestions for two routes from that entry point. The first is a short route that can be completed by most groups in 2 to 4 days. The second is a longer route that takes 4 to 8 days. It is important to understand that this book is merely an accumulation of *suggestions*. It does not describe *all* possible routes through the BWCAW. Quite the contrary, the routes that you could take are virtually infinite in number. You may wish to follow only a part of one route, or you may wish to combine two or more routes. ***Do not feel bound to the routes as they are described in this book.*** You may follow them precisely as written, but you may also use the suggestions simply as a basis for planning your own route.

Introductory remarks about each route tell you: 1) the *minimum* number of days to allow; 2) the length of the route; 3) the number of different lakes, rivers and creeks encountered, as well as the number of portages en route; 4) the difficulty (easier, challenging, most rugged), 5) the maps needed for the route, and 6) general comments, including to whom the route should appeal. Then each route is broken down into suggested days, giving the sequence of lakes, streams and portages, followed by points of special interest.

Example: Day 2 (13 miles): Little Trout Lake, p. 376 rods, **Little Indian Sioux River**, p. 32 rods, **river**, p. 32 rods, **river**, p. 12 rods, **river, rapids,**

river, **rapids**, **river**, p. 70 rods, **river**, p. 40 rods, **river**, p. 34 rods, **river**, p. 35 rods, **river**, p. 120 rods, **Otter Lake**. You will find this day to be a sharp contrast from the prior day of paddling on large lakes... etc.
Explanation: On the second day of this route, you will paddle across Little Trout Lake and then portage 376 rods to the Little Indian Sioux River. You will follow the river to Otter Lake, negotiating 8 portages and some rapids along the way. You will make camp on Otter Lake at a campsite that is marked by a red dot on the map. Comments about the day's route follow the outlined sequence of lakes, rivers and portages.

Most of the routes suggested are "loops"—they begin and end at (or within walking distance of) the same location. There is no need for car shuttles between two points. Other routes start at one entry point and end at another entry point far enough away to necessitate a shuttle. The name of each route indicates whether the trip is a "loop" (The Eddie Falls *Loop*) or requires a "shuttle"(The Three Rivers *Route*). If a shuttle is required, drop off your vehicle at the end of the route *prior* to starting the journey. That generally works better than scheduling a pre-determined pick-up time at the end of your trip. If your parked vehicle is waiting for you, you won't be under any pressure to arrive at a particular time.

Of course, any route may be made more difficult by completing it in fewer days than recommended, or made easier by adding days. If fishing is a priority for your trip, you should consider adding at least one day for every three days suggested in this guide. For longer trips, you may also want to add layover days to your schedule. The longer you are tripping, the more likely you are to encounter strong wind, foul weather, sickness or injury that could slow your progress. (Always carry an extra day's supply of food, too, for just that reason.) Furthermore, after three or four days of rugged trekking, you may simply want to rest for a day before continuing.
About the author's biases: The difficulty ratings for the routes in this book are subjective. Difficulty is relative. A route that is "most rugged" to one party may be merely "challenging" to another group. An "easier" route to most paddlers may be "most rugged" to an inexperienced group of paddlers who really had no idea what they were getting into when they entered the BWCA Wilderness. Two major factors contribute to the difficulty ratings in this book: 1) the average distance paddled per day, and 2) the length, frequency, and difficulty of the portages. An "average" day in the BWCAW includes about 8 to10 miles of paddling, interrupted by 5 or 6 portages, measuring 50 to 100 rods in length. This should challenge most visitors. Anything less is usually rated "easier." Trips with a great deal more paddling and/or longer or more frequent portages are rated "most rugged." The ratings are based on my 30 years

of Boundary Waters tripping and my experience with all age groups and experience levels.

Even more subjective is my opinion of what constitutes an interesting route and beautiful scenery. You may or may not agree, but it's background information that you may find useful in selecting your route. First, I prefer tiny creeks, narrow rivers and smaller lakes. Wind is less likely to be a problem and wildlife is often more visible. Such a route offers a much more intimate natural experience, in my opinion. Second, I like rocks and hills—lakes bordered by elevated terrain with exposed rock faces, and campsites with rock outcroppings on which to rest and contemplate the sunset and the moonrise. Almost every lake, swamp and bog in the Boundary Waters is beautiful in its own way. But to this author there is nothing more striking than a small or narrow lake surrounded by tall hills or ridges covered by a generous blend of pine, birch and aspen trees and trimmed with steep rock ledges or cliffs. Equally pleasing, however, is a tiny, meandering stream littered with lily pads and bordered by a tamarack bog. Why do these opinions matter to you? Because, if a route is described as having lovely scenery, you'll know what is meant by "lovely."

If fishing is your thing: General comments about the fishing potential for each suggested route are included. The serious angler will find more information about each lake in **Appendix IV**. All of the 185 BWCAW lakes in this book are listed alphabetically. Data about each lake were obtained from the Minnesota Department of Natural Resources, including overall size, littoral size (acreage of the lake that is less than 15 feet deep), maximum depth, and the game-fish species that are known to inhabit the lake.

About the use of rods: One rod equals 16½ feet. Since that is roughly the length of most canoes, it is the unit of linear measurement in canoe country. Both the Fisher maps and the McKenzie maps use this unit of measurement. Although the maps are topographic, the indicated number of rods tells little about the difficulty of the portages. Long trails may be quite easy, and short ones may be extremely rough. This guide will warn you about the rough ones. You may notice that the length of a portage on the maps sometimes differs from the length in this book. While traveling throughout the BWCA Wilderness, whenever I doubted the portage lengths shown on the maps, I did my own measurements. On the shorter portages, I counted my steps. A stopwatch was useful on the longer trails. Sometimes they are simply estimates based on my 30 years of experience walking across portages. Although there is no guarantee that my measurements are precise, there is no doubt in my mind that they are usually more accurate than those on the maps. You can decide for yourself. If you find an error, please let me know!

Maps

It would be nearly impossible to show detailed maps on the pages of this book. Instead, you will find a foldout map of the entire western region inside the back cover. Use this map to plan your trip. When actually taking your trip, however, I recommend using the water-resistant topographic maps published by the W. A. Fisher Company. Thirty-two "F-series" maps combine to cover all of the BWCA Wilderness and Canada's Quetico Provincial Park. The scale is 1½" to a mile, and there is sufficient overlap to provide smooth transitions from map to map. Designated USFS campsites are identified by red dots on the maps, which are updated annually. A disclaimer on each map reads *"This map is not intended for navigational use, and is not represented to be correct in every respect."* Nevertheless, these maps are published specifically for canoeists and are remarkably accurate and detailed.

The discussion of each route tells you which maps are needed. You can order them from:

W. A. Fisher Company
P.O. Box 1107
Virginia, MN 55792-1107
(218) 741-9544

Some routes are served better by McKenzie Maps, which are also topographic (scale 2" to 1 mile). They also provide excellent detail and use red dots to identify campsite locations. Some routes described in this book require as many as three Fisher maps but only one McKenzie map (and vice versa). When such is the case, it is pointed out in the introduction to the route. You can order them from:

McKenzie Maps
8479 Frye Road
Minong, WI 54859
(800) 749-2113

You can purchase both of these map series from an outfitter when you arrive in northeastern Minnesota. The maps are also available at many camping stores in the Twin Cities area, as well as in some other upper-Midwestern cities. You can also mail-order them by phone or e-mail from *Boundary Waters Catalog* (see the section *Equipment, Clothing and Food* earlier in this chapter).

When to Visit the Boundary Waters

What's the best time of year to schedule a BWCAW canoe trip? That depends on your group's priorities. (See *Climate* in Chapter 1.) If seeing animal wildlife ranks high on your list, *where* you travel may be more important than *when*. The same applies to those who seek quiet seclusion. But you can increase your chances of both viewing wildlife and not viewing other people by your choice of an entry date, as well as your choice of an entry point.

Over the past 30 years, there has been a substantial increase in the number of visitors to the BWCAW—the most heavily used wilderness in America. 19,732 overnight use permits were issued to visitors in 1982 from May 1 through September 30. That number grew to 27,319 permits in 1997—a 38% increase in 15 years. Visitation is now distributed fairly equally throughout the three summer months, but more and more people are enjoying the Boundary Waters in May and September. In 1997, the distribution of visitors was:

May	13%
June	23%
July	24%
August	26%
September	14%

You can increase your chance of avoiding other people and obtaining a BWCAW permit by considering the following:

* The busiest days for entry are Saturday, Sunday and Monday. If possible, start your trip on one of the other four days of the week.
* Memorial Day weekend, Independence Day weekend, Labor Day weekend and the month of August are the busiest times. In 1997, the 20 days of heaviest use all fell in the period from July 31 through August 30. If you can postpone your trip until September, you are bound to see far fewer people, virtually no biting insects, and a forest full of fall colors.
* Consider using an entry point that has traditionally ranked low in popularity. A majority of visitors use a very small minority of the entry points. For instance, *more overnight travel permits are issued for Moose Lake each summer than for the 40 least popular entry points combined!*

Obtaining Travel Permits

Any visitor in the Boundary Waters must have a BWCAW travel permit in possession. It allows you to enter the Wilderness only on the starting date and through the entry point specified on the permit. Once in the Wilderness, you are free to travel where you desire, as long as motor-use restrictions are not violated. This applies to daytime use as well as overnight use of the Wilderness, any time of the year.

There are two types of permit systems for BWCAW visitors. One is a self-issuing permit system for non-motorized daytime visits during the summer, as well as for all types of visits from October 1 through April 30, when there is no quota on the number of permits issued. This permit is free and does not require a reservation. The permits are available at most entry points. You simply fill out the form, leave the "official use copy" in the drop box there or return it to a Superior National Forest office, and keep the "visitor copy" with you at all times while in the BWCAW.

The other permit system is for overnight visitation as well as daytime motorboat use from May 1 through September 30. Entry quotas were established for overnight campers in order to reduce competition for the limited number of established campsites and to avoid unauthorized camping on undeveloped sites. The daily limit at each entry point (from as low as 1 to as many as 27) is based on the number of campsites available to visitors using the routes served by the entry point. The quotas pertain only to overnight campers during the 5-month canoeing season. There is a separate quota system for daytime use by visitors with motorboats. There are no limits on the number of BWCAW visitors after September 30 and before May 1.

Overnight User Fee

A fee is charged for camping in the Boundary Waters. Adults are charged $10 per person per trip (in 2002). Youths under 18 and Golden Age or Golden Access Passport holders are charged $5 per person per trip. For visitors who plan to use the BWCA Wilderness more than four times during the same summer, seasonal fee cards may be obtained at a cost of $40 per adult or $20 for youth and Golden Age or Golden Access Passport holders. The Seasonal Fee Card may be purchased by mail or by phone from the BWCAW Reservation Center (see Reservations below), or in person after April 30 from any Superior National Forest District Office. This card fulfills the fee requirement for the entire season. But it does not eliminate the need for obtaining a BWCAW travel permit.

Most of the funds that are generated by the camping fees stay in the Boundary Waters. The funds allow the Forest Service to hire more employees to work in the Wilderness, maintaining and rehabilitating campsites and portage trails, educating visitors about low-impact camping techniques, assisting people in trouble, and expanding the hours of operation at the permit-issuing stations.

Campsite on Eugene Lake

Reservations

All overnight travel permits are available through advance reservations for a nonrefundable processing fee of $12 per reservation (in 2002) plus a $20 deposit for your camping fee (in 2002). You don't have to make a reservation before arriving at the BWCA Wilderness. It is advisable, however, since quotas at many entry points do fill up early. A reservation assures you of a permit to enter the Wilderness on a specific day at a certain entry point.

Starting with the 1999 canoeing season, the BWCAW Reservation Center became part of the National Recreation Reservation Service (NRRS):

Mail: BWCAW Reservation Center
P.O. Box 462
Ballston Spa, NY 12020
Telephone Feb. 1–Sep. 30: (877) 550-6777 (toll free)
TDD telephone: (877) TDD-NRRS (toll free)
Fax: (518) 884-9951
Web site: www.bwcaw.org/ (good general information, including permit-issuing stations, recent changes, rules and regulations, an entry map, and contacts). Reservation requires login ID and password.

You may reserve a permit by mail, fax, phone or Internet. Reservation applications received by mail, fax or Internet through January 15 are then processed by lottery regardless of the order received. Applications received after January 15 are processed on a first-come-first-served basis. Telephone reservations are accepted starting February 1. Phone reservations are accepted only with the use of a valid American Express, Discover, MasterCard or VISA credit card during normal business hours (9:00 AM to 5:30 PM EST in 1999). Reservations may be made only at the BWCAW Reservation Center. Do not call the Superior National Forest headquarters or any of the District Offices to make reservations. Reservation requests must include the following information:

- Method of travel (paddle, hike or motorboat).
- Party size (maximum of 9 people).
- Number of watercraft (maximum of 4 boats).
- Name, address and phone number of the group leader.
- Names of up to three alternate group leaders who might use the permit in the group leader's absence.
- The desired entry point name and number.
- The desired entry date.
- The estimated exit date.
- The planned exit point.
- Whether or not the group is guided and, if so, the guide's name.
- Location where the permit will be picked up.
- Payment by check, money order or charge card (cash not accepted).

It is also a good idea to include an alternate entry date and an alternate entry point, in case your first choices are not available.

The reservation fee and the full amount of the camping fee for your party must be paid when you reserve your permit. Currently the total amount due when your reservation is made is $32 ($12 for the reservation and $20 for the camping fee). If your total fee is calculated to be less than $20 (i.e. for a single person or for a party with seasonal camping permits), you must still pay $20 plus the $12 processing fee when you make your reservation. The overpayment will be refunded after completion of your trip.

After making your reservation, the trip leader will receive a letter confirming that a BWCAW travel permit is reserved. Reservations made within the last 7 days before the trip will be processed, but no confirmation letter will be sent.

Picking Up Your Permit

An overnight travel permit must be picked up in person within 24 hours of the trip starting date at a designated USFS District Office or at an outfitter or business that is an official permit issuing station (cooperator). This face-to-face contact affords personnel at the issuing station an opportunity to inform visitors about BWCAW regulations, wilderness ethics and minimum-impact camping techniques. *Only the party leader or an alternate leader whose name appears on the application may pick up the permit.* Identification is required, and periodic checks may take place in the Wilderness. All cards (Golden Age, Golden Access or Seasonal Fee) must be presented when the permit is picked up to receive a discount. Otherwise, the full camping fee will be charged. Cooperators may charge an extra $2 fee for issuing each overnight permit. Office hours vary, so be sure to check with your permit pick-up location for its office hours. Also, if you don't have a reservation, you must pick up your permit at a time when the availability of permits can be confirmed by the BWCAW Reservation Center.

Any change to your permit, except group size, requires a new $12 reservation fee. Group size changes are made when the permit is picked up. If there are more than 2 people in your party , the cost difference will be collected then. Cash, checks and credit cards are accepted at all USFS District Offices. Only credit cards are accepted by non-Forest Service cooperators (outfitters or resorts). If the party size decreases, a refund will be made by the BWCAW Reservation Center after the trip.

Canceling a Permit Reservation

The entire camping fee will be refunded if your reservation is cancelled two or more days prior to the entry date. If the reservation is not cancelled in advance, or if you do not use the permit, you will forfeit the $20 deposit and the $12 reservation processing fee.

BWCAW Information

The BWCAW Reservation Center personnel are available *only* for making reservations and selling camping passes. For information about the BWCA Wilderness, contact the Superior National Forest headquarters or any of the Ranger District offices listed below. They can answer your questions but cannot process reservations. Normal business hours are 8:00 AM to 4:30 PM weekdays before May 1 and after September 30. During the summer permit-issuing season, the District offices are generally open from 6:00 AM to 8:00 PM (fewer hours at the Isabella Work Station). The hours do change from year to year, however, and they may vary from office to office. The Superior National Forest office in Duluth is open 8:00 AM to 4:30 PM on weekdays.

If you have access to the Internet, you'll find an excellent web site with Superior National Forest information, including the BWCA Wilderness, at:

www.superiornationalforest.org/bwcaw

It includes information about updates, rules, entry points and other web sites.

Superior National Forest
Attn: Forest Supervisor
8901 Grand Ave Place
Duluth, MN 55808-1102
(218) 626-4300

Entry Points	Closest District Ranger Station	Telephone Number
1, 9, 12, 14, 16	La Croix Ranger District 320 N. Highway 53 Cook, MN 55723	(218) 666-0020
4-33, 77	Kawishiwi Ranger District 118 S. 4th Ave East Ely, MN 55731	(218) 365-7600 5/1-9/30 (218) 365-7561
34, 35, 67, 75, 84	Isabella Work Station 9420 Highway 1 Isabella, MN 55607	(218) 323-7722

If you have not reserved a permit in advance, you may pick it up at any District Ranger office or cooperating business. It is advisable, however, to drop by one that is closest to your entry point. The personnel there are likely to be more familiar with your proposed route. They can alert you to high water or low water conditions, bear problem areas, suitable campsites, road conditions and other particulars.

National Forest Campgrounds

In the introduction to each entry point in this guidebook, the closest USFS campground is included for those who might want to camp near their starting point before their trip. You may reserve campsites up to 240 days in advance (360 days for group facilities) at 9 campgrounds on the Superior National Forest by calling the National Recreation Reservation Service (NRRS) at (877) 444-6777. Or you may use their Internet web site for reservations:

www.reserveusa.com

In addition to the usual campsite fee, you will also be charged $9.00 (in 2002) for reservation processing. The service charge is the same whether you make your reservation by phone, by Internet, or in person at one of the NRRS field sites.

A Final Word

Believe it or not, these age-old routes *do change* from year to year. In fact, they may change several times each year. A deep navigable channel between lakes in early June may be shallow rock-strewn rapids that require a portage in August. A creek-side portage indicated as 35 rods on the map may turn out to be 135 rods when the creek dries up during a drought. Sometimes portages that were dry in June are flooded in August after beavers dam a stream adjacent to the trail. When a portage becomes too eroded from over-use, the Forest Service sometimes constructs a new trail, which is usually longer than the original. Likewise, trails through wet and muddy bogs may be elevated on boardwalks when there are funds available for trail maintenance. Or bypasses may be routed to higher and dryer ground.

On the other hand, occasionally an author's memory and notes fail him and a mistake is made. Or a typographical error occurs during publication that is overlooked during the proofing process. So, if you find inaccuracies in this book, or if you have any comments or suggestions to improve subsequent editions, please write the author (in care of the publisher). Thank you!

Important

The descriptions in this guidebook are necessarily cast in general terms. Neither the descriptions nor the maps can be assumed to be exact or to guarantee your arrival at any given point. You must undertake only those trips and trip segments that you know are within your competence. Given these cautions, you can have a wonderful time in the BWCA Wilderness.

|3

Entry from the Echo Trail South and Highway 169

The Southwestern Area

THE SOUTHWESTERN PART OF THE BOUNDARY WATERS CANOE AREA
Wilderness contains six entry points. Five are easily accessible from the
Echo Trail. Another is reached from State Highway 1-169. Because of
its proximity to the other entry points in the southwestern area, however, it "fits" much better in this chapter than with the other entry
points from State Highway 1 in Chapter 6, which are southeast of Ely.
The southwestern area is a unique part of the BWCAW. It is isolated
from the rest of the Boundary Waters by the Echo Trail corridor.
Perhaps for that reason, it is often overlooked by visitors and contains
one of the least used parts of the Wilderness.

Ely is the largest of the small northern Minnesota towns that serve
visiting canoeists in the BWCAW's Western Region. Originally the commercial center for iron mining and logging operations, Ely evolved
gradually—sometimes reluctantly—into the Canoe Capital of America.
It is a modern, bustling community with two supermarkets, several
motels and automotive service stations, a good variety of restaurants, a
plethora of bars, a laundromat, a hospital, and surely the most canoe
trip outfitters per capita in the world. Located near the east edge of

town, at the intersection of Highways 1 and 169, is the Ely Chamber of Commerce. It occupies an attractive log building and is staffed by knowledgeable and friendly folks who can supply you with up-to-date information about Ely and the surrounding attractions, including nearby resorts and campgrounds.

The place to pick up your permit for most of the entry points in the Western Region is ½ mile east of the Chamber of Commerce. Currently, the Kawishiwi Ranger District, USFS, occupies a space in the International Wolf Center at the outskirts of town. Opened in June of 1993, the extraordinary "Wolves and Humans" exhibit found its home in Ely after entertaining more than 2.5 million people during a multi-year tour across North America. There is also a captive pack of four timber wolves living in a relatively natural environment where you can observe their interactions. You should definitely allow time (at least a couple of hours) either before or after your canoe trip to visit this fascinating and informative exhibit. It is located right next to the USFS office where the BWCAW permits are issued.

Entry points near the far west end of the region lie in the La Croix Ranger District and are closer to the town of Cook, where the USFS headquarters is located. Unless you are using an outfitter in Ely, you can save driving time for some entry points by picking up your permit at the visitors' center in Cook. Though much smaller than Ely, Cook does offer visitors all the essentials, including two modern supermarkets, several restaurants and gas stations, and a hospital. The USFS visitors' center is adjacent to Highway 53 in the middle of town.

The Echo Trail is a winding, hilly, scenic road that most people find delightful to drive, if they don't have to drive it every day. To get to it from the International Wolf Center, drive ½ mile east on State Highway 169. Turn left onto County Road 88 (Grant McMahan Blvd.) and follow this good highway for 2½ miles to its junction with County Road 116, which is most often referred to as the Echo Trail. (For directions from Cook to the northwest end of the Echo Trail, see Entry Point 12, Location.)

The Echo Trail winds its way north and west 46½ miles to County Road 24 near Echo Lake. The road surface is blacktop for the first 10 miles, but gravel the rest of the way. The curves do straighten out near the Moose River entry points and, from there on, you can make better driving time. Most of the Echo Trail is rather treacherous, though, so drive with care.

Entry Point 1—Trout Lake

SEASONAL PERMITS: 880

POPULARITY RANK: 11th

DAILY QUOTA: 14

LOCATION: Trout Lake is accessible from Vermilion Lake, about 15 airline miles due west of Ely. From the International Wolf Center, follow State Highway 169 west, through Ely and Tower, for 27½ miles to its junction with County Road 77, about 4½ miles west of Tower. Turn right on County Road 77 and follow this blacktop road northwest for 9.8 miles to a "Y" intersection of the Arrowhead Point and Moccasin Point roads. Veer left there and continue for the final 1.7 miles on the Moccasin Point Road (Co. Rd. 929) to the public landing. There you will find a large private parking lot operated by Moccasin Point Resort, with gasoline pumps, telephone booth, snack bar and store. A fee is charged to park there.

DESCRIPTION: Public campgrounds on or near Vermilion Lake's south shore are located at Tower-Soudan State Park, McKinley Park and Tower Park, all just north of Highway 1-169, just outside of Tower. There is also a national forest campground at Pfeifer Lake, 10 miles southwest of Tower. Any of these will provide you with a convenient place to spend the night prior to the canoe trip. All are less than 20 miles from the public access to Vermilion Lake. Camping fees are charged at all of them.

To access Trout Lake, you must first cross part of Vermilion Lake. Vermilion is a very popular lake, dotted with private cabins and resorts. It is particularly attractive to aquatic motorists, many of whom travel into Trout Lake, where there is a 25-horsepower limit on motor size.

The Trout Lake entry point is a paradox for the wilderness canoeist. It ranks high in popularity among all BWCAW entry points. Furthermore, nearly six out of ten overnight travel permits issued each summer are to motorboat operators. It also ranks 4th among all entry points for the number of day-use motor permits issued. In fact, of all entry points into the BWCA Wilderness, Trout Lake boasts the highest percentage of motorboat usage and the lowest percentage of paddlers. This may not sound too appealing for paddlers seeking solitude. But consider this. Motors are not permitted to travel *beyond* Trout Lake itself, and only about four out of ten overnight travel permits are issued to paddlers. So, in spite of a rather high daily quota, an average of only about two groups per day that actually enter the BWCAW here are capable of entering the wilderness *beyond* Trout Lake.

What does all this mean for you? On the one hand, you may encounter some noise and congestion, mostly in the form of motorboats, on Trout Lake. On the other hand, if you are seeking a quick escape to solitude, you can find it at the Trout Lake entry point if you don't mind sharing your first two large lakes with motorists *and* if you don't stop on Trout Lake itself. You can quickly pass through one of the busiest and noisiest lakes in the Boundary Waters and into one of the least traveled and most pristine areas in the Wilderness, offering as much peace and solitude as anywhere else in the BWCAW. If you can tolerate the first and last days of these two routes, you will surely find a wilderness trip from this entry point to be outstanding.

Trout Lake is also one of the most *available* entry points in the entire BWCA Wilderness. Although it ranks high in popularity, the supply of overnight travel permits is usually much greater than the demand for them. Throughout the quota season, only about 40% of the available permits are actually used. If you are looking at the last minute for a good wilderness canoe trip, and most other entry points are filled up, therefore, consider Trout Lake as a fine alternative.

ROUTE #1-1: **The Pine Creek Loop**

3 Days, 26 Miles, 4 Lakes, 2 Creeks, 4 Portages

DIFFICULTY: Easier

FISHER MAPS: F-1, F-8

INTRODUCTION: This short loop will give you an excellent taste of what the Boundary Waters can offer. Large lakes where motorboats are permitted lead to a more isolated and peaceful region restricted to paddlers—an area that receives relatively few human visitors and is home for much wildlife. From the boat landing on Vermilion Lake, the route first leads northeast to Trout and Little Trout lakes. It then follows tiny Pine Creek southeast to Pine Lake. Finally, it returns to the south end of Trout Lake and backtracks to Vermilion Lake.

A longtime favorite of anglers, Trout Lake contains lake trout, walleyes, northern pike and smallmouth bass, while Little Trout and Pine lakes are good sources of walleyes and northern pike. Stretching the loop over three full days should allow plenty of time to fish. Avid anglers may want to add a fourth day, however, to allow time to explore the waters of the more remote lakes just east of the loop. Strong paddlers with little or no interest in fishing could surely complete the loop in just two days. Beware the possibility of strong winds and high waves, however, on Trout and Vermilion lakes. That could slow travel considerably, or make it virtually impossible for awhile.

Day 1 (11 miles): Vermilion Lake, p. 40 rods, **Trout Lake, Little Trout Creek, Little Trout Lake.** Unless wind is a problem across the vast expanses of Vermilion and Trout lakes, this should be an easy beginning for this 3-day outing. Along the way, you'll see private cabins outside the BWCAW and (possibly) numerous motorboats until you reach Little Trout Creek, beyond which motors are not permitted.

There are two portages connecting Vermilion and Trout lakes. The 40-rod trail starts at the north end of a small bay and climbs a small hill en route to Portage Bay of Trout Lake. About ¼ mile east of this portage is a ½-mile-long portage used by trucks to haul motorboats between the lakes. A court ruling in 1992 closed that service from 1993 through 1998. But congressional legislation in 1998 reopened the portage to a motorized operation in 1999.

The creek connecting Little Trout and Trout lakes is very shallow, and there could be a beaver dam there to necessitate a quick lift-over. Don't panic if you see a number of canoes on Little Trout Lake. It seems that anglers often use motorboats to access campsites at the north end of Trout Lake. Then they paddle canoes into Little Trout Lake to fish. The campsites on the sandy shore of Little Trout Lake are well used, but not as attractive as many of those on Trout Lake. The shallow water in front of the sites may also be choked with aquatic vegetation after midsummer. If you don't mind sharing "your" lake with motorists, you might prefer to camp at the more attractive sites on Trout Lake. Even if you camp on Little Trout Lake, you are likely to hear motors on nearby Trout Lake right up until dark (and maybe thereafter).

Day 2 (7 miles): Little Trout Lake, Little Trout Creek, Trout Lake, p. 60 rods, **Pine Creek, Pine Lake.** Pine Creek is much deeper and wider than Little Trout Creek. The 60-rod portage at the mouth of the creek could be shortened to 40 rods when there is plenty of water in the creek. Try paddling up the creek past the first landing for 20 rods to the next landing on the right. The path is excellent—quite smooth and virtually level. The put-in at the other end, however, is awkward and muddy. Unless beavers are active, there may be no other obstructions along the course of the creek. When the water level is low, however, you may have to lift your canoe across a shallow, boulder-strewn section of the creek about a mile from the portage. You may also "bottom out" at the source of the creek, near Pine Lake. Of course, beavers may entirely alter the character of Pine Creek at any time. Expect the unexpected.

You'll find a scenic overlook at the summit of a high rock slope adjacent to the Chad Lake portage trail. A short climb leads to a panoramic view across Pine Creek valley. In mid-July, you might also find a wealth of blueberries on the rocky slope.

There are several good campsites on Pine Lake. The best are in the northwest part of the lake. The most private are in the southeast end. A couple small sand beaches along the east shoreline may be enticing to swimmers.

Be alert for wildlife. My party once witnessed three deer, one moose, two mink, several great blue herons, two loons, a soaring bald eagle and very few human beings. That was on the "busy" 4th of July weekend.

Day 3 (8 miles): Pine Lake, p. 260 rods, **Trout Lake,** p. 40 rods, **Vermilion Lake.** The 260-rod portage is not a particularly tough carry, but the length makes it a challenge to inexperienced or out-of-shape trippers. During the first 200 rods, the trail gradually climbs to nearly 90 feet above Pine Lake, before descending nearly that much in the final 60 rods to Trout Lake.

After negotiating the final portage (this time mostly downhill), you may want to reward your efforts by soaking your body in the gentle, scenic rapids that drains Trout Lake into Vermilion Lake.

ROUTE #1-2: The Cummings Lake Loop

           5 Days, 53 Miles, 14 Lakes, 2 Rivers, 3 Creeks, 22 Portages

DIFFICULTY: Most rugged

FISHER MAPS: F-1, F-8, F-9

INTRODUCTION: This is a good route for seasoned canoeists who don't mind hard work to achieve wilderness solitude. The route will take you from Vermilion Lake north through Trout and Little Trout lakes and then across a long portage to the Little Indian Sioux River. You will paddle east on this tiny, winding stream, through marshy terrain teeming with wildlife, to its headwaters at Otter and Cummings lakes. From the east end of Cummings Lake, you will turn south and then west, navigating the smaller lakes and streams that will return you to the busy motor route where you began.

Your first and last days will probably be shared with many others, but solitude will be yours to cherish in the rest of this interesting loop. Moose and deer are plentiful along the Little Indian Sioux River, and fishing is good in many of the lakes along the route. Try for bass in Otter, Cummings, Chad and Trout Lake. Or catch a walleye breakfast in Pine, Buck, Little Trout or Trout lakes. Northern pike are found in nearly all of the lakes on this route. And don't forget the name of your entry point; there are lake trout to be found in the depths of big Trout Lake.

Beware the possibility of low water in the Little Indian Sioux River, particularly during late summer or an unusually dry year. At times, it could be too low to carry a loaded canoe. You might get through, but it could take much longer than expected. Consult with the Forest Service before starting out on this route.

Day 1 (11 miles): Vermilion Lake, p. 40 rods, Trout Lake, Little Trout Creek, Little Trout Lake. (See comments for Day 1, Route #1-1.) If you encounter strong wind out of the north or west that makes crossing Trout Lake very difficult or impossible, you could reverse this route. You would bypass the main part of Trout Lake, and a north or west wind would be no problem until you reached Cummings Lake and began your journey back to Trout Lake.

Day 2 (13 miles): Little Trout Lake, p. 376 rods, Little Indian Sioux River, p. 32 rods, river, p. 32 rods, river, p. 12 rods, river, rapids, river, rapids, river, p. 70 rods, river, p. 40 rods, river, p. 34 rods, river, p. 35 rods, river, p. 120 rods, Otter Lake. You will find this day to be a sharp contrast to the prior day of paddling on large lakes. A day with nine portages is exhausting by any measure. And travel on the meandering Little Indian Sioux River is deceivingly slow. This is the price you must pay for wilderness solitude. You should see few, if any, other human beings this day after departing from Little Trout Lake. Enjoy the bountiful wildlife and absence of other paddlers along the river's

Little Trout Creek

course. I once witnessed six deer and a cow moose leisurely drinking from the river's swampy bank. Who knows how many other creatures watched us paddle silently through this winding wilderness?

The first long portage starts at a sandy beach that may be obscured by aquatic vegetation in the shallow water in front of the landing. It has a surprisingly good, virtually level path most of the way to the river, with only a few wet spots along the trail. The final 15 rods, however, are across a spongy bog at the edge of the river, where it may be impossible to avoid wet feet.

The remaining eight portages are sometimes hard to find and brushy. Most are dry, however, with fairly good paths, in spite of the infrequent use they receive. Although you are traveling upstream, most of the portages are quite level. Only the third portage (32 rods) has much elevation change—a rather steep climb about half way across. It is also one of the more scenic portages, with a good view across the rapids to a pine-covered ridge on the other side.

In addition to the seven portages along the river, you will also encounter two small rapids around which there are no portage trails—one just beyond the 12-rod portage and the other just before the 70-rod trail. In that long, winding stretch of river between those two portages, my wife and I encountered 27 beaver dams during the summer of 1998. Most of the dams could be paddled over without any difficulty, but a few required lift-overs. The 70-rod portage bypasses a shallow part of the river that is plagued with windfalls. The path along the south bank of the river is hard to see. Watch for tree blazes and rock cairns that mark the way.

If the only campsite on Otter Lake is occupied, you'll have to continue on to Cummings Lake. There are several nice sites from which to choose, including a large site on a beautiful, pine-covered rocky point just one half-mile east of the 5-rod portage. Claim the first vacant site you see. Cummings Lake entertains visitors from the Crab Lake entry point. The farther east and south you paddle, the more likely you'll find the campsites to be occupied.

Day 3 (11 miles): Otter Lake, p. 5 rods, **Cummings Lake,** p. 35 rods, **Korb River, Korb Lake, Korb River,** p. 1-10 rods, **river, Little Crab Lake, Lunetta Creek, Lunetta Lake,** p. 60 rods, **Lunetta Creek,** p. 48 rods, **creek, Schlamn Lake.** After the previous rugged day, this day should be easy. So enjoy it. Contrary to the previous nine portages, all of these trails are well used and well maintained. None is difficult, although the 35-rod path may be wet at the southeast end, due to a beaver dam that floods the trail. The length of the short portage along the Korb River depends on the water level, ranging from a mere lift-over in high water to a 10-rod carry in very low water.

Tamarack and spruce bogs border the Korb River. In early summer, you may see many pitcher plants growing along the river's bank. Later in the season, water lilies may occupy the entire surface of the stream. Beaver lodges are in abundance throughout both sections of the river. So don't be surprised if occasional dams pop up along the course of the river.

The final portage (48 rods) starts out at a grassy, wet landing and follows a brushy trail for the first 20 rods. It then joins the path of an old logging road for the final 28 rods back to the shore of the creek. Just before the end of the portage, use caution crossing the creek on rocks and boulders. There is no bridge across the creek.

Day 4 (10 miles): Schlamn Lake, p. 210 rods, **Glenmore Lake,** p. 195 rods, **Western Lake,** p. 80 rods, **Buck Lake,** p. 250 rods, **Chad Lake,** p. 260 rods, **Pine Creek, Pine Lake.** With a total of 995 rods of portages, this is another tough day, especially if you cannot carry all of your gear in just one trip. If you take two trips, you will be walking more than nine miles this day. The first trail (210 rods) gains about 75 feet in the first 80 rods, and then follows a rather scenic ridge that is covered by a mature forest of large aspens, Norway pines and spruce trees. There is a panoramic view across a swamp just before the steep descent to Glenmore Lake. Watch for a huge, old white pine near the center of the next long portage (195 rods), which has a wet, boggy spot nearby. The 250-rod trail is plagued with rocks and roots, but it has a lovely stand of Norway pines about half way across. The final (and longest) portage of the day starts out with a short, but steep incline, and is mostly uphill for the first 140 rods. Watch out for slippery spots on sloping rocks, especially when wet. At the end, the trail drops rather steeply down to Pine Creek. You'll find a scenic overlook at the summit of a high rock slope adjacent to the portage trail. A short climb leads to a panoramic view across Pine Creek valley. In mid-July, you might also find a wealth of blueberries on the rocky slope.

There are several good campsites on Pine Lake. The best are in the northwest part of the lake; the most private are in the southeast end. A couple of small sand beaches along the east shoreline may be enticing to swimmers.

Day 5 (8 miles): Pine Lake, p. 260 rods, **Trout Lake,** p. 40 rods, **Vermilion Lake.** (See comments for Day 3, Route #1-1.)

Entry Point 4—Crab Lake

SEASONAL PERMITS: 375

POPULARITY RANK: 21st

DAILY QUOTA: 4

LOCATION: Crab Lake is accessible from big Burntside Lake, a very popular and populated lake about four miles northwest of Ely. Several public boat landings are situated around Burntside Lake. The newest, most convenient to Ely, and best access is located along the south shore near the center of the lake. From its junction with Highway 1-169, 4¾ miles west of the International Wolf Center in Ely, drive north on County Road 88 for 2.3 miles to County Road 404 (the Van Vac Road). Turn left and drive 1.2 miles west on this good, scenic, black-topped road to a DNR public access. The boat landing is 0.2 mile north (right) of the Van Vac Road. A parking lot adjacent to the boat landing is large enough to accommodate as many as 15 vehicles. There is an outhouse between the parking lot and the boat landing.

If there is a strong west wind, you might prefer starting your trip at a different public landing, located at the southwest end of Burntside Lake. From Highway 1-169, 8¾ miles west of the International Wolf Center in Ely, drive north on County Road 404 (the Wolf Lake Road) for 2.2 miles. The road starts out with a blacktop surface but changes to gravel after 1.6 miles. It leads to an inconspicuous one-lane road on the right, which, in turn, leads 0.2 mile north to the shore of Burntside Lake. The turnoff to this rough and winding gravel road may not be marked, but it is shared by private property identified with Fire Number 3319. The landing has very little space for parking and even less room to turn around. That's why I recommend the more convenient and spacious public landing off the Van Vac Road if wind is not a problem.

DESCRIPTION: Camping is prohibited at both public landings. There is a nice campground at Bearhead Lake

State Park, however, that offers a good place to spend the night prior to your canoe trip. It has well water, hot showers, and a nice sand beach for swimming. The park is located 7 miles south of Highway 1-169, about midway between Ely and Tower-Soudan. A fee is charged there, both for camping and for access to the park.

The Crab Lake Entry Point is a good way into the BWCA Wilderness for canoeists who don't mind hard work to achieve wilderness solitude. Entering here, however, has two drawbacks. First, you must cross a large, populated lake where motorboats flourish. Second, there is a 1-mile portage at the entrance to the Wilderness. Although the long portage is not difficult, the length itself makes this a challenging way to start a canoe trip, when the food pack is bulging and your muscles are not.

Nevertheless, a surprising number of people each year enter the Boundary Waters at Crab Lake. In terms of popularity, it ranks among the top third of all entry points. With a quota of 4 permits each day, however, it is usually not difficult to get a reservation. Only 60% of the available permits are actually used each summer. Motorboats are not permitted.

Although Burntside Lake is populated and sometimes noisy, it is also one of the more beautiful lakes in the area. It has over a hundred pine-covered, rocky islands that make navigation a challenge to most paddlers. If you can find your way across Burntside Lake, you can find your way anywhere in the BWCA Wilderness. Keep your compass handy and learn how to use it before launching your canoe onto this incredible lake. If you can find your way to the Crab Lake portage and cross it without suffering cardiac arrest, you should have no problem with the rest of your canoe trip.

ROUTE # 4-1: The Buck Lake Loop

　　　　　　3 Days, 28 Miles, 10 Lakes, 1 River, 1 Creek, 12 Portages

DIFFICULTY: Most rugged

FISHER MAPS: F-8, F-9

INTRODUCTION: This route is not suggested for anyone wanting a leisurely weekend outing. It is a tough loop. From the northwest corner of big Burntside Lake, you will first head north through Crab Lake to

Cummings Lake. Then you will head west and cross a 1½-mile-long portage to Buck Lake. From Buck Lake, then, you will begin your easterly return to Burntside Lake via a chain of smaller lakes that entertain few visitors. Each day, you will encounter a portage measuring at least a mile. The reward is seeing relatively few other people in the region beyond Crab Lake.

If you have any time and energy left at the end of each daily journey, you might enjoy some good fishing opportunities along the route. Anglers find bass and northern pike in Crab, Little Crab, Lunetta and Cummings lakes. Buck and Western lakes are considered pretty good walleye lakes.

Day 1 (11 miles): Burntside Lake, p. 320 rods, **Crab Lake,** p. 20 rods, **Little Crab Lake, Korb River,** p. 1-10 rods, **river, Korb Lake, Korb River,** p. 35 rods, **Cummings Lake.** Burntside Lake is a beautiful start for any trip, in spite of the motorboats and human habitation throughout the lake. Many of the islands have cabins and boat houses on them. The many islands serve as useful wind barriers, if needed.

For the most part, the mile-long path to Crab Lake is remarkably smooth, unusually wide and very well maintained. In 1996 a new trail was constructed at the beginning of the portage. It crosses private land for the first 70 rods and has a 10-rod boardwalk across a bog. The remainder of the trail follows the path of an old roadway that is smooth enough and wide enough to ride a bicycle across (if bicycles were allowed in the Wilderness). About midway across the portage, the trail skirts the edge of a swamp and crosses a small creek on a log bridge. Then the trail climbs gradually for nearly 100 rods to the crest of a large hill 90 feet above the swamp, before descending gradually to the southeast end of Crab Lake.

Don't be discouraged if you encounter several other groups on the first portage or if you see that most of the campsites on Crab Lake are occupied. It seems that most of the visitors using this entry point travel no farther than Crab Lake. The lakes and rivers to the west and north still offer good havens for paddlers in search of wilderness tranquillity. The region into which you are heading has traditionally been one of the least visited parts of the entire BWCA Wilderness.

The 20-rod and 35-rod portages also have excellent paths, although the longer trail may be wet at the beginning, thanks to a beaver dam spanning the Korb River. Depending on the water level and beaver activity, the short portage along the upper (southern) section of the Korb River could be as long as 10 rods during very low water or as short as 1 rod during high water. Tamarack and spruce bogs border the

Korb River. In early summer, you may see pitcher plants growing there, too. Later in the season, water lilies may occupy the entire surface of the river. Beaver lodges are in abundance throughout both sections of the river.

For an 11-mile day of paddling, plan to camp near the center of Cummings Lake. A lovely campsite lies at the west end of a long, pine-covered, rocky peninsula.

Day 2 (8 miles): Cummings Lake, p. 480 rods, **Buck Lake,** p. 80 rods, **Western Lake,** p. 195 rods, **Glenmore Lake,** p. 210 rods, **Schlamn Lake.** You're day starts with a long portage—4½ miles of hiking if you need two trips to get all your gear across. That could occupy much of your morning. Fortunately, the trail isn't as bad as it might appear— mostly level with just a few small undulations. It has a pretty good path, although windfalls could obstruct it if a portage crew hasn't been there in awhile. The first half-mile is the best, as the trail passes through a forest of Norway pines and skirts close to two grassy bogs on the north (right) side of the trail. During the second half-mile, the trail skirts the edge of a beaver pond at the base of a pine-covered ridge.

Western Lake is bordered by dead spruce trees and so is the only campsite there—not an attractive setting. The beginning of the 195-rod trail out of Western Lake is hard to see among the many windfalls and other shoreline obstructions. The location on the map, however, is accurate. The trail gradually climbs uphill, then passes through a wet, boggy area, before descending to Glenmore Lake. A huge, old white pine is near the midpoint of the portage.

The final portage of the day is also the most scenic and has the best path. The trail first climbs to a high ridge overlooking a large beaver pond and swamp. It then levels off for most of the distance, before it drops down to Schlamn Lake. It passes through a mature forest of large aspens, tall Norway pines and spruce, and occasional maple trees. The path is quite smooth most of the way, but rougher near Schlamn Lake.

Schlamn is a boreal-looking lake, surrounded primarily by jack pines and spruce, as well as by bogs. The only campsite there sits on a pine-covered rock outcrop and has two fair tent sites.

Day 3 (9 miles): Schlamn Lake, Lunetta Creek, p. 48 rods, **creek,** p. 60 rods, **Lunetta Lake, Lunetta Creek, Little Crab Lake,** p. 20 rods, **Crab Lake,** p. 320 rods, **Burntside Lake.** You must paddle a quarter mile into Lunetta Creek before accessing the 48-rod portage. The trail starts out on the bed of an old road for the first 28 rods, soon crossing the small creek. There is no bridge over the creek, just large rocks on which to step. Step carefully! After 28 rods, the trail veers off the old road to the left on a brushy path, which ends at a grassy, wet and mucky landing.

The beginning of the next portage (60 rods) is easy to miss. Watch carefully for the junction of another small creek on the left. Paddle into that creek and watch immediately for the portage landing on the right. The trail has a good path. If you paddle past the portage landing, Lunetta Creek will basically dead-end in a large bog shortly thereafter. You will have to turn around and look for the portage a little harder the next time.

ROUTE # 4-2: The Little Trout Lake Loop

6 Days, 47 Miles, 14 Lakes, 2 Rivers, 2 Creeks, 23 Portages

DIFFICULTY: Most rugged

FISHER MAPS: F-8, F-9

INTRODUCTION: This route is not for weak or out-of-shape canoeists. From the northwest corner of big Burntside Lake, you will first head north through Crab Lake to Cummings Lake. Then the route veers toward the west and leads down the remote Little Indian Sioux River to Little Trout Lake. From there, you will steer southeastward to cross a chain of smaller lakes and streams that entertain few visitors, before returning to Crab and Burntside lakes. En route, you will cross seven portages that each measure more than one half-mile and three that measure at least a mile. Furthermore, you will be crossing more than a third of the portages (9) on just one day.

If you are up to the challenge, though, you are in for a delightful journey through a part of the BWCA Wilderness that hosts very few visitors. If, on the other hand, you're not in the very best shape or you are with a group of less experienced paddlers, you should consider adding a day to this route. Unofficial campsites are found at several places along the Little Indian Sioux River. To break up a long day on the river into two shorter days, you can do so by getting *prior authorization* from the USFS to spend a night in the Canthook Primitive Management Area (see Chapter 1), which includes part of the Little Indian Sioux River. Without prior authorization, however, you are not permitted to camp along the river.

Wildlife abounds along the winding Little Indian Sioux River, as do fish in many of the lakes along this route. There are smallmouth bass in Crab, Cummings, Otter, Chad and Trout lakes. Walleyes also populate Buck, Little Trout and Trout lakes. Northern pike are found in nearly all of the lakes on this route.

Beware the possibility of low water in the Little Indian Sioux River, particularly during late summer or an unusually dry year. At times, it could be too low to carry a loaded canoe. You might get through, but it could take much longer than expected. Consult with the Forest Service before starting out on this route.

Day 1 (6 miles): Burntside Lake, p. 320 rods, **Crab Lake,** p. 20 rods, **Little Crab Lake.** (See comments for Day 1, Route #4-1, paragraphs 1-3.) There is only one campsite on Little Crab Lake, and it is a popular one. It is a spacious site in a lovely stand of Norway pines with a sunset exposure. Claim it early. This part of the wilderness entertains frequent visitors. If that campsite is occupied, or if you prefer to get off the main route, you could detour to a nice (but smaller) campsite on Lunetta Lake. That would add an extra mile of paddling for this day, but there would be plenty of time to make it up tomorrow. Otherwise, if you continue on to Korb Lake, you could easily paddle right past the only campsite on that lake. It is situated atop a rock ledge high above the north shore of the lake.

Day 2 (8 miles): Little Crab Lake, Korb River, p. 1-10 rods, **river, Korb Lake, Korb River,** p. 35 rods, **Cummings Lake,** p. 5 rods, **Otter Lake.** (See comments for Day 1, Route #4-1, paragraph 4.) This is the easiest day of your trip, unless strong west wind is a problem on Cummings Lake. The object is to camp as close to the Little Indian Sioux River as possible, because there are no designated campsites along the river. If the only campsite on Otter Lake is occupied, you'll have to return to Cummings Lake. There are several nice sites from which to choose, including a large site on a beautiful, pine-covered rocky point just one half-mile east of the 5-rod portage.

Day 3 (13 miles): Otter Lake, p. 120 rods, **Little Indian Sioux River,** p. 35 rods, **river,** p. 34 rods, **river,** p. 40 rods, **river,** p. 70 rods, **river, rapids, river, rapids, river,** p. 12 rods, **river,** p. 32 rods, **river, p.** 32 rods, **river,** p. 376 rods, **Little Trout Lake.** With 9 portages this day (the last one over a mile long), this is by far the most rugged day of the trip. Not much traffic passes this way and the portage trails are sometimes hard to see. Most are brushy and windfalls could be problem. The portages are clustered into two groups: five portages and a rapids right away, then a long stretch of river paddling (perhaps 2 hours), followed by another rapids and four more portages. Most of the portages are quite level and dry, with fairly good paths. Only the first 32-rod portage (the 7th carry of the day) has any noticeable elevation change—a rather steep descent about half way along the trail. It is also one of the more scenic portages, with a good view across the rapids to a pine-covered ridge on the other side.

Soon after the next 32-rod portage, watch very carefully for the start of the long trail to Little Trout Lake. The remains of an old dock crib on the west (left) side of the river are the only indication of the beginning of the portage on the grassy bank of the river. It's easy to miss if you are not watching carefully. The trail starts out in a bog on a wet, spongy path for the first 15 rods, but it soon hits dry ground. It is quite level and has a surprisingly good path most of the way to Little Trout Lake, with only a couple of other boggy wet spots along the way. The put-in is at a sandy beach. You may have to walk your canoe out into the shallow, weedy lake before you can paddle away.

Don't panic at the end of this long day if you see several canoes on the lake. There is a good chance the anglers occupying them are camped on Trout Lake nearby. The campsites are generally better on Trout Lake, but if it's late in the day, you should claim the first site you see on Little Trout Lake.

Day 4 (7 miles): Little Trout Lake, Little Trout Creek, Trout Lake, p. 60 rods, Pine Creek, p. 260 rods, Chad Lake, p. 250 rods, Buck Lake. Although this is a much easier day than the previous day, those two long portages do create a challenge. The creek connecting Little Trout and Trout lakes is very shallow, and there could be a beaver dam obstructing your path that requires a lift-over. Pine Creek, on the other hand, is plenty deep and much wider. The 60-rod portage could be shortened to 40 rods when there is plenty of water at the mouth of the creek. Try paddling up the creek past the first landing for 20 rods to the next landing on the right. The path is excellent—quite smooth and virtually level. The put-in at the other end, however, is awkward and muddy.

The first long portage starts just to the east (right) of a steep rock slope. The trail first climbs rather steeply to a rocky ridge. It has a good path, but it is slippery when wet. The last half of the trail, however, is generally downhill with a path that is plagued with rocks and roots, as well as a couple of muddy spots. There is a short, steep drop at the end. Use caution on the slippery rock!

The last portage starts out with a fairly steep but short climb to detour past a swamp. Then it follows a fairly good path on a gentle slope up and over a low hill. The midpoint of the trail is highlighted by a lovely stand of tall Norway pines. The remainder of the path has rocks and roots. The put-in at Buck Lake is quite shallow and rocky.

The only Buck Lake campsite shown on the 1997 Fisher map is across from the portage landing. It is a nice site for one tent, on a rock ledge with a west exposure. It affords a nice view of the pine-covered rocky slope on the other side of this long and narrow lake. There is another USFS campsite farther down the lake, across from the portage to Western Lake that was not showing on the Fisher map.

Day 5 (7 miles): Buck Lake, p. 80 rods, **Western Lake,** p. 195 rods, **Glenmore Lake,** p. 210 rods, **Schlamn Lake, Lunetta Creek,** p. 48 rods, **creek,** p. 60 rods, **Lunetta Lake, Lunetta Creek, Little Crab Lake.** The first portage climbs over a hill, then skirts the edge of a bog on a fair path.

Western Lake is bordered by dead spruce trees and so is the only campsite there—not an attractive setting. The beginning of the 195-rod trail out of Western Lake is hard to see among the many windfalls and other shoreline obstructions. The location on the map, however, is accurate. The trail gradually climbs uphill, then passes through a wet, boggy area, before descending to Glenmore Lake. A huge, old white pine is near the midpoint of the portage.

The longest portage of the day is also the most scenic and has the best path. The trail first climbs to a high ridge overlooking a large beaver pond and swamp. It then levels off for most of the distance, before it drops down to Schlamn Lake. It passes through a mature forest of large aspens, tall Norway pines and spruce, and occasional maple trees. The path is quite smooth most of the way, but rougher near Schlamn Lake.

You must paddle a quarter mile into Lunetta Creek before accessing the 48-rod portage. The trail starts out on the bed of an old road for the first 28 rods, crossing the small creek soon after the start. There is no bridge over the creek, just large rocks on which to step. Step carefully! After 28 rods, the trail veers off the old road to the left on a brushy path, which ends at a grassy, wet and mucky landing.

The beginning of the next portage (60 rods) is easy to miss. Watch carefully for the junction of another small creek on the left. Paddle into that creek and watch immediately for the portage landing on the right. The trail has a good path. If you paddle past the portage landing, Lunetta Creek will basically dead-end in a large bog shortly thereafter. You'll simply have to turn around and look for the portage a little harder.

Day 6 (6 miles): Little Crab Lake, p. 20 rods, **Crab Lake,** p. 320 rods, **Burntside Lake.** This should all look familiar from your first day. This time, however, the long trail connecting Crab and Burntside lakes is mostly downhill after a gradual climb at the beginning. After what you have experienced so far on this route, it's an easy last day.

Entry Point 6—Slim Lake

SEASONAL PERMITS: 150

POPULARITY RANK: 36th

DAILY QUOTA: 2

LOCATION: Slim Lake is 8 miles northwest of Ely, 2 miles west of the Echo Trail and ½ mile north of Burntside Lake. To get there, follow County Road 116 (the Echo Trail) 8.9 miles north and west from County Road 88. Turn left onto County Road 644 (the North Arm Road) and follow this winding road (first black-topped, then gravel) southwest for 2.3 miles to the public access for Burntside Lake on the left. A primitive, one-lane road leads north (right) from there for 0.2 mile to its end, where a beaver dam has flooded the road.

DESCRIPTION: A small parking area accommodates 3-4 vehicles. From there, a short boardwalk across the boggy creek marks the beginning of a good 80-rod portage trail to the east shore of Slim Lake. It has a wide and easy path on the former roadbed that ascends gently to the lake, skirting a creek and a beaver pond on the left side of the trail.

Slim is a slender, pretty lake with a rocky shoreline covered by Norway pines and birch trees. It is an easily accessible entry point that entertains as many day-use visitors as those with overnight travel permits. Although only two groups of campers per day may enter the wilderness here, the demand for these permits is even less than the supply. Less than half of the available overnight travel permits are used each summer. While Slim Lake ranks high among entry points for the number of day-use visitors, many of the permits are issued to hikers who can access only the south end of the lake.

Motors are prohibited through this entry point. Although it is close to one of the most popular lakes in the area—Burntside Lake— you will quickly escape into a genuine feeling of wilderness solitude and will experience a high-quality expedition via either of the two routes suggested below. Both of the suggested routes end by crossing Burntside Lake. It could be bustling with motorized traffic, and there are several private cabins, resorts and camps along the final six miles of the expeditions. All that activity might seem dismal for these otherwise high-quality wilderness trips, were it not for the exceptional beauty of that island-studded lake.

Camping is prohibited at the access to Slim Lake. Fenske Lake Campground, located just 3 miles away toward Ely on the Echo Trail, provides a good place to spend the night before your canoe trip. A fee is charged for camping there.

ROUTE #6-1: The Big Moose Loop

4 Days, 31 Miles, 12 Lakes, 2 Rivers, 12 Portages

DIFFICULTY: Most rugged

FISHER MAP: F-9

INTRODUCTION: This is a good route for anyone who likes quiet, isolated lakes and who doesn't mind hard work to get to them. The short, rugged journey will take you northwest from the Slim Lake portage, through a lightly traveled chain of lakes, to the north edge of this part of the BWCA Wilderness at Big Moose Lake. Turning south, then, you will cross a long portage to enter Cummings Lake. From there, you will meander through a series of smaller lakes and streams to exit the BWCAW across a mile-long portage to Burntside Lake. Following its north shoreline, you will finally paddle back to your origin at the Slim Lake portage.

Do not attempt this route unless you are in the very best physical condition. When finished, you will have spent as much time walking on portage trails as you did paddling on the adjoining lakes. Three portages exceed 1½ miles and a fourth is exactly a mile. That is *one big portage* each day. It is largely *because* of these portages, however, that this route is so enticing to the strong wilderness enthusiast. Only a dedicated canoeist will tackle the route. You will see few, if any, other canoeists along that portion of the route within the BWCA Wilderness, where motors are not allowed. You will feel truly isolated from the rest of the world, even though you will never be more than 5 miles from a road or a resort.

Anglers will find northern pike, walleyes, smallmouth bass and pan fish along the route, and the persistent angler may even pull lake trout from the depths of Burntside Lake.

Day 1 (6 miles): P. 80 rods, **Slim Lake**, p. 77 rods, **Rice Lake**, p. 130 rods, **Hook Lake**, p. 600 rods, **Big Rice Lake.** Portages total 887 rods this day. That's 2,661 rods (over 8 miles) of walking if you cannot transport all of your gear in one carry. All portages, except the first, are very lightly traveled. The second portage (77 rods) starts out on grass-covered boulders and crosses a creek twice. Walk carefully on the rocky, grassy path. You may have trouble seeing the pathway during your 600-rod trek to Big Rice Lake. The trail gains about 50 feet elevation during the first half-mile, but descends over a hundred feet during the final mile to Big Rice Lake. Walk quietly and you may see moose along the trail. You will surely see more *tracks* of moose than of other people.

Big Rice is a very shallow lake (maximum of 5 feet deep) that is bordered by bog along the west shoreline. If the only campsite on the lake is occupied, you will have to proceed down the Portage River to Lapond Lake, where there is another campsite. Anglers may want to try their luck for the big northern pike that inhabit Big Rice Lake.

Day 2 (7 miles): **Big Rice Lake, Portage River,** p. 35 rods, **river, Lapond Lake, Portage River,** p. 145 rods, **Duck Lake,** p. 480 rods, **Big Moose Lake.** This day may appear easy compared to the first day, with only three portages totaling 660 rods. But that is still over 6 miles of walking if you need two trips to get your gear across the portages. Most of this day you'll be paddling on shallow water in a region dominated by bog—when you're not walking, that is.

All of the portages are seldom used, and windfalls may slow your treks considerably, particularly during the spring (before the portage crews are out). The first short portage bypasses small rapids where the Portage River drops 12 feet. It appears to be popular among bald eagles as a fishing spot in early spring. When the water level is low, you may have to use a 2-rod "lift-over" portage to get back onto the river from the west side of Lapond Lake.

The first 45 rods of the 145-rod portage are through a spruce bog. The rest of the trail is dry, however, and it ends at a rock outcropping that affords a good place for lunch or a snack before continuing. It's about the only place on Duck Lake where you could "pull over," since muskeg borders most of the southern and western shorelines. The final long trail also begins on muskeg for about 50 rods, then climbs over a couple of hills en route to the east shore of Big Moose Lake.

There are a couple of nice campsites near the north end of Big Moose Lake. Don't delay in claiming one. Other paddlers have access to this big lake via the Moose River and the Big Moose Lake Trail.

Anglers should find walleyes in the lake, and they might even find a few smallmouth bass and northern pike.

Day 3 (9 miles): Big Moose Lake, p. 600 rods, **Cummings Lake,** p. 35 rods, **Korb River, Korb Lake, Korb River,** p. 1-10 rods, **river, Little Crab Lake.** You get to stretch your legs on another long portage right away this day. If you cannot carry all your gear in just one trip, you'll be walking over 5½ miles before lunch. The trail is not as bad as it might seem, though. It begins and ends on a rather hilly note, but follows the crest of a rather level ridge along most of its course. The path is generally good, but, as on the portages the previous day, it could be plagued with windfalls if a portage crew has not been there in awhile.

After that first carry (which could take all morning) the going should be easy. The 35-rod path may be wet at the southeast end, however, due to a beaver dam that floods the trail. The length of the short portage along the Korb River depends on the water level, ranging from a mere lift-over in high water to a 10-rod carry in low water.

Tamarack and spruce bogs border the Korb River. In early summer, you may see many pitcher plants growing along the river's bank. Later in the season, water lilies may occupy the entire surface of the stream. Beaver lodges are in abundance throughout both sections of the river. So don't be surprised if occasional dams pop up along the course of the river.

There is only one campsite on Little Crab Lake, and it is a popular one. It is a spacious site in a lovely stand of Norway pines with a sunset exposure. Claim it early. This part of the wilderness entertains frequent visitors from the Crab Lake Entry Point. If that campsite is occupied, or if you prefer to get off the main route, you could paddle west through Lunetta Creek to another nice (but smaller) campsite on Lunetta Lake. That will add about a mile of paddling, but no more portages. There are also several nice campsites on Crab Lake, but there is consistent demand for those sites. This is the busiest part of the entire loop that is within the BWCAW.

Day 4 (9 miles): Little Crab Lake, p. 20 rods, **Crab Lake,** p. 320 rods, **Burntside Lake.** Your final portage is appropriate for this route—one full mile. Compared to the previous long trails, however, this one will surely seem easy. After climbing gently for the first 60 rods, it's all downhill. Most of the descent is during the next 100 rods, when the trail drops about 90 feet to skirt the edge of a beaver swamp. After crossing a small creek on a log bridge, then, the trail continues on a more gradual descent to the northwest shore of Burntside Lake. Most of the trail follows the path of an old roadway that is smooth enough and wide enough to ride a bicycle across (if bicycles were allowed in the Wilderness). A new trail, however, was constructed across private land for the final 70 rods, including a 10-rod boardwalk over a bog.

Burntside Lake is populated with many private cabins and several resorts, and you will probably hear motorboats along the final 6 miles of this route. But the lake is also one of the most beautiful lakes in the area, with over a hundred pine-covered, rocky islands. The many islands serve as useful wind barriers, if needed. It is a confusing lake, so watch your map carefully for the channel that veers northeast from the main body of big Burntside Lake to its North Arm.

You can leave your canoe and gear at the boat landing adjacent to the Echo Trail. Then walk ¼ mile up the one-lane road to get your car at the Slim Lake parking spot.

ROUTE #6-2:	**The Giant Portages Loop**
	7 Days, 57 Miles, 20 Lakes, 2 Rivers, 3 Creeks, 28 Portages
DIFFICULTY:	Most rugged
FISHER MAP:	F-8, F-9
INTRODUCTION:	If you want to escape from summer crowds, and tough physical challenges don't discourage you, this is the route to choose. The rugged journey will take you northwest from the Slim Lake portage, through a lightly traveled chain of lakes, to the north edge of this part of the BWCA Wilderness at Big Moose Lake. After portaging south to Cummings Lake, then, you will steer west and follow the meandering Little Indian Sioux River to the long portage that connects the river to Little Trout Lake. After one night in a busy part of the Wilderness, you will then paddle and portage southeast through a chain of lightly traveled smaller lakes until you exit the Boundary Waters at the Crab Lake portage. From there, six more miles of paddling will return you to the Slim Lake portage at the north end of big Burntside Lake.

As on the previous route, when finished you will have spent as much time walking on portage trails as paddling on the adjoining lakes and streams. Nine portages exceed half a mile, and five of those are at least a mile. It is largely because of these portages, however, that this route

Beaver dam on the Little Indian Sioux River

is so enticing to the strong wilderness tripper. Only a dedicated (some might say "crazy") canoeist will tackle this route. It is not unusual to see no other canoeists along much of the route where motors are prohibited.

If you are up to the challenge, though, you are in for a delightful journey through a part of the BWCA Wilderness that hosts very few visitors. If, on the other hand, you're not in the very best shape or with a group of less experienced paddlers, you should consider adding a day to this route. Unofficial campsites are found at a several places along the Little Indian Sioux River. To break up a long day on the river into two shorter days, you can get *prior authorization* from the USFS to spend a night in the Canthook Primitive Management Area (see Chapter 1), which includes part of the Little Indian Sioux River. Without prior authorization, however, you are not permitted to camp along the river.

Anglers will find northern pike, walleyes, smallmouth bass and pan fish along the route, and the persistent angler might even pull lake trout from the depths of Trout and Burntside lakes.

Beware the possibility of low water in the Little Indian Sioux River, particularly during late summer or an unusually dry year. At times, it could be too low to transport a loaded canoe. You might get through, but it could take much longer than expected. Consult with the Forest Service before starting out on this route.

Day 1 (6 miles): P. 80 rods, **Slim Lake**, p. 77 rods, **Rice Lake**, p. 130 rods, **Hook Lake**, p. 600 rods, **Big Rice Lake**. (See comments for Day 1, Route #6-1.)

Day 2 (7 miles): **Big Rice Lake, Portage River**, p. 35 rods, **river, Lapond Lake, Portage River**, p. 145 rods, **Duck Lake**, p. 480 rods, **Big Moose Lake**. (See comments for Day 2, Route #6-1.)

Day 3 (8 miles): **Big Moose Lake**, p. 480 rods, **Cummings Lake**, p. 5 rods, **Otter Lake**. You get to stretch your legs on another long portage right away this day. The trail is not as bad as it might seem, though. It begins and ends on a rather hilly note, but follows the crest of a rather level ridge for most of its course. The path is generally good, but, as on the portages the previous day, it could be plagued with windfalls if a portage crew has not been there in awhile.

If the only campsite on Otter Lake is occupied, you'll have to return to Cummings Lake. There are several nice sites from which to choose, including a large site on a beautiful, pine-covered rocky point just one half-mile east of the 5-rod portage. There are no designated campsites along the Little Indian Sioux River. Try to camp as close to Otter Lake as possible to enable an early start down the Little Indian Sioux River the next day.

Day 4 (13 miles): **Otter Lake**, p. 120 rods, **Little Indian Sioux River**, p. 35 rods, **river**, p. 34 rods, **river**, p. 40 rods, **river**, p. 70 rods, **river, rapids, river, rapids, river**, p. 12 rods, **river**, p. 32 rods, **river**, p. 32 rods, **river**, p. 376 rods, **Little Trout Lake**. (See comments for Day 3, Route #4-2.)

Day 5 (7 miles): **Little Trout Lake, Little Trout Creek, Trout Lake**, p. 60 rods, **Pine Creek**, p. 260 rods, **Chad Lake**, p. 250 rods, **Buck Lake**. (See comments for Day 4, Route #4-2.)

Day 6 (7 miles): **Buck Lake**, p. 80 rods, **Western Lake**, p. 195 rods, **Glenmore Lake**, p. 210 rods, **Schlamn Lake, Lunetta Creek**, p. 48 rods, **creek**, p. 60 rods, **Lunetta Lake, Lunetta Creek, Little Crab Lake**. (See comments for Day 5, Route #4-2.)

Day 7 (9 miles): **Little Crab Lake**, p. 20 rods, **Crab Lake**, p. 320 rods, **Burntside Lake**. (See comments for Day 4, Route #6-1.)

Entry Point 7—Big Lake

SEASONAL PERMITS: 75

POPULARITY RANK: 51st

DAILY QUOTA: 2

LOCATION: Big Lake is located 12 miles northwest of Ely, just south of the Echo Trail. Drive north on the Echo Trail 17.3 miles from County Road 88, one mile past the turnoff to Lodge of Whispering Pines. Turn left onto Forest Road 1027, which leads 0.3 mile south to the boat landing on the north shore of Big Lake. A small parking lot adjacent to the landing will accommodate 10-12 vehicles. An outhouse is nearby.

Drive with caution on the narrow, winding Echo Trail, particularly for the last 7½ miles. Traffic is not heavy, but there is nearly always some, because of two resorts on Big Lake and more than a dozen BWCAW entry points along the road.

DESCRIPTION: The public campground at Fenske Lake, 10 miles closer to Ely on the Echo Trail, provides a good place to spend the night before your canoe trip. A fee is charged to camp there.

Big Lake is the most "available" canoeing entry point in the western region of the Boundary Waters. Only a quarter of its available permits are actually used during the quota season. Although motors are not allowed to enter the BWCAW from Big Lake, Big Lake itself is outside the wilderness boundary. There are two resorts and a few cabins on the north shore. In spite of that, it is a peaceful entry point. Once you leave the big lake, you aren't likely to see many other paddlers in this region—either campers or day-trippers. So, if you are looking for a quiet, easily accessible wilderness retreat, or if other entry points are booked up, consider Big Lake as your starting point.

ROUTE # 7-1: The Big Rice Route

2 Days, 13 Miles, 6 Lakes, 1 River, 1 Creek, 5 Portages

DIFFICULTY: Challenging

FISHER MAPS: F-9

INTRODUCTION: This short route leads south from Big Lake, through an interesting variety of canoeing terrain, to the Slim Lake entry point. Along the way, you will experience lakes ranging in size from quite large to very small, a narrow, winding stream, and one of the longest portages in the region. Were it not for that long, rugged portage, the route would be quite easy.

From the southwest corner of Big Lake, you will follow the Portage River south, through Lapond Lake, to Big Rice Lake. Most of the next morning will be spent on a portage measuring nearly 2 miles. Then, after catching your breath, you will head east across Hook and Rice lakes to Slim Lake. The route ends near the south end of Slim Lake, about 13 miles by road from the starting point. So you will have to make prior arrangements to leave your vehicle at the Slim Lake Entry Point.

You will be paddling most of the time on shallow water where northern pike lurk beneath the surface. Anglers may also find walleyes in Big and Slim lakes.

Day 1 (7 miles): Big Lake, creek, Portage River, Lapond Lake, Portage River, p. 35 rods, river, Big Rice Lake. This day offers a lovely introduction to the BWCA Wilderness. Much of Big Lake's shoreline is cloaked with middle-aged Norway pines and some scattered large white pines, all of which yield to a boggy shoreline of muskeg and scattered spruce trees at the southwest end of the lake. A tiny creek there leads west to the Portage River.

When the water level is low in the river, it may be necessary to take a 2-rod portage ("lift-over") at the point where it drains Lapond Lake. Both Lapond and Big Rice lakes are quite shallow (maximum of 5 feet) and bordered to a large extent by spruce bogs. During much of the canoeing season, they may, at first glance, look more like meadows than lakes—nearly covered with vegetation (including lily pads and wild rice). Each lake has only once campsite, but there is seldom any competition for them.

If you get a late start and don't mind portaging, you can probably access Lapond Lake quickest by taking the 150-rod portage from the southwest end of Big Lake. It climbs over a low hill on a fairly good path and ends at a small peninsula on the north shore of Lapond Lake. A lovely campsite with space for three or four tents lies in a pine grove on the east shore of that shallow lake.

Day 2 (6 miles): **Big Rice Lake,** p. 600 rods, **Hook Lake,** p. 130 rods, **Rice Lake,** p. 77 rods, **Slim Lake,** p. 80 rods. That first portage of the day is what makes this short route "challenging." Otherwise, it would be an easy trip. The long trail gains 120 feet in several short ascents during the first mile, then gradually descends about 50 feet during the final half-mile. Seldom used, it may be brushy and plagued with windfalls at times.

If you decide to get this over with on the first day (or if the only campsites on Lapond and Big Rice lakes are already occupied and you *must* forge onward), you will find a very pretty campsite near the south end of Hook Lake. There are not enough tent sites there, however, to accommodate a large group of campers.

During late summer, Rice Lake may be nearly clogged with wild rice. The rocky trail connecting Rice and Slim lakes crosses a small creek twice and ends in a small field of grass-covered boulders. Watch your step!

Slim is a lovely lake with a rocky shoreline that is covered mostly with Norway pines and birch trees. A few maples also add bright red color to the autumn foliage. An excellent footpath connects the southeast shore of the lake with a small parking lot a quarter mile to the east. If time permits and the season is right, you might want to pick blueberries before ending your trip. During mid-summer, there is often a wealth of berries atop the bare, rocky ridge bordering Slim Lake, just north of the portage to Burntside Lake.

You could further delay the end of your canoe trip by taking a short side trip first. An outstanding panorama can be seen from a high, rock ridge ¼ mile south of Slim Lake, referred to locally as "Old Baldy." A blazed trail begins at a Forest Service campsite on the south shore of the lake. It winds its way around the south tip of the lake and up through the thickly wooded hillside. Watch carefully for a spur trail to the left that leads up to the rocky summit. The main trail continues on for nearly a mile to County Road 644 across from Camp Du Nord.

ROUTE # 7-2: The Big Trout Route

6 Days, 51 Miles, 16 Lakes, 2 Rivers, 4 Creeks, 23 Portages

DIFFICULTY: Most rugged

FISHER MAPS: F-8, F-9

INTRODUCTION: This physically challenging route covers much of the BWCA Wilderness region south of the Echo

Trail. Because of tough, long portages that discourage the casual canoeist, along with quotas
that allow only a few groups per day into this
region, it is a good place to escape from the summer crowds.

From Big Lake, the route first takes you southwest through Duck and
Big Moose lakes to Cummings Lake, in the heart of this region. From
this land of big lakes and long portages, you will then escape westward
by paddling down the winding Little Indian Sioux River. Where the
river bends north, you will portage farther west to Little Trout Lake.
After paddling south to big Trout Lake, you will steer eastward and follow a chain of smaller, lightly traveled lakes and creeks to exit the
Boundary Waters at the Crab Lake portage. The final six miles of this
journey will be along the north shore of Burntside Lake. You'll take out
at the northeast end of the lake near the Slim Lake portage, where your
vehicle should be waiting to transport you back to "reality."

When finished, you will have spent as much time on portages as
on water. Four of the trails measure at least a mile, and six more are
longer than half a mile each. On the fringe of the Wilderness, you may
encounter some noise from motorboats and some competition for
campsites (Crab and Little Trout lakes, in particular). In the isolated
interior part of this region, however, you are not likely to see or hear
many other travelers, though you may see moose, deer and many other
types of wildlife.

For anyone who likes to go where few others dare, and to whom
portages are welcome challenges rather than dreaded obstacles, this
route is a good choice. Along the way, if there is any energy left at the
end of each day, the anglers in your group will have excellent opportunities to ply the waters for walleyes, northern pike and smallmouth
bass.

If you are not in the very best shape or with a group of less experienced paddlers, you should consider adding a day to this route.
Unofficial campsites are found at several places along the Little Indian
Sioux River. To break up a long day on the river into two shorter days,
you can get *prior authorization* from the USFS to spend a night in the
Canthook Primitive Management Area (see Chapter 1), which includes
part of the Little Indian Sioux River. Without prior authorization, however, you are not permitted to camp along the river.

Beware the possibility of low water in the Little Indian Sioux
River, particularly during late summer or an unusually dry year. At
times, it could be too low to carry a loaded canoe. You might get
through, but it could take much longer than expected. Consult with
the Forest Service before starting out on this route.

The route ends about 13 miles from the starting point, so you will have to arrange to leave your vehicle at the take-out point on Burntside Lake (see the directions to the Slim Lake Entry Point). Or, if you prefer, you could extend this route two more days by adding the reverse of Route #7-1, thus making the journey a complete loop. If that is your choice, you could spend your sixth night at a USFS campsite in the narrow channel of Burntside Lake that leads to the North Arm.

Day 1 (7 miles): Big Lake, creek, Portage River, p. 145 rods, **Duck Lake,** p. 480 rods, **Big Moose Lake.** Like the first day of the previous route, this is a day of canoeing contrasts, with big and small lakes, tiny streams and a very long portage. When you arrive at the junction of the unnamed creek and the Portage River, bear left and watch for the portage trail leading to Duck Lake less than ¹⁄₁₀ mile from the creek junction. The trail continues westbound at a point where the river bends to the south. Be prepared for wet feet as the trail crosses a spruce bog for the first 45 rods. It then climbs over a low rise through a deteriorating forest plagued with windfalls, and ends at a nice rock outcropping on the east shore of Duck Lake. The final long trail also begins on muskeg for about 50 rods, then climbs over a couple of hills en route to the east shore of Big Moose Lake.

There are a couple of nice campsites near the north end of Big Moose Lake. Don't delay in claiming one. Other paddlers have access to this big lake via the Moose River and the Big Moose Lake Trail. Anglers should find walleyes in the lake, and they might even find a few smallmouth bass and northern pike.

Day 2 (8 miles): Big Moose Lake, p. 480 rods, **Cummings Lake,** p. 5 rods, **Otter Lake.** (See comments for Day 3, Route #6-2.)

Day 3 (13 miles): Otter Lake, p. 120 rods, **Little Indian Sioux River,** p. 35 rods, **river,** p. 34 rods, **river,** p. 40 rods, **river,** p. 70 rods, **river, rapids, river, rapids, river,** p. 12 rods, **river,** p. 32 rods, **river,** p. 32 rods, **river,** p. 376 rods, **Little Trout Lake.** (See comments for Day 3, Route #4-2.)

Day 4 (7 miles): Little Trout Lake, Little Trout Creek, Trout Lake, p. 60 rods, **Pine Creek,** p. 260 rods, **Chad Lake,** p. 250 rods, **Buck Lake.** (See comments for Day 4, Route #4-2.)

Day 5 (7 miles): Buck Lake, p. 80 rods, **Western Lake,** p. 195 rods, **Glenmore Lake,** p. 210 rods, **Schlamn Lake, Lunetta Creek,** p. 48 rods, **creek,** p. 60 rods, **Lunetta Lake, Lunetta Creek, Little Crab Lake.** (See comments for Day 5, Route #4-2.)

Day 6 (9 miles): Little Crab Lake, p. 20 rods, **Crab Lake,** p. 320 rods, **Burntside Lake.** (See comments for Day 4, Route #6-1.)

Entry Point 8—Moose River South

SEASONAL PERMITS: 74

POPULARITY RANK: 52nd

DAILY QUOTA: 1

LOCATION: The Moose River begins its winding course at the northwest corner of Big Moose Lake, 15 miles northwest of Ely, and slowly meanders north for about 10 miles to Nina Moose Lake. The Echo Trail crosses the river about midway between the two lakes. One access, a mile north of the Echo Trail, serves trippers paddling toward Nina Moose Lake via the Moose River North entry point. To find the public access for canoeists who wish to paddle south to Big Moose Lake, drive 22.2 miles northwest on the Echo Trail from County Road 88 to its intersection with Forest Route 464. Turn left there and follow F.R. 464 (a 1-lane road with turnouts) an additional 3½ miles to the Moose River. Watch for moose along the road. This is a good area in which to see them.

Designated parking space, just east of the bridge, is limited to about 3 vehicles. There is seldom much competition for the space.

DESCRIPTION: The Moose River is a narrow, shallow, meandering stream. During dry periods, its navigation could be awkward, but probably not impossible. Unlike its northern counterpart, the Moose River South entry point entertains few Wilderness visitors, including day-trippers. That is due, most likely, to the long portages leading east and south from Big Moose Lake. Nevertheless, with only one permit issued each day, you should make your reservation early if your trip will start on Friday, Saturday, Sunday or Monday. About half of the available permits are issued each summer, and many of those are for weekends.

Among those few who do enter the Wilderness here, only a small percentage continue beyond Big Moose Lake, which is a pleasant weekend destination in itself. Consequently, a high-quality wilderness experience can be found on either of the routes described below. Motorboats are not allowed to enter the BWCAW here.

The Lake Jeanette Campground is 12 miles farther west on the Echo Trail from its junction with Forest Route 464. The Fenske Lake Campground is not much farther away, located 8 miles up the Echo Trail from County Road 88, about 18 miles from this entry point. Either one provides a convenient place to spend the night prior to the start of your trip. A camping fee is charged at both USFS campgrounds.

ROUTE # 8-1: The Duck Lake Route
2 Days, 12 Miles, 3 Lakes, 2 Rivers, 1 Creek, 4 Portages

DIFFICULTY: Challenging

FISHER MAPS: F-9

INTRODUCTION: This short route could probably be completed in just one long day by strong and experienced paddlers. Spread over two full days, however, it is a more tolerable—but still challenging—route for most canoeists. With ambitious hikers or avid anglers in your group, you might even want to add a third day. From F.R. 464, you will first meander up the Moose River to Big Moose Lake, with two portages along the way. From there, you will negotiate a long portage to Duck Lake, and then another, shorter portage to the Portage River. After passing through a tiny creek joining the Portage River with Big Lake, you will paddle across the west side of Big Lake to the public landing at the lake's north end.

You should have a car waiting for you at the Big Lake landing. Otherwise someone will have to walk 8½ miles back to the Moose River South entry point (not unreasonable if you have a jogger in your group).

You probably won't see many people along this route while in the BWCA Wilderness, but there is a pretty good chance of seeing a moose or two anywhere along the route. Big Lake lies outside the Boundary

Waters and is the only part of the route where motorboats are permitted. It has two resorts and a few private cabins along the north shore.

There are good populations of walleyes in Big Moose and Big lakes. Anglers might also hook some northern pike or smallmouth bass. Don't waste your bait, however, in shallow Duck Lake.

Day 1 (5 miles): Moose River, p. 160 rods, **river,** p. 60 rods, **Big Moose Lake.** This is a short day of paddling through an area frequented by moose. The first long portage is a good "shakedown" for the longer carry awaiting you the next day. If you find it nearly unbearable, you might want to reconsider continuing on the route to Big Lake. The trail bypasses several rapids by climbing over two low hills on a fairly good path. The final portage is much easier, with very little gain in elevation.

Big Moose Lake has several campsites dispersed along its rocky shoreline. If you still have energy left after setting up camp and if you enjoy hiking, you could explore two good trails—one at each end of the lake. The Big Moose Lake Trail extends two miles from the north end of the lake to a small parking lot 0.3 mile south of Forest Route 464. At the opposite end of the lake, a portage trail leads almost two miles south to Cummings Lake. Allow a couple of hours to hike either trail.

Day 2 (7 miles): Big Moose Lake, p. 480 rods, **Duck Lake,** p. 145 rods, **Portage River, creek, Big Lake.** These two portages are seldom used and could be plagued with windfalls if a portage crew has not been across them recently. The first long trail surmounts two hills en route to Duck Lake. The final 50 rods are across wet, spongy muskeg in a spruce bog. The final portage starts on a rock outcropping, and the path is basically dry for the first 100 rods; but the final 45 rods are also across a wet spruce bog.

After you put in at the Portage River, paddle east (left on the river) for less than $\frac{1}{10}$ mile and watch for the junction of the unnamed creek that continues eastbound to Big Lake. As you enter the lake, you'll be leaving the BWCA Wilderness.

ROUTE # 8-2:   The Big Moose and Buck Route
6 Days, 46 Miles, 13 Lakes, 4 Rivers, 3 Creeks, 19 Portages

DIFFICULTY: Challenging

FISHER MAPS: F-8, F-9

INTRODUCTION: If you like variety and don't mind a few long portages along the way, you will surely find this delightful route to be exceptional. Time spent is about equally divided among lakes, streams and portages. From F.R. 464, you will first meander up the Moose River to Big Moose Lake, taking two portages along the way. From there, you will negotiate a long portage south to Cummings Lake and then continue southbound to Little Crab Lake. At that point, you will turn west and follow a chain of small lakes to Trout Lake at the southwest corner of the BWCA Wilderness. From there, the route leads north through Little Trout Lake, across a mile-long portage and then down the Little Indian Sioux River. After your final night on Bootleg Lake, you'll continue north-bound on the Little Pony and Little Indian Sioux rivers to the Echo Trail.

Strong and experienced paddlers could surely complete this route in five days, perhaps even four. There are enough long portages along the way, however, to slow an average group of canoeists to a pace of 7 to 8 miles per day. Eight of the portages are more than half a mile long, and two exceed a mile. If completed in less than six days, the route would be labeled "rugged." With avid anglers or less experienced canoeists in your group, consider adding a 7th day. You could either make each day a little shorter and easier, or you could schedule a layover day for rest and relaxation in the middle of your expedition.

With so much paddling on creeks and rivers, you will have a good chance of viewing wildlife along the route. Moose, in particular, are prevalent in this region. While most of the route is very lightly traveled, your second and fourth nights will be in more heavily visited parts of the Wilderness. Motorboats are prohibited from the entire route except Trout Lake.

If there are anglers in your group, they will have good opportunities to catch all of the major game fish, including lake trout on big Trout Lake. Walleyes and northern pike are found in most of the lakes, while bass inhabit the waters of Big Moose, Little Crab, Little Trout and Bootleg lakes, as well as some of the lakes in between.

Of course, you should make prior arrangements to shuttle your car to the Little Indian Sioux River South entry point. This route ends 7½ miles by road from its origin.

Day 1 (5 miles): Moose River, p. 160 rods, **river,** p. 60 rods, **Big Moose Lake.** (See comments for Day 1, Route #8-1.) If you prefer fishing rather than hiking, you should have no problem finding walleyes in Big Moose Lake. There are also northern pike and smallmouth bass in the lake.

Day 2 (9 miles): Big Moose Lake, p. 600 rods, **Cummings Lake,** p. 35 rods, **Korb River, Korb Lake, Korb River,** p. 1-10 rods, **river, Little Crab Lake.** (See comments for Day 3, Route #6-1.) Before retiring for the night, the anglers in your group may want to cast their lines for the northern pike or bass that inhabit Little Crab Lake.

Day 3 (7 miles): Little Crab Lake, Lunetta Creek, Lunetta Lake, p. 60 rods, **Lunetta Creek,** p. 48 rods, **creek, Schlamn Lake,** p. 210 rods, **Glenmore Lake,** p. 195 rods, **Western Lake,** p. 80 rods, **Buck Lake.** To most folks, this day would be considered pretty tough, with 593 rods of portages. But on this route, it's not a bad day, with all of these portages adding up to less than just your *first* portage on the previous day. All of the trails have fairly good paths, in spite of the relatively light use they receive each summer.

The second portage (48 rods), however, starts out at a grassy, wet landing and follows a brushy trail for the first 20 rods. It then joins the path of an old logging road for the final 28 rods back to the shore of the creek. Just before the end of the portage, use caution crossing the creek on rocks and boulders. There is no bridge across the creek. Lunetta Creek doesn't look like much on the map, but it is always deep enough to float a canoe.

The next portage (210 rods) gains about 75 feet in the first 80 rods, and then follows a rather scenic ridge that is covered by a mature forest of large aspens, Norway pines and spruce trees. There is a panoramic view across a swamp just before the steep descent to Glenmore Lake. Watch for a huge, old white pine near the center of the next long portage (195 rods), which has a wet, boggy spot nearby.

The Fisher map (revised 1997) shows only one campsite on Buck Lake, on the south shore not far from the next portage to Chad Lake. It is a small site on a rock ledge with good space for only one tent. Another USFS campsite lies on the north shore of the lake, however, close to the portage from Western Lake. Buck Lake is a good source of walleyes and northern pike.

Day 4 (7 miles): Buck Lake, p. 250 rods, **Chad Lake,** p. 260 rods, **Pine Creek,** p. 60 rods, **Trout Lake, Little Trout Creek, Little Trout Lake.** The 250-rod trail is cluttered with rocks and roots, but it has a lovely stand of Norway pines about half way across. The longest portage of the day starts out with a short but steep incline, and is mostly uphill for the first 140 rods. Watch out for slippery spots on sloping rocks, especially when wet. At the end, the trail drops rather steeply down to Pine Creek. There is a scenic overlook at the summit of a high rock slope adjacent to the portage trail. A short climb leads to a panoramic view across Pine Creek valley. In mid-July, you might also find a wealth of blueberries on the rocky slope.

Pine Creek is generally deep and wide. The 60-rod portage at the mouth of the creek could be shortened to 40 rods when there is plenty of water in the creek. The path is excellent—quite smooth and virtually level—after the awkward and muddy landing, that is. If the creek's water level appears to be high, you can re-enter the creek at the first landing you come to, and then paddle down the final 20 rods of creek to Trout Lake. If the water level is low, however, you'll have to carry your gear all the way to Trout Lake.

The creek connecting Little Trout and Trout lakes is very shallow, and there could be a beaver dam there to necessitate a quick lift-over. Don't panic if you see a number of canoes on Little Trout Lake. It seems that anglers often use motorboats to access campsites at the north end of Trout Lake. Then they paddle canoes into Little Trout Lake to fish for the walleyes, smallmouth bass and northern pike that lurk beneath its surface. The campsites on the sandy shore of Little Trout Lake are well used, but not as attractive as many of those on Trout Lake. The shallow water in front of the sites may also be choked with aquatic vegetation after mid-summer. If you don't mind sharing "your" lake with motorists, you might prefer to camp at the more attractive sites on Trout Lake. Even if you camp on Little Trout Lake, you are likely to hear motors on nearby Trout Lake right up until dark (and maybe thereafter). This will likely be the noisiest part of the entire route. Trout is the only lake on this route where motorboats are permitted.

Day 5 (8 miles): Little Trout Lake, p. 376 rods, **Little Indian Sioux River,** p. 200 rods, **Bootleg Lake.** The first long portage starts at a sandy beach that may be obscured by aquatic vegetation in the shallow water in front of the landing. It has a surprisingly good, virtually level path most of the way to the river, with only a few wet spots along the way. The final 15 rods, however, are across a spongy bog at the edge of the river where it may be impossible to avoid wet feet.

Travel on the meandering Little Indian Sioux River is deceivingly slow. You should see few, if any, other human beings this day after departing from Little Trout Lake. Enjoy the bountiful wildlife and absence of other paddlers along the river's course.

Watch carefully for the beginning of the 200-rod portage to Bootleg Lake. You will find it at a bend in the river where its general course changes from northeastward to northwestward. The path receives very little use, and it may be overgrown and blocked by occasional windfalls. The trail climbs gradually for the first 120 rods to nearly 100 feet above the river, then descends more steeply to the shore of Bootleg Lake. Rock cairns mark the path along a rocky ridge about midway across the trail. In addition to the two official USFS campsites on Bootleg Lake, there is also an unofficial site on the south shore of this boot-shaped lake—but use it only if the other two sites are occupied.

Day 6 (10 miles): Bootleg Lake, p. 60 rods, **Little Pony River,** p. 60 rods, **river, Little Indian Sioux River,** p. 120 rods, **river,** p. 8 rods, **river.** This will be a long day of paddling down the gradually widening, deepening and straightening channels of the two rivers. The Little Pony is a much smaller river than the Little Indian Sioux. When the water is high, the second 60-rod portage may be reduced to only 15 rods. The river is very shallow and rocky below that 15-rod portage, but you may be able to walk your canoe between the close, grassy banks of the river on the firm sand bottom. Also when the water level is high, you may be able to shorten the 100-rod portage to about 60 rods by taking out of the river about 40 rods downstream from the main portage landing. Use caution, however, if you choose this alternative, since you will be flirting with fast water at the top of the major rapids.

Entry Point 9—Little Indian Sioux River South

SEASONAL PERMITS: 26

POPULARITY RANK: 60th

DAILY QUOTA: 1/2 (1 group every other day)

LOCATION: The Little Indian Sioux River begins its winding course at the west end of Otter Lake, about 15 miles northwest of Ely. It flows west for about 6 miles, then turns north and eventually flows into Loon Lake on the Canadian border. The entire river except that part in the immediate vicinity of the Echo Trail is contained within the BWCAW. The upper part of the river (south of the Echo Trail) is accessible via this entry point, while the Little Indian Sioux River North entry point (#14) serves the lower (northern) part. To get to the boat landing, drive north from County Road 88 on the Echo Trail for 29.9 miles. Access to the river is below the bridge on the left side of the road. A small parking lot on the north (right) side of the road, just past the bridge, will accommodate half a dozen vehicles.

DESCRIPTION: This entry point is unique. It is the only entry point in the entire BWCA Wilderness where entry is allowed every other day. That is because there simply are not enough campsites south of the Echo Trail to support a new group entering every day. The result is a very quiet, lightly traveled route into the Wilderness. Motors are not permitted, and very few paddlers venture in for just a day trip. Nevertheless, don't wait to make your reservation. With so few permits issued each summer, you could have difficulty finding an available permit for the most popular days of the summer. In 1997, this entry point ranked 10th among all entry points filled the greatest number of days (due in large part to the fact that half of all summer days are unavailable in the first place.).

The Jeanette Lake Campground, 4½ miles west of the Little Indian Sioux River via the Echo Trail, is a good place to spend the night prior to your canoe trip. This will enable an early start the following morning—and you will need it. This small campground often fills up, especially on weekends. So get there early, or you may have to drive on to the Echo Lake Campground, near the west end of the Echo Trail.

This entry point leads into one of the least traveled, most pristine areas within the BWCA Wilderness, offering as much solitude and bountiful wildlife as you would every hope to encounter. The Little Indian Sioux River provides a good opportunity for the quiet paddler to view moose, deer, beaver, waterfowl, and other wildlife. It is most suitable early in the summer, when the water level is normally high. During the latter part of the summer, or during a dry year, the upper (southern) part of the river could be too shallow for navigation with loaded canoes. You might get through, but it could take much longer than expected. Consult with the Forest Service before starting out on this route.

Regardless of the date, you will surely see few, if any, other canoes on this slow, meandering stream.

ROUTE #9-1: **The Little Rivers Loop**

2 Days, 25 Miles, 1 Lake, 2 Rivers, 8 Portages

DIFFICULTY: Challenging

FISHER MAPS: F-8, F-16

INTRODUCTION: This is a good route on which to escape from crowds on holidays or busy weekends. It is challenging because of the distance traveled in two days, rather than because of any particularly tough portages. From the Echo Trail, you will first paddle south on the Little Indian Sioux and Little Pony rivers to camp on Bootleg Lake. After a night's rest, you will portage westward to reenter the Little Indian Sioux River. Then you will meander your way north to your origin at the Echo Trail, after backtracking the lower (northern) 6½ miles of the river.

The first three miles of this route are shown on map F-16, but not on F-8. If you want to save a few bucks, you really don't need the F-16 map to find your way along the Little Indian Sioux River. If you prefer to know exactly where you are at any given moment, however, you'll want to include F-16 in your map case.

Water level should not be a problem anywhere on this part of the Little Indian Sioux River. Low water on the Little Pony River, however, could present some problems late in the summer or during unusually dry years.

Because of the long days of paddling required to access Bootleg Lake, you might find it more enjoyable to spend two nights there. Stretching the trip over three full days affords anglers an opportunity to search the depths of Bootleg Lake for the northern pike, smallmouth bass and bluegills that reside there.

If the first day of travel is about as much as you can handle, it might be a good idea to simply return the way you came. Otherwise, you may find the second day of this route to be downright rugged, with 13 miles of paddling after a 200-rod portage. Unfortunately, there are no campsites along the river to enable this route to be equally divided into three days instead of just two.

Day 1 (10 miles): Little Indian Sioux River, p. 8 rods, river, p. 100 rods, **river, Little Pony River,** p. 60 rods, **river,** p. 60 rods, **Bootleg Lake.** Travel up the Little Indian Sioux River can be deceivingly slow. Although there is very little current to slow your progress, a strong south wind may be a hindrance in this wide-open valley. The first short portage is around Sioux Falls, a lovely cascade just above the confluence of Urho Creek on the west side of the river.

The Little Pony is a much narrower river than the Little Indian Sioux. If the water level is high enough, that first 60-rod portage may be reduced to only 15 rods. The river is very shallow and rocky, however, just below the 15-rod portage. If you cannot paddle through it, you may be able to simply walk your canoe between the close grassy banks of the river, which has a firm sand bottom.

In addition to the two official USFS campsites on Bootleg Lake, there is an unofficial site at the south end of the lake, which could be used for an emergency—*only* if the other sites are occupied and you have no other legal options.

Day 2 (15 miles): Bootleg Lake, p. 200 rods, **Little Indian Sioux River,** p. 20 rods, **river,** p. 100 rods, **river,** p. 8 rods, **river.** That first long portage receives very little use, and it could be overgrown or blocked by windfalls if a portage crew has not been along in awhile. It ascends over 80 feet during the first 80 rods, and then gradually descends the rest of the way down to the soggy shore of the river. Rock cairns mark the way along a rocky ridge about midway along the trail.

After the portage you will be paddling for over 13 miles on the meandering river. Allow plenty of time to enjoy the aquatic environment along its marshy shores. This day will take even longer than the first day.

ROUTE #9-2:	**The Bootleg Buck Route**
	6 Days, 45 Miles, 13 Lakes, 4 Rivers, 3 Creeks, 19 Portages
DIFFICULTY:	Challenging
FISHER MAPS:	F-8, F-9 (F-16 optional)
INTRODUCTION:	This excellent route will take you through a seldom visited part of the Boundary Waters, frequented more by moose, deer, beavers and other wildlife than by human beings. From the boat access off the Echo Trail, you will first paddle south on the Little Indian Sioux and Little Pony rivers to Bootleg Lake. From that isolated lake, you will portage back to the Little Indian Sioux River and follow that narrowing stream farther south to a one-mile portage connecting the river with Little Trout Lake. After a night in a noisy corner of the BWCA Wilderness, you'll follow Pine Creek back into a quieter region and work your way east through a chain of smaller lakes and streams to Little Crab Lake. At that point, the route steers north through Cummings Lake and across the route's longest portage to Big Moose Lake. From there it is a short paddle down the meandering Moose River to end at Forest Route 464, 7½ miles by road from your origin.

Along this route, you will experience virtually all that the BWCAW can offer—big and small lakes, a long and winding river, tiny creeks, and portages of all sizes. It is a challenging route, even for experienced wilderness paddlers, with eight portages measuring more than half a mile. Two are more than a mile. Don't even *think* about taking this route unless you are in the best physical condition and an experienced canoe camper. If you are up to the task, however, you will surely find this route to a delightful journey that you will long remember.

The anglers in your group will have plenty of opportunities to catch most of the game fish for which the BWCAW is renowned. Walleyes and northern pike inhabit many of the lakes along this route. Several lakes are also good sources of smallmouth bass. If you spend some time on big Trout Lake, you might even find an elusive lake trout.

The first three miles of this route are shown on map F-16, but not on F-8. If you want to save a few bucks, you really don't need the F-16 map to find your way along the Little Indian Sioux River. If you prefer to know exactly where you are at any given moment, however, you'll want to include F-16 in your map case.

Day 1 (10 miles): Little Indian Sioux River, p. 8 rods, **river,** p. 100 rods, **river, Little Pony River,** p. 60 rods, **river,** p. 60 rods, **Bootleg Lake.** (See comments for Day 1, Route #9-1.)

Day 2 (7 miles): Bootleg Lake, p. 200 rods, **Little Indian Sioux River,** p. 376 rods, **Little Trout Lake.** That first long portage receives very little use, and it could be overgrown or blocked by windfalls if a portage crew has not been along in awhile. It ascends over 80 feet during the first 80 rods, and then gradually descends the rest of the way down to the soggy shore of the river. Rock cairns mark the way along a rocky ridge about midway along the trail.

Watch very carefully for the start of the long trail to Little Trout Lake. The remains of an old dock crib on the west (right) side of the river are the only indication of the beginning of the portage on the grassy bank of the river. It's easy to miss! Perhaps the best way to find it is to look near the end of a part of the river that is flanked by wide-open bogs. You'll be approaching a wooded region with some elevated terrain bordering the river. If you miss the portage, you will soon come to a 32-rod portage. Turn around there and try again.

The long trail starts out in a bog on a wet, spongy path for the first 15 rods, but it soon hits dry ground. It is quite level and has a surprisingly good path most of the way to Little Trout Lake, with only a couple of other boggy wet spots along the way. The put-in is at a sandy beach. You may have to walk your canoe out into the shallow, weedy lake before you can paddle away.

Don't panic at the end of this day if you see several canoes on the lake. There is a good chance the anglers occupying them are camped on Trout Lake nearby. It seems that anglers often use motorboats to access campsites at the north end of Trout Lake. Then they paddle canoes into Little Trout Lake to fish. The campsites on the sandy shore of Little Trout Lake are well used, but not as attractive as many of those on Trout Lake. If it's late in the day, you should probably claim the first open site you see. Don't be alarmed if you hear motorboats right up until dark (and maybe beyond). Trout is the only lake on this route where motorboats are permitted.

Day 3 (7 miles): Little Trout Lake, Little Trout Creek, Trout Lake, p. 60 rods, **Pine Creek,** p. 260 rods, **Chad Lake,** p. 250 rods, **Buck Lake.** (See comments for Day 4, Route #4-2.)

Day 4 (7 miles): Buck Lake, p. 80 rods, **Western Lake,** p. 195 rods, **Glenmore Lake,** p. 210 rods, **Schlamn Lake, Lunetta Creek,** p. 48 rods, **creek,** p. 60 rods, **Lunetta Lake, Lunetta Creek, Little Crab Lake.** (See comments for Day 5, Route #4-2.)

Day 5 (9 miles): Little Crab Lake, Korb River, p. 1-10 rods, **river, Korb Lake, Korb River,** p. 35 rods, **Cummings Lake,** p. 600 rods, **Big Moose Lake.** Depending on the water level and beaver activity, the short portage along the upper (southern) section of the Korb River could be as long as 10 rods in low water or simply a "lift-over" in high water. Tamarack and spruce bogs border the Korb River. In early summer, you may see pitcher plants growing there, too. Later in the season, water lilies may occupy the entire surface of the river. Beaver lodges are in abundance throughout both sections of the river. The 35-rod portage has an excellent path, although it may be wet at the beginning because of a beaver dam spanning the river.

The day ends with the longest portage of the entire route. If you cannot carry all your gear in just one trip, you'll be walking over 5½ miles, which could take up to three hours. The trail is not as bad as it might seem. It begins and ends on small hills, but it follows the crest of a rather level ridge along most of its course. The path is generally good, but it could be cluttered with windfalls if a portage crew has not been there in awhile.

Big Moose Lake has several nice campsites. Don't delay in claiming one, since campers have access to this lake from both the Moose River South and Big Moose Lake Trail entry points.

Day 6 (5 miles): Big Moose Lake, p. 60 rods, **Moose River,** p. 160 rods, **river.** This is a short day of paddling and portaging through an area frequented by moose, so keep a watchful eye. The final portage bypasses several rapids by climbing over two low hills on a fairly good path. After what you've been through on this route, it's an easy day, indeed.

|4

Entry from the Echo Trail North

The Northwestern Area

THE NORTHWESTERN PART OF THE BOUNDARY WATERS CANOE AREA Wilderness includes the region from the Echo Trail north to the Canadian border. The seven entry points that serve this area are easily accessible from the Echo Trail. They entertain far more visitors than do the entry points on the south side of the road, perhaps because of their proximity to the Canadian border.

Ely is the main commercial center that serves most visiting canoeists, and the International Wolf Center is the most convenient place to pick up your permit if you are passing through Ely. Entry points near the far-western end of the region lie closer to the town of Cook, however, where the La Croix Ranger Station is located. Unless you are using an outfitter in Ely, you may save driving time for some entry points by picking up your permit at the visitors' center in Cook. (See the introduction to Chapter 3 for more information about Ely, Cook and the Echo Trail itself.)

BOUNDARY WATERS CANOE AREA-WESTERN REGION

Entry Point 12—Little Vermilion Lake

SEASONAL PERMITS: 483

POPULARITY RANK: 16th

DAILY QUOTA: 14 (including 12A—Lac La Croix only)

LOCATION: Little Vermilion Lake is the westernmost canoe-ing entry point for the BWCA Wilderness, about 36 airline miles northwest of Ely. It is accessible from Crane Lake, two miles to the west (five miles by water trails), at the north end of County Road 24. To get there from Ely, follow the Echo Trail 46.5 miles northwest to its end at a T-inter-section with County Road 24. Turn right and drive 6 more miles north on Co. Rd. 24, a good blacktop road, to its junction with County Road 425. Then turn right again and continue on 425, a gravel road, for 1½ miles to the DNR public boat landing on the right side of the road.

If you are coming from the La Croix Ranger Station in Cook, rather than from Ely, drive north on Highway 53 for 17 miles to the village of Orr. Turn right onto County Road 23 and follow that good blacktop road northeast for 16½ miles to Buyck, where the highway continues northbound as County Road 24. The junction of County Road 425 is 10 miles north of Buyck. Allow nearly an hour for the drive from Cook to Crane Lake, and at least 1½ hours for the longer drive from Ely.

DESCRIPTION: A large parking lot adjacent to the boat landing has ample space for 38 vehicles with trailers and half a dozen more spaces for cars without trailers. A water pump and an outhouse are nearby. The boat landing provides access to the easternmost bay at the south end of Crane Lake. There is another boat access in "downtown" Crane Lake, across from the Voyageur National Park visitors' center at the end of County Road 24. A small fee is charged for parking there. The boat landing there provides access to the westernmost bay at the south end of Crane Lake.

Crane Lake is a popular gateway to much more than simply the BWCA Wilderness. It is also an access to the southeast end of Voyageurs National Park, to the west end of Quetico Provincial Park, and to the Canadian side of the international boundary waters. The unincorporated village of Crane Lake is home to only about a dozen year-around residents, but the tiny community is bustling with activity during the summer months. The south shore of the lake is populated with several resorts and private cabins. There is also a U.S. Customs station for boaters and canoeists entering the United States from Canada.

Little Vermilion Lake is actually much busier than its BWCAW statistics indicate. It is part of a frequently used route to the Canadian side of popular Lac La Croix. In fact, the lake is divided between the two nations. The west side of Little Vermilion Lake lies in America's BWCA Wilderness, while the east side of the lake is part of Canada. Motorboats are permitted on both sides of the boundary, and there are two mechanized portages along the route to Lac La Croix. There are no daily quotas for boat traffic on the Canadian side of the border, which is not part of any park or designated wilderness area.

If you don't mind the sound of motorboats and sea planes, and you are willing to paddle a few miles to find wilderness tranquility, this entry point has a good deal to offer. The large quota here makes it often available when other entry points leading to the same general area are booked up. Less than one-fourth of the available camping permits were actually used in 1997. You will find little peace and quiet during the first two days of either route described below. Nevertheless, once you depart from the Canadian border, it won't take long to find respite from the sights and sounds of civilization in a lovely part of the Boundary Waters just south of the border.

The Echo Lake Campground is the closest USFS campground to the Crane Lake access. It is located about a mile north of the Echo Trail from a point ¾ mile east of County Road 24. A fee is charged to camp there.

ROUTE #12-1: The Two Rivers Route

               3 Days, 28 Miles, 6 Lakes, 2 Rivers, 6 Portages

DIFFICULTY: Easier

FISHER MAPS: F-15, F-16, F-22

INTRODUCTION: This interesting route offers a good introduction to the BWCA Wilderness for neophytes who might take comfort in knowing that civilization is never too far away. From Crane Lake, you will first paddle north to Sand Point Lake. From there, you will veer toward the southeast and follow the Canadian boundary through Little Vermilion Lake and up the Loon River to Loon Lake. At that point, this route will take you south, following the Little Indian Sioux River through the Pauness lakes to end at the Echo Trail, 24½ miles by road from your origin.

Much of this route, from Crane Lake all the way to Loon Lake, is open to motorboats. After you leave the Canadian border, you won't hear motorboats. But you also won't escape from other canoes, as you enter a part of the Wilderness served by the popular Little Indian Sioux River North entry point. Although the route lacks the remote "wilderness character" that is found from most other entry points along the Echo Trail, it is a lovely route, nevertheless. It is also an easy journey for those who might not be up to the rigors of long or frequent portages.

Anglers will find a good variety of game fish in the lakes along this route, from small pan fish to big lake sturgeon (both found in Sand Point Lake). Walleyes, northern pike and smallmouth bass also inhabit the large lakes along the Canadian border.

Of course, you should drop off a car at the Little Indian Sioux River North Entry Point before starting this journey. Otherwise, it would be a long walk back to Crane Lake.

Day 1 (9 miles): Crane Lake, King William's Narrows, Sand Point Lake, Little Vermilion Narrows, Little Vermilion Lake. On a busy summer day, Crane Lake is a veritable highway for motorboats, jet skis, pontoon planes and houseboats. Crane and Sand Point lakes are also highly susceptible to the effects of a strong northwest wind. If such a wind is forecast, get an early start, when the wind is normally calm, to get across these two lakes before the wind becomes a problem. Even on a calm day, however, big waves from the wakes of motorboats may be a hazard.

All three of these lakes are part of the Namakan Reservoir, a huge body of water composed of interconnected lakes along the Canadian border. There can be a dramatic fluctuation in water level throughout the reservoir from year to year and season to season. Though fluctuations are quite noticeable when the water level is low, you won't experience any ill effects from them until you reach the south end of Little Vermilion Lake at the mouth of the Loon River.

The first two lakes are bordered by a rocky, pine-covered shoreline that has numerous cabins, lake homes and resorts. It is a beautiful area, especially in the two narrows between the first three lakes. Motorboats

At a Loon Lake campsite—at the end of a long day

share much of this route with canoeists, and traffic is especially heavy from the Crane Lake landing to Sand Point Lake. By comparison, Little Vermilion Lake may seem rather quiet, with periods of stillness and tranquillity between the occasional passing of motorboats. It is another lovely lake with a pine-covered, rocky shoreline.

Competent paddlers should have no trouble arriving at Little Vermilion Lake in just half a day of paddling, unless wind is a problem. To continue on, however, would make this a *big* day, since there are no designated campsites along the Loon River. So claim your campsite early and enjoy an afternoon of fishing or hiking. There are several nice campsites.

If you feel like stretching your legs after nine miles of paddling, the Herriman Lake Trails can be accessed at a sand beach near the south end of the lake. Thirteen miles of foot trails penetrate the region southwest of Little Vermilion Lake.

If you'd like to escape from the motor route this night, consider a short detour to camp on Dovre Lake. The 40-rod portage leads west from near the middle of Little Vermilion Lake. It's a fairly steep climb to Dovre Lake, where you'll find a campsite at the west end of the portage amidst a pretty grove of Norway pines. There are several tent sites but, unfortunately, the fire grate is right alongside the portage trail. A more distant campsite is on the south shore. From there, you would have direct access to the Herriman Lake Trails.

Day 2 (11 miles): Little Vermilion Lake, Loon River, p. 12 rods, river, p. 80 rods, Loon Lake. When the water level is high, the wide mouth of the Loon River looks like an extension of Little Vermilion Lake, and it presents no problem to paddlers. When the water level is low, however, that part of the river may be too shallow to even paddle a canoe straight across it. When such is the case, you may have to wind your way over the deepest channel of the river. Use your map as a guide and follow the winding course of the international border, which is, in fact, the deepest channel of the Loon River. When the water level is *extremely* low (as it was in the spring of 1998), the shallowest part of the river actually turns into mud flats, at which time it is easier to see the channel where you must paddle.

Farther upstream, the Loon River is fringed closely by a forest of aspen, birch, spruce and pine trees—atypical of most winding rivers in the Boundary Waters Canoe Area, which are most often bordered by wide bogs. Just prior to reaching the 12-rod portage around "56 rapids," you will see a break in the forest on the south side of the river. It is the site of a former 1920's logging camp known as "Camp 56" and operated by the Rainy River Lumber Company. Nearby, on the north shore of the river, you may see a couple of eagle nests near the tops of two old pines. The portage may not be necessary around "56 rapids" when the water level is high enough that you can simply paddle (hard) up through the swift current.

At the 80-rod Loon Lake Portage, which bypasses Loon Falls, there is a small resort that operates a mechanized railway to haul motorboats to the west end of Loon Lake. For half the price of a motorboat ($10 in 1998), you can have your loaded canoe hauled up this portage on a rail car. The uphill portage on the south side of the railway is not difficult, but it could be muddy in places.

There are several nice campsites near the mouth of the Little Indian Sioux River (approximately 11 miles from the middle of Little Vermilion Lake). Again, you may have to share "your" lake with motorboats, as well as with other canoeists that converge on Loon Lake from three other directions. Don't expect total peace and quite here. Since most motor traffic travels north to Lac La Croix, however, it is usually quietest at the south end of the lake or in East Loon Bay.

Day 3 (8 miles): Loon Lake, Little Indian Sioux River, p. 110 rods, river, Lower Pauness Lake, p. 40 rods, Upper Pauness Lake, Little Indian Sioux River, p. 60 rods, river, p. 40 rods. Soon after breaking camp, you will be heading into a more tranquil part of the BWCA Wilderness. Wildlife abounds along the marshy shores of the Little Indian Sioux River, so keep a watchful eye.

The first portage (and longest carry of the entire route) bypasses one of the most spectacular scenic attractions in the western region of the Boundary Waters. Devil's Cascade plunges 75 feet through a deep granite gorge below Lower Pauness Lake. The trail ascends over 90 feet during the first 40 rods, then levels out at the top of a high ridge. There, near the midpoint of the trail, you'll cross the Devil's Cascade Trail, where there is a wide, grassy place to park your canoe and gear. From there, follow the hiking trail 100 feet west (right) to a panoramic overlook above the cascade.

There are two portages connecting the Pauness lakes. The shallow southeast ends of the lakes may be choked after mid-summer with aquatic vegetation that makes it more difficult to access the shorter trail. The longer portage (40 rods) passes over a low hill on an excellent path.

The 60-rod Elm Portage goes around scenic rapids with a small waterfall near the middle. The good uphill path skirts close to the river on a low ridge that affords excellent views of the rapids and falls below.

The final portage (40 rods) leads from the bank of the river to a large parking lot north of the Echo Trail. The trail ascends more than 80 feet and crosses a sloping rock ledge that is quite slippery when wet. Use caution on this steep slope.

ROUTE #12-2: The Lac La Croix Route

7 Days, 65 Miles, 16 Lakes, 2 Rivers, 3 Creeks, 19 Portages

DIFFICULTY: Challenging

FISHER MAPS: F-15, F-16, F-22, F-23

INTRODUCTION: This interesting route offers tastes of all types of canoeing experiences, including large and small lakes, long rivers and tiny creeks, short and longer portages, some sites of historical significance, and a good opportunity to see wildlife along the way. First you will paddle north from Crane Lake to Sand Point Lake. Then you will follow the international boundary southeast through Little Vermilion Lake and up the Loon River to Loon Lake. Continuing along the Canadian border, you will then paddle north to Lac La Croix and follow this giant horseshoe-shaped lake north, then east, and finally south for 16 miles to the mouth of Pocket Creek. At that point, you will steer west and return to Loon Lake via a chain of smaller lakes and streams that parallels the border a few miles south of Lac La Croix. From Loon Lake, then, you will follow the meandering Little Indian Sioux River south to end this lovely route at the Echo Trail, 24½ miles by road from your origin.

Although most of this route is easy, the series of frequent portages between Pocket and East Loon lakes warrants a rating of "challenging." During the first four days and 42 miles of this route, you'll cross only five portages, and the longest is only 80 rods. During the final three days and 23 miles of your journey, however, you'll encounter 14 portages, four of which are longer than 100 rods.

Water level should not be a critical factor on this route, although very low water could necessitate some artful dodging along the Loon River and a portage around "56 rapids," which may not be necessary when the river is high. Finger and Pocket creeks could also pose a minor problem for heavily loaded canoes in very low water.

Most of this route is heavily used during the summer months. Only that part between Pocket Creek and East Loon Lake, which is the only part of the route where motors are prohibited, receives light to moderate visitation. Attractive scenery compensates for the noise and congestion found along the rest of the route.

Anglers will find that northern pike inhabit most of the lakes along this route. Walleye and smallmouth bass may also be found in Crane and Little Vermilion lakes, as well as in Lac La Croix, where lake trout are also present.

If you have time to add an 8th day to this trip, Pocket Lake is a good place to enjoy a layover after the 4th day. That would afford you an opportunity to explore the fascinating southeast end of Lac La Croix. There you will find two points of historical interest. On the west shore of Canada's Irving Island, there is a fine display of old Indian rock paintings—the largest display of pictographs in the Quetico-Superior region. About a mile farther south, then, you will see Warrior Hill, also on the Canadian shoreline. This was once the testing ground for the bravery and strength of Ojibway braves who ran from the lake's edge to the summit of the rocky precipice. On the way back, you might also enjoy a side trip into Lady Boot Bay, considered by many visitors to be the most beautiful part of Lac La Croix.

Day 1 (9 miles): Crane Lake, King William's Narrows, Sand Point Lake, Little Vermilion Narrows, Little Vermilion Lake. (See comments for Day 1, Route #12-1.)

Little Vermilion Lake campsite

Day 2 (11 miles): Little Vermilion Lake, Loon River, p. 12 rods, river, p. 80 rods, Loon Lake. (See comments for Day 2, Route #12-1.)

Day 3 (12 miles): Loon Lake, p. 50 rods, Lac La Croix. In the west half of Lac La Croix, you will see countless small islands that make navigation difficult at times. If necessary, use your compass to establish a general heading and focus your attention on major landmarks and the larger islands. Your only portage of the day is an easy trek on a good path up a gradual slope to the southwest shore of Lac La Croix. As at the previous portage, there is a mechanized railway on which to transport motorboats.

The BWCA Wilderness Act of 1978 prohibits motorboats on the US side of Lac La Croix in all but its southwest end. The restriction, of course, does not apply to the Canadian half of the lake. So you are still likely to hear motorboats in nearly all parts of this gigantic lake.

Don't miss the small display of Indian rock paintings along the US shoreline, just north of the portage. Along the Canadian shoreline, you will see a couple of resorts, as well as an Indian village at the source of the Namakan River. It lies in the Neguaguon Lake Indian Reserve, adjacent to Quetico Provincial Park.

Plan to camp in the vicinity of Forty One Island, to make this a 12-mile day. Don't expect a quiet evening in seclusion. There is a busy resort less than a mile north of the island, and seaplanes may land there throughout the day. For a little more peace and privacy, if time permits, you might consider portaging south to either Gun Lake (80 rods) or Takucmich Lake (20 rods) to spend the night.

Day 4 (10 miles): Lac La Croix, p. 15 rods, Pocket creek, p. 15 rods, Pocket Lake. Because of the ever-present threat of wind on Lac La Croix, it is best to allow for two full days to paddle from one end to the other. A strong head wind is always a retarding menace, but also beware the strong *tail* wind. When starting across a wide-open expanse of water with a strong wind at your back, the lake ahead of you may appear relatively calm and quite safe. As you proceed farther and farther out from the lee side of a sheltering shoreline, however, you will find that the waves grow higher and higher. Suddenly you may find your canoe in rougher water than you can handle, resulting in either a swamped or a capsized canoe. Wind can be either a friend or a foe, depending on how much respect you have for it and how much good judgment you demonstrate in its presence. It is always best to paddle close to the shoreline of a large lake. Not only is it safer, it is also far more interesting.

The short portage from Lac La Croix to Pocket Creek may vary from 15 rods to 20 rods, depending on the water level in Pocket Creek. The trail bypasses small rapids and a beaver dam that maintains the water depth in Pocket Creek. The next short portage at the other end of Pocket Creek may not be necessary when the water level is high in the creek. Try paddling right up through the narrow, shallow channel.

Day 5 (8 miles): Pocket Lake, Finger Creek, p. 90 rods, Finger Lake, p. 2 rods, Thumb Lake, p. 200 rods, Beartrack Lake, p. 30 rods, Little Beartrack Lake, p. 30 rods, Eugene Lake, p. 45 rods, Steep Lake, p. 120 rods, South Lake. On this day you will pass through a chain of picturesque lakes, bordered by forests of pine and spruce, with rocky shorelines and occasional cliffs. The short portage between Finger and Thumb lakes is little more than a quick lift-over. The longest and most challenging carry of the day (200 rods) gradually ascends to nearly 100 feet above Thumb Lake on a good path during the first 90 rods. Then the path is nearly level the rest of the way to Beartrack Lake.

If time and energy are plentiful, you might enjoy a short side trip on the portage from the north end of Little Beartrack Lake to Gun Lake. This rough and rocky trail passes along the shadowy base of a steep ridge that towers more than 100 feet above the portage. Stow your canoe and gear near the portage landing (but not blocking it) and enjoy a slow hike through this unique setting.

Resting near a Loon Lake campsite

You will see extensive wind damage to the forest along the west side of Little Beartrack Lake and the south half of Eugene Lake—the only unattractive part of this chain of lovely lakes. Before portaging north from Steep Lake, take time to explore the fascinating cliffs that adorn its northeast shoreline.

The final portage of the day has the most dramatic change in elevation. Fortunately, you are headed in the right direction. After a short climb for the first 15 rods from Steep Lake, it's all downhill, dropping over 170 feet to the southeast end of South Lake. There is a dandy campsite with two good tent sites in the narrows between South and North lakes.

Day 6 (7 miles): South Lake, p. 52 rods, Section 3 Pond, Slim Creek, p. 52 rods, Slim Lake, p. 173 rods, Little Loon Lake, Loon Lake. The first two portages have good paths and are mostly level, although the first one ascends 40 feet during the first 25 rods. You'll find the start of the second carry about 60 rods into the tiny creek on the west (right) bank. The biggest challenge of the day is found on the last, long portage. The trail ascends over 50 feet during the first 60 rods and then drops more than 130 feet to the north end of Little Loon Lake. The footing is treacherous on the rough, slippery path. It is plagued with rocks and roots, as well as some muddy spots.

You'll find several nice campsites in East Loon Bay, as well as near the mouth of the Little Indian Sioux River. If it's a warm day and a refreshing swim is in order, you may want to take advantage of one of the good sand beaches in East Loon Bay.

Day 7 (8 miles): Loon Lake, Little Indian Sioux River, p. 110 rods, river, Lower Pauness Lake, p. 40 rods, Upper Pauness Lake, Little Indian Sioux River, p. 60 rods, river, p. 40 rods. (See comments for Day 3, Route #12-1.) Of course, if you prefer, you could make this a complete loop by adding an extra day and backtracking from Loon Lake to Crane Lake.

Entry Point 14—Little Indian Sioux River North

SEASONAL PERMITS: 670

POPULARITY RANK: 14th

DAILY QUOTA: 6

LOCATION: The Little Indian Sioux River begins its winding course about 15 miles northwest of Ely, at the west end of Otter Lake. It flows west for about 6 miles, then turns north, and eventually flows into Loon Lake on the Canadian border. The entire river, except that part in the immediate vicinity of the Echo Trail, is contained within the BWCA Wilderness. The upper part of the river is accessible via the Little Indian Sioux River South entry point (#9), while this entry point serves the lower, northern part of the river. To get to the access from Ely, follow the Echo Trail northwest from County Road 88 for 30 miles. About 0.1 mile past the river's bridge, turn right and follow an access road 0.3 mile north to its end at a large parking lot. From there, a 40-rod portage leads farther north to the river.

DESCRIPTION: The Jeanette Lake Campground, located 4½ miles farther west on the Echo Trail, is the closest USFS facility to this entry point. It provides a good place to spend the night before your trip, enabling an early start the next morning. A fee is charged to camp there. Try to get there early to find a vacant campsite at this popular campground.

Unlike its southern counterpart, and in spite of its remote location, the Little Indian Sioux River North is one of the three busiest entry points along the Echo Trail. In 1997, it also ranked 16th among all BWCAW entry points with quotas filled the greatest number of days. Nearly ¾ of its available permits are used each summer. Be sure to make your reservation early if you plan to enter the Wilderness here. Motorboats are not allowed.

The Little Indian Sioux River provides relatively easy access to big Lac La Croix on the Canadian border, known for its good fishing and attractive scenery. It also affords access to a lovely region south of the Canadian border where you'll find a chain of smaller lakes, fewer people and very nice scenery. Although it's a challenge to access these lakes, they are well worth the effort needed to get there.

ROUTE #14-1: **The Four Rivers Route**

3 Days, 25 Miles, 10 Lakes, 4 Rivers, 16 Portages

DIFFICULTY: Challenging

FISHER MAPS: F-16

INTRODUCTION: This interesting route starts and ends on rivers joined in the middle by a chain of lakes that entertain fewer visitors than the rivers at either end. From the boat landing just north of the parking lot, you will first paddle northwest down the Little Indian Sioux River to Upper Pauness Lake. From there the route heads east across a chain of lovely lakes and lengthy portages to Oyster Lake. From the east shore of Oyster Lake, then, you will begin a southbound journey on three small rivers and across two lakes to end your expedition at the Moose River North entry point, a little more than eight miles by road from your origin.

This is a good route for anyone wanting to experience a brief but fine taste of the Boundary Waters in a region that abounds in wildlife. For those who paddle quietly and watch carefully, it is a good place to view moose. Whereas both the Little Indian Sioux River North and Moose River North entry points are quite popular, you are bound to see several other canoeing parties on the first and last days of your journey. The middle portion of the route between Shell and Oyster lakes, however, is a better place to find solitude. Motorboats are not permitted on any part of the route.

Don't consider this route unless you are in pretty good physical condition. Four portages exceed half a mile, and a fifth is exactly half a mile. The trails are usually in good condition, but there are some notable hills on the longest portages that could be exhausting for an out-of-shape desk jockey.

Anglers will find all kinds of game fish in the lakes along this route. Walleyes and northern pike inhabit most of the lakes, and small-mouth bass and pan fish may be found in some. With luck, you might also pull a lake trout from the depths of Oyster Lake.

Day 1 (9 miles): P. 40 rods, **Little Indian Sioux River,** p. 60 rods, **river, Upper Pauness Lake,** p. 40 rods, **Lower Pauness Lake,** p. 216 rods, **Shell Lake,** p. 15 rods, **Little Shell Lake,** p. 4 rods, **Lynx Lake.** You'll be heading downhill for the first half of this day, as you follow the Little Indian Sioux River northwest to the Pauness lakes. If you paddle quietly and the wind is in your favor, you may be treated to the sight of a moose along the placid river. Other forms of wildlife also abound in the river valley.

Use caution on that very first portage from the parking lot to the river. It descends more than 80 feet and crosses a sloping rock ledge that may be slippery, especially when wet.

The 60-rod Elm Portage follows a scenic downhill path close to the river that overlooks a small waterfall and rushing rapids. Immediately after putting back into the river, look to the west (left) for another scenic waterfall where Jeanette Creek pours over a rock shelf and into the Little Indian Sioux River.

Between the Pauness lakes, you will have a choice of two portages. When the water level is low, or when the aquatic weeds are abundant in the southeast ends of the two lakes, it may be easier to access the longer trail (40 rods). It follows a good path over a small hill.

After completing the portage, take time for a short detour to the north end of Lower Pauness Lake, where Devil's Cascade plunges 75 feet through a deep granite gorge. Cache your canoe and gear well off the trail to not block the way for other canoeists using the landing. Then hike north on the portage. Near the midpoint of the portage, at the crest of a hill, you'll cross the Devil's Cascade Trail. Follow this hiking trail 100 feet west (left) to a panoramic overlook above the cascade. It is a great place to eat lunch or take a break.

The 216-rod portage connecting Lower Pauness and Shell lakes is mostly level and has an excellent path. The beginning of the portage, however, may be muddy when water is low. It is also somewhat difficult to see when aquatic plants growing in the shallow water in front of the landing are abundant during late summer. About a third of the way across the portage, you'll cross the Devil's Cascade Trail. Then, about ⅔ of the way across, you will skirt the edge of a swamp on the south (right) side of the portage trail. Watch for moose.

When the water level is normal or high, you should be able to paddle through the short, shallow creek connecting Little Shell and Lynx lakes. Even when the water is low, you can probably lift your canoe over some rocks in the creek to avoid the 4-rod portage. If you choose to keep your feet dry, you'll find the portage on the north side of the creek.

Day 2 (8 miles): Lynx Lake, p. 260 rods, **Ruby Lake,** p. 10 rods, **Hustler Lake,** p. 300 rods, **Oyster Lake,** p. 60 rods, **Oyster River,** p. 180 rods, **Agnes Lake.** If your shoulders aren't sore already, they surely will be by the end of this day. With five portages totaling 810 rods in length, you will be walking over 7½ miles this day if you must make two trips to get all your gear across. The portages have excellent, well-maintained paths, and none is particularly difficult—just long. The first climbs nearly 130 feet during the first 120 rods and then gradually descends about 70 feet to the south shore of Ruby Lake.

After a brief respite on Ruby and Hustler lakes, you'll arrive at the longest portage of the entire journey. Fortunately, it is mostly downhill. After climbing over 60 feet during the first 80 rods, the trail descends nearly 140 feet during the final 200 rods, including a rather steep drop near the end.

Navigating the upper part of the Oyster River between the two portages should pose no problem during a normal year. The stretch below the 180-rod portage, however, may be more of a muddy challenge, especially during late summer or a dry year. The portage bypasses that part of the river and offers the most direct route to Agnes Lake. After a short climb during the first 25 rods, the trail is then nearly level for the next 100 rods, followed by a gradual descent to the west shore of Agnes Lake.

While you may not see many other paddlers between Shell and Oyster lakes, the number of campers on Agnes Lake may surprise you. Most of them access this lake from the Moose River North entry point to the south. Try to claim you campsite early this afternoon. There are several nice sites. For the anglers in your group, there is a good population of walleyes inhabiting Agnes Lake. Make sure that your food pack is hung well this night. Black bears are traditional pests in this area.

Day 3 (8 miles): Agnes Lake, Nina Moose River, p. 96 rods, **river,** p. 70 rods, **river, Nina Moose Lake, Moose River,** p. 25 rods, **river,** p. 20 rods, **river,** p. 160 rods. This day should seem easy compared to the previous day. Although you will be traveling upstream, the opposing current is usually not a problem, except in early spring or following a torrential downpour. The portages have good, sandy paths, and they are well used and well maintained. None is difficult, including the final long carry.

On the west shore of Nina Moose Lake, you may still see evidence of a 1971 fire that ravaged 25 square miles of woodlands between there and the Little Indian Sioux River. As you approach the south end of that lake, don't let your course stray too far east. If you do, you may find yourself paddling up the Portage River instead of the Moose River. Both lead south to the Echo Trail, but the Moose River is a much more "user friendly" course to follow, and that's where your car will be.

About a mile up the Moose River, you will paddle close to a hill that rises 150 feet above the east (left) bank. A steep climb there will take you to a scenic overlook across the Moose River valley. Use caution on the steep slope, especially if it's wet.

The final half-mile portage gradually climbs more than 60 feet on a very good path. It passes through a predominately young forest, accented by some giant red and white pines, and ends at a large parking lot one mile north of the Echo Trail.

ROUTE #14-2: The Sioux Hustler Loop

6 Days, 45 Miles, 23 Lakes, 1 River, 4 Creeks, 28 Portages

DIFFICULTY: Challenging

FISHER MAPS: F-16

INTRODUCTION: This is a wonderful route for canoeists who prefer a variety of canoeing experiences. The loop includes most of the smaller lakes that are "encased" within the huge horseshoe of Lac La Croix. From the boat landing just north of the parking lot, you will first paddle northwest down the Little Indian Sioux River to Upper Pauness Lake. From there the route heads east across a chain of lovely lakes and lengthy portages to Oyster Lake. At that point, you will steer north to Pocket Lake through a chain of lakes and creeks that see fewer visitors than most of the other lakes on this route. From Pocket Lake, then, you will head west to penetrate perhaps the prettiest part of this loop, where smaller lakes are bordered by some steep cliffs and rocky, pine-covered shorelines. At South Lake you will turn south and head for Loon Lake for a quick glimpse of Canada. Then you will paddle up the

Little Indian Sioux River and through the
Pauness lakes to return to the parking lot at the
Echo Trail.

Although you are not likely to escape completely from other people
anywhere along this route, it is certainly a more peaceful part of the
Wilderness than nearby Lac La Croix. The only part of the loop on
which motorboats are allowed is Loon Lake. The other lakes and
streams are reserved strictly for paddlers.

Although you will be challenged by several long portages (six
longer than half a mile), the portage paths are maintained in excellent
condition. Most of the carries (16) are less than ¼ mile. And most of
the lakes are small enough that wind should not be a serious problem.
A few fascinating creeks also add variety to the route. Overall, this is a
very nice loop that most groups should be able to complete easily in
six days. A layover day, however, is suggested in the middle of the route
for a side trip to Lac La Croix, or to rest weary muscles from the strain
of those first long portages.

Campsite on Pocket Lake

Cliffs at the north end of Steep Lake

Anglers should probably spread the loop over 7 or 8 days, to allow plenty of time to explore the lakes for their resident populations of walleyes, northern pike, smallmouth bass and lake trout.

Day 1 (7 miles): P. 40 rods, **Little Indian Sioux River,** p. 60 rods, **river, Upper Pauness Lake,** p. 40 rods, **Lower Pauness Lake,** p. 216 rods, **Shell Lake.** (See comments for Day 1, Route #14-1, paragraphs 1-6. There is no need for a detour this day to view Devil's Cascade. You will portage around it on the last day of this loop.)

Day 2 (7 miles): **Shell Lake,** p. 15 rods, **Little Shell Lake,** p. 4 rods, **Lynx Lake,** p. 260 rods, **Ruby Lake,** p. 10 rods, **Hustler Lake,** p. 300 rods, **Oyster Lake.** When the water level is normal or high, you should be able to paddle through the short, shallow creek connecting Little Shell and Lynx lakes. (See comments for Day 2, Route #14-1, paragraphs 1 and 2.)

Day 3 (8 miles): **Oyster Lake,** p. 65 rods, **Rocky Lake,** p. 85 rods, **Green Lake,** p. 120 rods, **Ge-be-on-e-quet Lake,** p. 23 rods, **Ge-be-on-e-quet Creek, Pocket Creek,** p. 15 rods, **Pocket Lake.** This day is much easier than the previous day. Although the portages may be more overgrown, they continue to have good paths. The longest trail (120 rods) climbs over a low hill at the beginning and then descends nearly 100 feet, including a rather steep drop for the final 20 rods.

Two large beaver dams on Ge-be-on-e-quet and Pocket creeks kept the water level high in both creeks during the very dry summer of 1997. The 3-foot-high dam on Ge-be-on-e-quet Creek requires a lift-over. You won't see the dam on Pocket Creek. It is located at the beginning of the portage from Pocket Creek to Lac La Croix. If that dam continues to hold the water at a high level, the 15-rod portage to Pocket Lake may not be necessary. Try paddling right up through the narrow, shallow channel.

Campsites along this chain of lakes are generally small, most with only one good tent site, until you reach Pocket Lake. There you will find a beautiful campsite at the top of a large outcrop of ledge rock sloping up from the water on the west shore of Pocket Lake. It has plenty of space for three or four tents. Anglers may find walleyes, northern pike and smallmouth bass swimming nearby.

Pocket Lake is a good place to enjoy a layover day. It would afford you an opportunity to explore the fascinating southeast end of Lac La Croix. There you will find two sites of historical interest. On the west shore of Canada's Irving Island, there is a fine display of old Indian rock paintings—the largest display of pictographs in the Quetico-Superior region. About a mile farther south, then, you will see Warrior Hill, also on the Canadian shoreline (8 miles from your Pocket Lake

Lower Pauness Lake

99

campsite). Legends suggest that this was once the testing ground for the bravery and strength of Ojibway braves who ran from the lake's edge to the summit of the rocky precipice. On the way back, you might also enjoy a side trip into Lady Boot Bay, considered by many visitors to be the most beautiful part of Lac La Croix. This day requires a good deal of paddling (at least 16 miles), but there are only two short portages (15 rods each) along Pocket Creek.

Day 4 (8 miles): Pocket Lake, Finger Creek, p. 90 rods, Finger Lake, p. 2 rods, Thumb Lake, p. 200 rods, Beartrack Lake, p. 30 rods, Little Beartrack Lake, p. 30 rods, Eugene Lake, p. 45 rods, Steep Lake, p. 120 rods, South Lake. (See comments for Day 5, Route #12-2.)

Day 5 (7 miles): South Lake, p. 52 rods, Section 3 Pond, Slim Creek, p. 52 rods, Slim Lake, p. 173 rods, Little Loon Lake, Loon Lake. (See comments for Day 6, Route #12-2.) Motorboats are permitted on Loon Lake, and it is part of a popular route connecting Crane Lake with Lac La Croix. Since most of the motor traffic travels along the Canadian border, it is usually quietest at the south end of the lake or in East Loon Bay.

Day 6 (8 miles): Loon Lake, Little Indian Sioux River, p. 110 rods, river, Lower Pauness Lake, p. 40 rods, Upper Pauness Lake, Little Indian Sioux River, p. 60 rods, river, p. 40 rods. (See comments for Day 3, Route #12-1.)

Entry Point 16 — Moose River North

SEASONAL PERMITS: 856

POPULARITY RANK: 12th

DAILY QUOTA: 7

LOCATION: The Moose River begins at the northwest corner of Big Moose Lake, 15 miles northwest of Ely, and slowly winds its way north for about 10 miles to Nina Moose Lake. The Echo Trail crosses the river about 4 miles south of Nina Moose Lake. To get to the public access, follow the Echo Trail northwest for 23.2 miles from County Road 88. Just before the road crosses the river, Forest Route 206 spurs off to the north. Turn right there and drive one more mile to the large public parking lot at the road's end. From there a portage trail continues northbound to the Moose River. (Note: A mile before F.R. 206, you will see a sign pointing to the Moose River via Forest Route 464, south of the Echo Trail. Do not turn there; that road leads to the access serving the Moose River South entry point.)

DESCRIPTION: The Moose River is a good entry point for anyone who prefers the natural intimacy of a tiny stream. It is quite narrow and shallow, meanders considerably, and is almost choked with vegetation along its marshy banks for the first few miles. Access to the river is ½ mile north of the parking lot. The good, wide, relatively smooth portage trail begins at a small kiosk and gradually descends 50 feet to the bank of the river. Along the way, it passes through a mostly young forest, but watch for scattered giant red and white pines that predate modern history. You may also see signs of moose and wolves along the trail.

The Moose and Portage rivers share the same entry point number. Most BWCAW visitors enter via the Moose River, which is much easier than its neighboring route to the east. Motorboats are not permitted in the Wilderness on either river. This is the second-most-popular entry point along the Echo Trail. It is also one of the most difficult for which to get a permit. During the 1997 quota season (May 1 through September 30), its quota was filled to capacity nearly 80% of the time—8th among all entry points filled the greatest number of days. So, if you are planning to start your trip here, make your reservation as early as possible.

The Fenske Lake Campground, 8 miles north of County Road 88 on the Echo Trail, is a good place to spend the night before your canoe trip. Or you could stay at the Jeanette Lake Campground, 12 miles farther west on the Echo Trail. A fee is charged for camping at either USFS campground. You will have a better chance of finding a vacant campsite at Fenske Lake. The smaller Jeanette Lake Campground is often full, especially on weekends.

ROUTE #16-1: The Ramshead Lake Loop

2 Days, 15 Miles, 3 Lakes, 2 Rivers, 1 Creeks, 11 Portages

DIFFICULTY: Challenging

FISHER MAPS: F-16

INTRODUCTION: This is a good weekend route for anyone who likes paddling on small, winding streams, camping on a lake that entertains relatively few visitors, and taking a few long portages to achieve that quick isolation. From the Moose River portage, you will first follow the Moose River north to Nina Moose Lake. The Nina Moose River will then transport you farther north to the outlet of Ramshead Creek. At that point, you will depart from the popular river route leading to the Canadian border and steer your course west to Ramshead Lake. After a night on that quiet lake, you will portage to Lamb Lake and then back to Nina Moose Lake. Finally, you will backtrack along the Moose River to your origin at the Moose River parking lot.

More than half of this route is on rivers and creeks. The other half is divided among three lakes and 11 portages. If you are not in good physical condition, this route may seem more "rugged" than "challenging," since four of the portages are at least half a mile. All of the trails, combined, total more than 1,000 rods. If you need two trips to get your gear across the portages, you'll be walking nearly 10 miles during these two days.

You may see many other canoes on the Moose and Nina Moose rivers, but don't worry. Most will be traveling to or from Agnes Lake and Lac La Croix. Few people venture to Ramshead Lake.

Day 1 (9 miles): P. 160 rods, **Moose River,** p. 20 rods, **river,** p. 25 rods, **river, Nina Moose Lake, Nina Moose River,** p. 70 rods, **river,** p. 96 rods, **river, Ramshead Creek,** p. 160 rods, **creek, Ramshead Lake.** Most of your first day will be spent paddling downstream on two of the more interesting rivers in the western region of the BWCA Wilderness. In late summer or during dry years, you may scrape the sandy bottom of the Moose River in a few places soon after putting in. Small beaver dams also may obstruct traffic on slow streams like these. Quick lift-overs may be required in addition to the designated portages along the route.

On the west shore of Nina Moose Lake, you may see the charred evidence of a 1971 fire that ravaged 25 square miles of woodlands between the Moose River and the Little Indian Sioux River.

All of the portages this day are relatively easy, including the first and last half-mile treks. Most have smooth, sandy pathways that slope gently downhill. The only exception is the final portage, which ascends about 30 feet along the south shore of Ramshead Creek. Soon after the portage, you'll encounter a large beaver dam spanning the creek.

There are several campsites on Ramshead Lake—usually more than enough to accommodate the demand for them. One of the nicer sites rests on the east shore of the lake amidst a stand of Norway pines where a rock shelf slopes into the water. There is only one good place for a tent there, however. Ramshead is a shallow lake that is noted for its good population of northern pike.

Day 2 (6 miles): Ramshead Lake, p. 100 rods, **Lamb Lake,** p. 220 rods, **Nina Moose Lake, Moose River,** p. 25 rods, **river,** p. 20 rods, **river,** p. 160 rods. The southern route out of Ramshead Lake is shorter than the northern route leading to it. But it also necessitates a longer portage. Both of the trails to and from Lamb Lake receive far less use than the portages along the Moose and Nina Moose rivers. They may be overgrown with grass and shrubs and somewhat difficult to see at times. The 220-rod portage is also cluttered with rocks, and it may be muddy. After climbing more than 60 feet during the first 60 rods, it is mostly level or sloping gradually downhill the rest of the way to Nina Moose Lake.

As you paddle across the south end of Nina Moose Lake, don't let your course stray too far east. If you do, you may find yourself paddling

Moose River

up the Portage River instead of the Moose River. Both lead south to the Echo Trail, but the Moose River is a much more "user friendly" course to follow. And you won't have a car waiting for you at the Portage River parking lot.

About a mile up the Moose River, you will paddle close to a hill that rises 150 feet above the east (left) bank. A steep climb there will take you to a scenic overlook across the Moose River valley. Use caution on that steep slope, especially if it's wet.

ROUTE #16-2: The Green Rocky Oyster Loop

5 Days, 43 Miles, 10 Lakes, 4 Rivers, 3 Creeks, 20 Portages

DIFFICULTY: Challenging

FISHER MAPS: F-16

INTRODUCTION: This is a nice route for canoeists who prefer a good mixture of stream and lake paddling, portages that are challenging but not too rugged, and plenty of interesting scenery to view along the way. From the Moose River portage, you will first follow the Moose and Nina Moose rivers north to Agnes Lake. You will continue northbound to Lac La Croix, where you'll see some fascinating historic sites on the Canadian shoreline. After paddling across the southeast end of Lac La Croix, you will enter Pocket Creek and follow it west to Pocket Lake. From there, you will steer south through a chain of lovely, smaller lakes to Oyster Lake. The Oyster River will then transport you back to Agnes Lake and then southwest via the Moose River and Ramshead Creek to Ramshead Lake. After a final night on that quiet lake, you will portage to Lamb Lake and then back to Nina Moose Lake. Finally, you will backtrack along the Moose River to your origin at the Moose River parking lot.

When your trip is completed, you will have paddled on nearly as many streams as lakes. You'll probably see a fair number of other paddlers on the northbound part of the route. Lac La Croix, in particular, is a popular destination for canoeists. It is also the only part of the route where motorboats are permitted (on the Canadian side of the lake). The southbound part of the route, on the other hand, hosts fewer visitors. While you may never totally escape from other campers, you may find a higher degree of solitude at your last three campsites.

Anglers may find most species of fish known to the Boundary Waters along this route, including lake trout in Lac La Croix and Oyster lakes, and big northern pike in Ramshead Lake. Walleyes and smallmouth bass are also present in several of the lakes. If fishing is a priority, you should probably add a sixth day to this route and plan to travel no more than 6-to-8 miles each day.

Day 1 (9 miles): P. 160 rods, **Moose River**, p. 20 rods, **river**, p. 25 rods, **river**, **Nina Moose Lake, Nina Moose River**, p. 70 rods, **river**, p. 96 rods, **river**, **Agnes Lake**. (See comments for Day 1, Route #16-1, paragraphs 1-2.) There are several nice campsites on Agnes Lake. Don't delay in claiming one. This is a popular overnight stop for paddlers, as well as a destination in itself. Bears are traditional pests in this area. Hang your food pack well. If you hang it properly and maintain a clean campsite, you should have nothing to fear.

Day 2 (13 miles): **Agnes Lake**, p. 24 rods, **Boulder River**, p. 65 rods, **Lac La Croix, Pocket Creek**, p. 15 rods, **creek**, p. 15 rods, **Pocket Lake**. In terms of miles traveled, this will be the longest day of your canoe trip. The portages are short and easy, however, and you should make good time paddling across the southeast end of Lac La Croix (if there isn't a strong north wind). If you prefer a couple of extra miles of paddling to a 65-rod portage, follow the shallow, meandering course of the Boulder River from the 24-rod portage to Boulder Bay of Lac La Croix. When water levels are low, however, it is best to take the 65-rod portage.

Motorboats are permitted on the Canadian side of Lac La Croix, and this part of that huge lake is also popular among canoeists on both sides of the border. You'll see why it is. Beginning about 1½ miles north of Boulder Bay, on the Canadian shoreline, are two fascinating historical sites. First, on the south-facing shore of Irving Island is a steep rock slope known as Warrior Hill. Legends suggest that it was once the testing ground for the bravery and strength of Ojibway braves who ran from the lake's edge to the summit of the steep hill. About a mile farther north, at two locations, there are sheer granite cliffs that retain the fading red-brown remnants of pictographs. Painted long ago by Ojibway Indians who inhabited the area, this is the largest display of Indian rock paintings in the Quetico-Superior region.

The short portage from Lac La Croix to Pocket Creek may vary from 15 to 20 rods, depending on the water level in Pocket Creek. The trail bypasses some small rapids and a beaver dam that maintains the water depth in Pocket Creek. The next short portage, at the other end of Pocket Creek, may not be necessary at all when the water level is high in the creek. Try paddling right through the narrow, shallow channel. There is a beautiful campsite at the top of a large outcrop of ledge rock sloping up from the water on the west shore of Pocket Lake. It has plenty of space for three or four tents. Anglers may find walleyes, northern pike and smallmouth bass swimming nearby.

If it is getting late and you're still on Lac La Croix, it might be a good idea to simply spend the night on that lake, somewhere near the mouth of Pocket Creek. Then, the next morning, skip Pocket Lake altogether. It's not essential for this route to camp on Pocket Lake. I simply prefer the peace and quite found on the smaller lake, where motorboats are not permitted. Although you shouldn't see motorboats on the US side of Lac La Croix, you certainly may *hear* the low drone emanating from the Canadian side.

Day 3 (8 miles): Pocket Lake, p. 15 rods, **Pocket Creek, Ge-be-on-e-quet Creek,** p. 23 rods, **Ge-be-on-e-quet Lake,** p. 120 rods, **Green Lake,** p. 85 rods, **Rocky Lake,** p. 65 rods, **Oyster Lake.** This day is much shorter than the previous day. It should prove to be the part of the route where you'll see the fewest other paddlers. Although the portages may be more overgrown than those you've traversed so far, they continue to have good paths.

A large beaver dam on Ge-be-on-e-quet Creek kept the water level high in that creek during the very dry summer of 1997. You'll encounter the 3-foot-high dam soon after leaving Pocket Creek. It requires a steep lift-over. The short portage at the source of the creek (23 rods) gains 45 feet in elevation.

The longest carry of the day (120 rods) also ascends steeply for the first 20 rods, gaining more than 70 feet in elevation. It continues on a more gradual uphill slope for the next 30 rods, then levels out and eventually descends to the north shore of Green Lake. The first 20 rods of the next portage (85 rods) are also uphill, but the rest of the trail descends gradually to Rocky Lake.

Campsites along this chain of lakes are generally small, most with only one good tent site, until you reach Oyster Lake. There you will find several good sites, most on the cedar-lined south and east shore of the lake. The best and most popular campsites are on the long peninsula that separates the northern bay from the main part of the lake. Try to claim your campsite early this afternoon. While you may not see many other paddlers between Pocket and Rocky lakes, the number of campers on Oyster Lake may surprise you.

With a maximum depth of 130 feet, Oyster Lake contains populations of lake trout, northern pike and smallmouth bass.

Day 4 (7 miles): Oyster Lake, p. 60 rods, **Oyster River,** p. 180 rods, **Agnes Lake, Nina Moose River, Ramshead Creek,** p. 160 rods, **creek, Ramshead Lake.** Navigating the upper part of the Oyster River between the two portages should pose no problem during a normal year. The stretch below the 180-rod portage, however, may be more of a muddy challenge, especially during late summer or a dry year. The portage bypasses that part of the river and offers the most direct route to Agnes Lake. After a short climb during the first 25 rods, the trail is then nearly level for the next 100 rods, followed by a gradual descent to the west shore of Agnes Lake. If its early in the summer and the water level appears high in the Oyster River, you can probably bypass Agnes Lake and paddle directly to the Nina Moose River.

The final portage of the day ascends about 30 feet along the south shore of Ramshead Creek. Soon after the portage, you'll encounter a large beaver dam spanning the creek.

There are several campsites on Ramshead Lake—usually more than enough to accommodate the demand for them. One of the nicer sites rests on the east shore of the lake amidst a stand of Norway pines where a rock shelf slopes into the water. There is only one good place for a tent there, however. Ramshead is a shallow lake that is noted for its good northern pike population.

Day 5 (6 miles): Ramshead Lake, p. 100 rods, **Lamb Lake,** p. 220 rods, **Nina Moose Lake, Moose River,** p. 25 rods, **river,** p. 20 rods, **river,** p. 160 rods. (See comments for Day 2, Route #16-1.)

Entry Point 19—Stuart River

SEASONAL PERMITS: 98

POPULARITY RANK: 43rd

DAILY QUOTA: 1

LOCATION: The headwaters of the Stuart River are about 15 airline miles northwest of Ely, just north of Big Lake. The lazy little river flows slowly north for about 6 miles to Stuart Lake, 4 miles south of the Canadian border. Access to the river is across a 1½-mile portage from the Echo Trail, 17.4 miles northwest from County Road 88. This is one mile past the turnoff to Lodge of Whispering Pines.

DESCRIPTION: A small parking lot next to the Echo Trail will accommodate 4-5 vehicles. The Fenske Lake Campground, 10 miles closer to Ely on the Echo Trail, is a good place to spend the night before your canoe trip. That will enable an early start the following morning—and you may need it. A fee is charged to camp there.

The Stuart River is perhaps the quietest of all the canoeing entries that lead north from the Echo Trail. Only one overnight travel permit is available each day, but the demand is even less than that limited supply. Nearly 4 out of 10 available permits are not used each summer. So this entry point offers a good alternative if your destination is the Canadian border region north of the Echo Trail and the more popular entry points to the east and west are already booked up. You are not likely to see many daytime visitors, probably because of the physical exertion required to access the Stuart River.

The long portage from the parking lot to the river is mostly downhill, but it is still a rugged way to start a canoe trip. Beyond it, there are no designated campsites along the tiny, shallow river—not until persistent paddling and five more portages have taken you to Stuart Lake. Motors are not allowed on the river, and few canoes utilize it either. Consequently, this BWCAW entry point offers quick access to the kind of pristine wilderness that might take several days to find from many other entry points.

During a very dry year or late in the summer, the river may be too shallow in the final stretch leading into Stuart Lake—even when it appears fine in the upper (southern) stretches. Consult with the Forest Service or a local outfitter.

Route #19-1: The Five Rivers Route

3 Days, 26 Miles, 4 Lakes, 5 Rivers, 15 Portages

Difficulty: Challenging

Fisher Maps: F-9, F-16

Introduction: This is a wonderful route for anyone who prefers paddling on little, meandering streams instead of a chain of lakes. But it is also for strong trippers who don't mind portages ranging up to 1½ miles in length. After portaging from the parking lot to the Stuart River, you will follow that winding stream north to Stuart Lake. From there you will portage west to the Dahlgren River and then follow that stream north to Lac La Croix. After a side trip from Boulder Bay to a display of Indian rock paintings on the Canadian shore of Lac La Croix, you will then portage southwest to Agnes Lake. From there, the Nina Moose and Moose rivers will carry you south to a parking lot for the Moose River North entry point, one mile north of the Echo Trail and almost 7 miles by road from your origin.

Although your nights are spent on two lakes, most of your travel will be on tiny, meandering streams. Few other paddlers will share the first half of the route, northbound to Boulder Bay of Lac La Croix. The southbound route to the Moose River parking lot, however, will likely be shared with many other canoeists. Motorboats are not permitted on any part of the main route, although you might encounter them on a side trip to the Canadian border.

Strong, experienced canoeists should have no problem completing the route in three days, especially if only one trip is need on each portage to get all the gear across. A fourth day might be in order, however, if you want more time to explore Lac La Croix (see Day 2, paragraph 2 below), or to fish along the way.

You should leave a car at the Moose River North parking lot, unless you plan to end your canoe trip with a long hike back to the Stuart River parking lot.

Day 1 (8 miles): P. 480 rods, **Stuart River,** p. 85 rods, **river,** p. 52 rods, **river,** p. 74 rods, **river,** p. 14 rods, **river,** p. 74 rods, **Stuart Lake.** That first long portage from the parking lot has a good path that is mostly level to gently undulating for the first 220 rods. The trail then descends more than a hundred feet over the next 100 rods to cross the first of two creeks. If the water level in the second creek (Swamp Creek) is high enough to make crossing it a problem (too wide to step over and too deep to walk through), you can probably put in there and shorten the portage by about 50 rods. Paddle northeast (right) on Swamp Creek to the Stuart River, then turn left and follow the Stuart River downstream past the end of the portage landing.

Beaver dams may occasionally obstruct the shallow, winding, weedy Stuart River. Thanks to Nature's "corps of engineers," you may find the water level a bit to low as you approach the final portage. Plan on wet feet.

Portages total 779 rods this day. That's over 7 miles of walking if you need two trips to get your gear across them. If you should get a late start and Stuart Lake is too far for the first night, an alternate destination could be White Feather Lake, where there is an unofficial campsite on its north shore. To camp there, however, you must get *prior authorization* from the USFS to spend a night in the Sundial Lake Primitive Management Area (see Chapter 1), which includes White Feather Lake. It is accessible through a short stream that connects it to the Stuart River just southeast of the 52-rod portage.

You may see the charred remains of the White Feather Fire along the west side of the Stuart River near White Feather Lake. In 1996, that lightning-caused fire burned 4,750 acres east of the Stuart River. While this area was already a good place to see moose, the fire created even more browse for these creatures. They should continue to prosper here for years to come.

There are several nice campsites on Stuart Lake. The closest is a nice site at the south end of a large island in the south end of the lake. If the anglers in your group have energy left at the end of this long day, they may find some walleyes and northern pike lurking beneath the surface of Stuart Lake.

Day 2 (10 miles): Stuart Lake, p. 118 rods, **Dahlgren River,** p. 140 rods, **Boulder River, Lac La Croix,** p. 65 rods, **Boulder River,** p. 24 rods, **Agnes Lake.** This is another delightful day of paddling on two more rivers, with an opportunity for a side trip to a fascinating historical site. The two portages along the Dahlgren River are not difficult. The first passes over a low hill and through a lovely stand of old-growth pines. A small waterfall highlights the setting at the west end of the portage. The longest portage of the day (140 rods) gradually descends nearly 50 feet to the Boulder River.

This route leads north to Boulder Bay of Lac La Croix. From there, if you have the time and energy, a side trip north to the Canadian border may be in order. Beginning about 1½ miles north of Boulder Bay, on the Canadian shoreline, are two fascinating historical sites. First, on the south-facing shore of Irving Island is a steep rock slope known as Warrior Hill. It was once the testing ground for the bravery and strength of Ojibway braves who ran from the lake's edge to the summit of the steep hill. About a mile farther north, at two locations, there are sheer granite cliffs that retain the fading red-brown remnants of pictographs. Painted long ago by Ojibway Indians who inhabited the area, this is the largest display of Indian rock paintings in the Quetico-Superior region. Motorboats are permitted on the Canadian side of Lac La Croix, and this is also a popular destination for canoeists. The side trip will add about 6 miles of paddling on that big and beautiful lake. If you're short on time or energy, but you still want to explore this area, it might be a good idea to add a fourth day to the route and camp in the vicinity of Fish Stake Narrows.

Otherwise, if you prefer to not take the side trip, you could also bypass Boulder Bay. After completing the 140-rod portage, paddle west (left) on the Boulder River directly to the 24-rod portage to Agnes Lake.

There are several nice campsites on Agnes Lake. Don't delay in claiming one. This is a popular overnight stop for paddlers, as well as a destination in itself. Bears are traditional pests in this area. Hang your food pack well. If you hang it properly and maintain a clean campsite, you should have nothing to fear.

Day 3 (8 miles): Agnes Lake, Nina Moose River, p. 96 rods, **river**, p. 70 rods, **river, Nina Moose Lake, Moose River**, p. 25 rods, **river**, p. 20 rods, **river**, p. 160 rods. (See comments for Day 3, Route #14-1.)

ROUTE #19-2: The Iron Shell Oyster Route

8 Days, 66 Miles, 28 Lakes, 6 Rivers, 3 Creeks, 37 Portages

DIFFICULTY: Challenging

FISHER MAPS: F-9, F-16

INTRODUCTION: This is a terrific route for anyone who likes good variety, including large and small lakes, tiny creeks and wide rivers, and portages of all shapes and sizes. From the Stuart River portage, you will first follow the river north to Stuart Lake. From there, you will portage through a chain of small lakes leading to the Canadian border at Iron Lake. After taking a short side trip to beautiful Curtain Falls, you will then follow the Canadian border northwest to Lac La Croix, where you'll find a fascinating display of Indian rock paintings. From big Lac La Croix, you will then negotiate your way through a chain of lovely lakes that leads west to South Lake. From that point, the route leads south to Loon Lake and then up the Little Indian Sioux River. After viewing Devil's Cascade, you will steer east from Lower Pauness Lake and cross a chain of mid-sized lakes leading to Agnes Lake. From there, the Nina Moose and Moose Rivers will carry you south to a parking lot for the Moose River North entry point, one mile north of the Echo Trail and almost 7 miles by road from your origin.

With waterfalls, rapids, pictographs and sheer rock cliffs to view along the way, there is no time for boredom along this interesting route. Motorboats are permitted on the Canadian side of Lac La Croix and on Loon Lake. The rest of the route is strictly for paddlers.

Curtain Falls between Crooked Lake and Iron Lake

An average group of competent paddlers should have no problem completing the trip in eight days. A group of anglers or an inexperienced party of paddlers should add an extra day. Anglers may find virtually every type of fish known to the Boundary Waters, including walleyes, northern pike, smallmouth bass, lake trout and pan fish.

Of course, you need to leave a car at the end of this route, unless you plan to end your canoe trip with a long walk back to the Stuart River parking lot.

Day 1 (8 miles): P. 480 rods, **Stuart River,** p. 85 rods, **river,** p. 52 rods, **river,** p. 74 rods, **river,** p. 14 rods, **river,** p. 74 rods, **Stuart Lake.** (See comments for Day 1, Route #19-1.)

Day 2 (6 miles): Stuart Lake, p. 320 rods, **Fox Lake,** p. 60 rods, **Rush Lake,** p. 67 rods, **Dark Lake,** p. 72 rods, **Iron Lake.** In terms of miles traveled, this is the shortest day of the route. With portages totaling 519 rods, however, it is far from easy. If two trips are needed to get your gear across the portages, you'll be walking nearly 5 miles on this 6-mile stretch. The first trail is long, but fairly level to gently undulating after a short climb at the beginning. The last three are much shorter, but each surmounts a small hill.

Claim your campsite early on Iron Lake (6 miles to Three Island). This is a popular destination for anglers and sightseers alike. Then paddle to the northeast end of the lake to view Curtain Falls, which cascades a total of 29 feet on its way from Crooked Lake to Iron Lake. It is, by far, the most spectacular waterfall in the western part of the BWCA Wilderness—well worth a side trip. Along the way, the anglers in your group may want to ply the water for some of the walleyes, northern pike or smallmouth bass that inhabit Iron Lake. You're bound to hook a walleye or two in the rapids below the falls.

Day 3 (10 miles): Iron Lake, Bottle River, Bottle Lake, p. 80 rods, **Lac La Croix.** If wind is not a problem, this should be the easiest day of your trip, affording you an opportunity to enjoy some interesting sites along the way. The only portage of the day (Bottle Portage) bypasses a 23-foot drop in the Bottle River by cutting across a large Canadian peninsula. The wide trail is well used but not well maintained, with muddy potholes throughout the path.

After cleaning the mud off your boots and legs, enjoy a leisurely paddle across the scenic southeast end of Lac La Croix. Beginning less than two miles northwest of the portage are two fascinating historical sites. First, on the south-facing shore of Irving Island is a steep rock slope known as Warrior Hill. Legends relate that it was once the testing ground for the bravery and strength of Ojibway braves who ran from the lake's edge to the summit of the steep hill. Then, about a mile farther north, at two locations, there are sheer granite cliffs that retain the fading red-brown remnants of pictographs. Painted long ago by Ojibway Indians who inhabited the area, this is the largest display of Indian rock paintings in the Quetico-Superior region.

You may see or hear a few motorboats on the Canadian side of the border throughout this day. Guides from the Lac La Croix First Nation, an Ojibway community living on the northern shore of Lac La Croix, use them. By agreement with the Canadian government, the guides are permitted to use motorboats up to 10 horsepower on 10 lakes each year from a list of 20 lakes in the western third of Quetico Provincial Park. Bottle and Iron lakes are among those 20 lakes. Motorboats are also permitted for anyone on the Canadian side of Lac La Croix, and this part of that huge lake is also popular among canoeists on both sides of the border.

For a 10-mile day, plan to camp near the southwest corner of Coleman Island. It is a couple of miles south and west of the Canadian border in a quieter part of the lake. For an even quieter evening, you could paddle 2 miles off the main route to Lady Boot Bay, which is arguably the most beautiful part of Lac La Croix—and definitely the quietest.

Day 4 (9 miles): Lac La Croix, p. 15 rods, **Pocket Creek,** p. 15 rods, **Pocket Lake, Finger Creek,** p. 90 rods, **Finger Lake,** p. 2 rods, **Thumb Lake,** p. 200 rods, **Beartrack Lake,** p. 30 rods, **Little Beartrack Lake,** p. 30 rods, **Eugene Lake.** On this day you will pass through a chain of picturesque lakes, bordered by forests of pine and spruce, with rocky shorelines and occasional cliffs. The short portage from Lac La Croix to Pocket Creek may vary from 15 rods to 20 rods, depending on the water level in Pocket Creek. The trail bypasses small rapids and a beaver dam that maintains the water depth in Pocket Creek. The next short portage, at the other end of Pocket Creek, may not be necessary when the water level is high in the creek. Try paddling right up through the narrow, shallow channel.

The short portage between Finger and Thumb lakes is little more than a quick lift-over. The longest and most challenging carry of the day (200 rods) gradually ascends to nearly 100 feet above Thumb Lake on a good path during the first 90 rods. Then the path is nearly level the rest of the way to Beartrack Lake.

You will see extensive wind damage to the forest along the west side of Little Beartrack Lake and the south half of Eugene Lake—the only unattractive part of this chain of lakes. The campsite near the north end of Eugene Lake escaped the effects of that tumultuous storm. Anglers will find northern pike in the deep water of Eugene Lake.

Day 5 (9 miles): Eugene Lake, p. 45 rods, **Steep Lake,** p. 120 rods, **South Lake,** p. 52 rods, **Section 3 Pond, Slim Creek,** p. 52 rods,

Moonrise over Oyster Lake

Slim Lake, p. 173 rods, **Little Loon Lake, Loon Lake.** Before portaging north from Steep Lake, take time to explore the striking cliffs that adorn its northeast shoreline.

The portage to South Lake has the most dramatic change in elevation of any along this entire route. Fortunately, you are headed in the right direction. After a short climb from Steep Lake for the first 15 rods, it's all downhill, dropping over 170 feet to the southeast end of South Lake.

The next two portages have good paths and are mostly level, although the first one ascends 40 feet during the first 25 rods. You'll find the start of the second carry about 60 rods into the tiny creek on the west (right) bank. The biggest challenge of the day is found on the last long portage. The trail ascends over 50 feet during the first 60 rods and then drops more than 130 feet to the north end of Little Loon Lake. The footing is treacherous on the rough, slippery path. It is plagued with rocks and roots, as well as some muddy spots.

You'll find several nice campsites in East Loon Bay, as well as near the mouth of the Little Indian Sioux River. If it's a warm day and a refreshing swim is in order, you may want to take advantage of one of the good sand beaches in East Loon Bay. Motorboats are permitted on Loon Lake, but most of them stay along the Canadian border in the main part of the lake.

Day 6 (8 miles): Loon Lake, Little Indian Sioux River, p. 110 rods, **Lower Pauness Lake,** p. 216 rods, **Shell Lake,** p. 15 rods, **Little Shell Lake,** p. 4 rods, **Lynx Lake.** Soon after breaking camp, you will be heading into a more tranquil part of the BWCA Wilderness. Wildlife abounds along the marshy shores of the Little Indian Sioux River, so keep a watchful eye.

The first portage passes a spectacular scenic attraction. Devil's Cascade plunges 75 feet through a deep granite gorge below Lower Pauness Lake. The trail ascends over 90 feet during the first 40 rods, then levels out at the top of a high ridge. There, near the midpoint of the trail, you'll cross the Devil's Cascade Trail, where there is a wide, grassy place to park your canoe and gear. From there, walk on the hiking trail 100 feet west (right) to a panoramic overlook above the cascade.

The 216-rod portage connecting Lower Pauness and Shell lakes is mostly level and has an excellent path. The beginning of the portage, however, may be muddy when the water is low. It is also somewhat difficult to see when aquatic plants growing in the shallow water in front of the landing are abundant during late summer. About a third of the way across the portage, you'll cross the Devil's Cascade Trail. Then, about ⅔ of the way across, you will skirt the edge of a swamp on the south (right) side of the portage trail. Watch for moose.

When the water level is normal or high, you should be able to paddle through the short, shallow creek connecting Little Shell and Lynx lakes. Even when the water is low, you can probably lift your canoe over some rocks in the creek to avoid the 4-rod portage. You'll find the portage on the north side of the creek if you choose to keep your feet dry.

There is a nice campsite for a larger group on an elevated rock ledge near the west end of Lynx Lake. It has plenty of room for three or four tents with exposure to both the sunrise and the sunset.

Day 7 (8 miles): Lynx Lake, p. 260 rods, **Ruby Lake,** p. 10 rods, **Hustler Lake,** p. 300 rods, **Oyster Lake,** p. 60 rods, **Oyster River,** p. 180 rods, **Agnes Lake.** (See comments for Day 2, Route #14-1.)

Day 8 (8 miles): Agnes Lake, Nina Moose River, p. 96 rods, **river,** p. 70 rods, **river, Nina Moose Lake, Moose River,** p. 25 rods, **river,** p. 20 rods, **river,** p. 160 rods. (See comments for Day 3, Route #14-1.)

Entry Point 20 — Angleworm Lake

SEASONAL PERMITS: 145

POPULARITY RANK: 37th

DAILY QUOTA: 2

LOCATION: As the loon flies, Angleworm Lake lies about 12 miles northwest of Ely. The signed trailhead ("Angleworm Trail") and small parking lot are on the east (right) side of the Echo Trail, 13 miles north of County Road 88.

DESCRIPTION: The Fenske Lake Campground, 5 miles closer to Ely along the Echo Trail, is a good place to spend the night before your trip. There are 16 campsites, well water and a small swimming beach. A camping fee is charged.

It doesn't take a long study of the map to understand why this entry point ranks low in popularity. On the other hand, the fact that 145 groups were willing to brave the initial 2-mile portage in 1997 is a tribute to beauty of Angleworm Lake. No doubt, if Angleworm Lake were easily accessible to canoeists, it would surely be one of the most popular entry points along the Echo Trail.

As it is, you may see as many hikers as canoeists on the trail leading to Angleworm Lake. Most of the hikers are there for the day only, but canoeists have some competition from backpackers for the campsites on Angleworm and Home lakes. A 10-mile footpath encircles Angleworm, Home and Whiskey Jack lakes. It branches off from the long portage ¼-mile south of Angleworm Lake. Considered by many to be one of the finest hiking trails in the Ely area, the Angleworm Trail follows high rock ridges with scenic overlooks, passes through impressive stands of large red and white pines, and frequently drops down to touch the shore of Angleworm Lake. At those points, paddlers also have access to the trail. They provide good opportunities to stretch your legs and gain a unique perspective of the long lake on which you're paddling.

To further discourage canoeists from using this lovely entry point, there is also no easy exit. The only outlets are by way of either a 1½-mile portage southeast to Trease Lake or a ⅔-mile portage north to Gull

Lake (after a 40-rod carry to Home Lake). Consequently, Angleworm Lake is not an entry point for the inexperienced or for anyone who is not in the best physical condition.

If you don't mind the hard work, though, this is a wonderful way to escape from the summer crowds. Angleworm Lake attracts an average of nearly one canoeing group per day during the summer quota season—less than half the daily quota. So, if you are determined to paddle to the Canadian border region north of the Echo Trail and the other entry points are booked up, this one just might be available.

In addition to the two routes described below, you can also access from Angleworm Lake the two routes suggested for the South Hegman Lake entry point.

ROUTE #20-1: **The Sterling Creek Route**

3 Days, 26 Miles, 11 Lakes, 2 Rivers, 1 Creek, 21 Portages

DIFFICULTY: Most rugged

FISHER MAPS: F-9, F-16, F-17

INTRODUCTION: This route is a wonderful choice for strong and experienced canoeists who want to quickly escape from other people and who are willing to work hard for their wilderness tranquility. After the long portage to Angleworm Lake, you will continue northbound on a chain of small lakes from Angleworm to Thunder Lake. Then you'll steer northwest from Beartrap Lake and follow the Beartrap River downstream to Sunday Lake. Sterling Creek will then carry you west to a short chain of small lakes that entertain very few visitors. After a final night on Stuart Lake, you will paddle south up the Stuart River to end at the Echo Trail, about 4½ miles by road from your origin.

The middle of this route passes through the Sundial Lake Primitive Management Area (see Chapter 1). Portages are not maintained by the Forest Service between Beartrap Lake and Stuart Lake, and camping is not permitted there without a special permit. Wildfire consumed 4,750 acres of forest in that PMA in 1996.

This is one of the most difficult short routes in this guide. Several long, seldom-used portages will test your strength and stamina. The

reward is peaceful seclusion in a region that receives very little canoeing traffic at any time. The route is not suitable for an average group of
paddlers and certainly not recommended for inexperienced parties. If
you cannot carry your canoe and all of your gear across portages in just
one trip, three days probably isn't long enough. By adding a fourth day,
it is much more bearable for most groups. A fifth day might even be
appropriate for some parties.

This is not a complete loop. Unless you are willing to hike 4½
miles back to the Angleworm trailhead, plan to have a car waiting at
the Stuart River parking lot (see Entry Point 19).

Warning: *When water levels are low, two of the streams on this route
may be too shallow for navigation of a loaded canoe. Sterling Creek is capable of nearly drying up and the lower (northernmost) stretch of the Stuart
River can be quite shallow during late summer.*

Day 1 (7 miles): P. 640 rods, **Angleworm Lake,** p. 48 rods, **Home
Lake,** p. 260 rods, **Gull Lake,** p. 40 rods, **Mudhole Lake,** p. 60 rods,
Thunder Lake. Don't let the first half of the 2-mile portage fool you.
The whole trail has an excellent, well-maintained path, but the second
half is a lot more rugged than the beginning. During the first half-mile
from the parking lot, the trail crosses nearly level to gently undulating
terrain on an excellent path that was once part of a USFS forest route
leading all the way to the Canadian border. It then descends during the
second half-mile more than 150 feet into the Spring Creek valley. After
crossing the small creek and adjacent marsh on a long boardwalk, the
trail abruptly ascends more than 100 feet to a high rocky ridge overlooking the valley. Parts of the trail continue to use the path of the old
Forest Route while other parts utilize more recently cut hiking trails.
These steep, rocky trail segments are more scenic for hikers, but they
are far more difficult for those who must carry a canoe. About 100 rods
after crossing Spring Creek, the trail passes through an open marsh and
crosses another short boardwalk with beaver ponds on both sides of
the trail. 120 rods farther up the trail (about ¼ mile before the end of
the portage), you'll come to the junction of three trails. A portage to
Trease Lake leads to the south (hard right). The east branch of the
Angleworm Trail (for hikers) leads east, while the portage continues in
a northeast direction. Just ¼ mile farther, watch for a short spur trail
branching off to the right from the hiking trail. It leads down to the
south end of Angleworm Lake. This is a long portage to cross only
once. If you need two trips to get all of your gear across, you'll be walking 6 miles before you ever dip a paddle in the water this day. And, by
the end of this day, you will have walked nearly 10 miles.

If you've had enough for one day after that first portage, you'll
find several good campsites on Angleworm Lake. There are 4 sites

On the Beartrap River

along the west shore of the lake accessible to backpackers. The nicest sites, however, are on the east shore of the lake. If you can make it a little farther, there is a nice canoeists on Home Lake. Another site for backpackers lies in a lovely stand of tall pines just north of the lake, 20 rods west of the portage trail to Gull Lake.

The long portage from Home Lake has a good path that starts out with a gradual climb for the first 70 rods, followed by a steeper descent for the next 60 rods. The last half of the trail is nearly level or gently undulating, ending at a rock outcrop on the west shore of Gull Lake. At 12 rods from Home Lake a trail spurs off to the left from the portage trail that leads to the backpacker campsite. Stay to the right for the portage to Gull Lake. You will cross the Angleworm Trail 30 rods from Home Lake. There are some large, very old white pines along the portage, including one that must surely be over 300 years old.

The other short portages are quite easy compared to what you've already crossed. The 40-rod path leading north from Gull Lake, however, may be muddy at the beginning, because of a large beaver dam that keeps the water level high. Don't delay in claiming your campsite for the evening. The chain of lakes lying north and east of Home Lake entertains far more visitors than do Angleworm and Home lakes.

Day 2 (11 miles): Thunder Lake, p. 5 rods, **Beartrap Lake,** p. 200 rods, **Beartrap River,** p. 65 rods, **river,** p. 20 rods, **river, Sunday Lake,** p. 17 rods, **Beartrap River, Sterling Creek,** p. 160 rods, **creek,** p. 8 rods, **Sterling Lake,** p. 148 rods, **Bibon Lake,** p. 10 rods, **Nibin Lake,** p. 180 rods, **Stuart Lake.** This is a long day of paddling and portaging, with three portages each exceeding half a mile. If you are the first expedition through the area after a windstorm, windfalls could seriously obstruct your path on any of the portages. Even if you're not the first one through, don't expect the trails to be groomed in this primitive management area.

The first long portage is mostly downhill, descending over 100 feet to the Beartrap River after a short climb from Beartrap Lake. The river is shallow, weedy and extremely tiny until it joins with Spring Creek about ¼ mile after the portage. You may encounter several beaver dams between the 20-rod portage and Sunday Lake, with a few requiring lift-overs.

During dry periods, Sterling Creek may be too low to carry a loaded canoe. Indeed, it could be virtually dry by August. People very seldom use the portages between Sunday and Stuart lakes, and the paths are often quite difficult to see. You will probably see more moose tracks than human footprints. The roughest of the portages is the 148-rod trail, which climbs a steep hill separating Sterling and Bibon lakes. The other two half-mile carries are not as exhausting as the shorter one.

If this all sounds like too much for one day, you could shorten the route 3 miles by camping on Sterling Lake. To do so, however, you must get prior authorization from the Forest Service to camp in the Sundial Lake PMA (see Chapter 1).

Day 3 (8 miles): Stuart Lake, p. 74 rods, **Stuart River,** p. 14 rods, **river,** p. 74 rods, **river,** p. 52 rods, **river,** p. 85 rods, **river,** p. 480 rods. Beaver dams are scattered along the Stuart River, and during low-water periods you may have to step out of your canoe on occasion, particularly at the lower (north) end of the shallow, winding stream. Watch for moose throughout the day. This is a very good area in which to see them. None of the first five portages is difficult—particularly after what you have already experienced. That's good, because you'll need your energy for the final carry.

Should you get a late start this morning or find it necessary to make an early camp, you'll find an unofficial campsite on the north shore of White Feather Lake. To camp there, however, you must get prior authorization from the USFS to spend a night in the Sundial Lake Primitive Management Area (see Chapter 1), which includes White Feather Lake. It is accessible through a short stream that connects it to the Stuart River just southeast of the 52-rod portage. You may see the charred remains of the White Feather Fire along the west side of the Stuart River near White Feather Lake. While this area was already a good place to see moose, the fire created even more browse for these creatures. They should continue to prosper for years to come.

If the water level is high, you might be able to shorten the final long portage by about 50 rods. Paddle 25 rods past the portage landing on the Stuart River to the mouth of Swamp Creek on the right. Continue paddling up this tiny creek for about 65 rods to its intersection with the Stuart River portage. Land on the south (left) bank and start your portage there. After crossing another small creek, the trail ascends more than 100 feet during the ensuing 100 rods. The final 220 rods of the portage are mostly level to gently undulating. The trail has a good path all the way from the river to the small parking lot next to the Echo Trail.

ROUTE #20-2: The Green Iron Gun Loop

8 Days, 76 Miles, 26 Lakes, 5 Rivers, 5 Creeks, 38 Portages

DIFFICULTY: Most rugged

FISHER MAPS: F-9, F-16, F-17

INTRODUCTION: This is a terrific route for seasoned canoeists in good physical condition who want a variety of canoeing experiences. After the long portage to Angleworm Lake, you will continue northbound on a chain of small lakes from Angleworm to Thunder Lake. Then you'll steer northwest from Beartrap Lake and follow the Beartrap River downstream to Sunday Lake. Sterling Creek will then carry you west to a short chain of small lakes that entertains very few visitors. At Stuart Lake you will then steer northwest and follow the Dahlgren and Boulder rivers to Agnes Lake. The Oyster River will then carry you farther west to Oyster Lake. At that point, you will turn north and cross a chain of small lakes leading to Pocket Lake. That's when the easiest part of the journey begins. From the mouth of Pocket Creek, you'll enter Lac La Croix and paddle east to the Canadian border. After viewing a couple of historic sites there, you will follow the international boundary southeast to Friday Bay of Crooked Lake. From there, you'll reenter a region of smaller lakes and tiny creeks that lead back to your origin at Angleworm Lake.

Along the way, you will be entertained by two lovely waterfalls, a large display of prehistoric Indian rock paintings, and scenery that includes large lakes and tiny creeks. The label of "rugged" for this route is well deserved, but only because of the first two and last two days of the expedition. The middle part of the loop ranges from challenging to easy. Because of the beginning and the end, however, only seasoned canoeists in top physical condition should embark on this journey.

Part of this route passes through the Sundial Lake Primitive Management Area (see Chapter 1). The Forest Service does not maintain portages between Beartrap Lake and Stuart Lake, and camping is not permitted there without a special permit. Wildfire consumed 4,750 acres of forest in that PMA in 1996. While this area was already a good place to see moose, the fire created even more browse for these creatures. They should continue to prosper for years to come.

If you're behind schedule after the second day, or if 8 days in the Wilderness is just too long for your summer vacation, a couple of good shortcuts are possible. You could eliminate two days of travel by heading directly to Iron Lake from Stuart Lake (see comments for Day 2, Route #20). Or you could take a longer route to Iron Lake via the Dahlgren River to Lac La Croix, then east through Bottle Lake. Either way, though, you'll still have two rugged days at the beginning and two more at the end of this exhausting route.

This probably isn't the kind of route that most dedicated anglers would consider. If you have enough energy left at the end of each day to cast a line, however, you'll find plenty of game fish in the lakes along this route. Walleyes, northern pike, smallmouth bass, black crappies and even lake trout may be found in the water beneath your canoe.

Warning: *When water levels are low, at least one of the streams on this route may be too shallow for navigation of a loaded canoe. Sterling Creek is capable of nearly drying up by late summer or during a very dry year.*

Day 1 (7 miles): P. 640 rods, **Angleworm Lake,** p. 48 rods, **Home Lake,** p. 260 rods, **Gull Lake,** p. 40 rods, **Mudhole Lake,** p. 60 rods, **Thunder Lake.** (See comments for Day 1, Route #20-1.)

Day 2 (11 miles): Thunder Lake, p. 5 rods, **Beartrap Lake,** p. 200 rods, **Beartrap River,** p. 65 rods, **river,** p. 20 rods, **river, Sunday Lake,** p. 17 rods, **Beartrap River, Sterling Creek,** p. 160 rods, **creek,** p. 8 rods, **Sterling Lake,** p. 148 rods, **Bibon Lake,** p. 10 rods, **Nibin Lake,** p. 180 rods, **Stuart Lake.** (See comments for Day 2, Route #20-1.)

Day 3 (10 miles): Stuart Lake, p. 118 rods, Dahlgren River, p. 140 rods, **Boulder River, Lac La Croix,** p. 65 rods, **Boulder River,** p. 24 rods, **Agnes Lake.** This is a delightful day of paddling on two more rivers, but much easier than the preceding two days. The two portages along the Dahlgren River are not difficult. The first passes over a low

Portaging from Rocky Lake to Green Lake

hill and through a lovely stand of old-growth pines. A small waterfall highlights the setting at the west end of the portage. The longest portage of the day (140 rods) gradually descends nearly 50 feet to the Boulder River.

There are several nice campsites on Agnes Lake. Don't delay in claiming one. This is a popular overnight stop for paddlers, as well as a destination in itself. Bears are traditional pests in this area. Hang your food pack well. If you hang it properly and maintain a clean campsite, you should have nothing to fear.

Day 4 (11 miles): Agnes Lake, p. 180 rods, **Oyster River,** p. 60 rods, **Oyster Lake,** p. 65 rods, **Rocky Lake,** p. 85 rods, **Green Lake,** p. 120 rods, **Ge-be-on-e-quet Lake,** p. 23 rods, **Ge-be-on-e-quet Creek, Pocket Creek,** p. 15 rods, **Pocket Lake.** After the first portage, you'll leave most of the traffic behind, especially north of Oyster Lake. All of the portages have good paths. The longest trail (120 rods) climbs over a low hill at the beginning and then descends nearly 100 feet, including a rather steep drop for the final 20 rods.

Two large beaver dams on Ge-be-on-e-quet and Pocket creeks kept the water level high in both creeks during the very dry summer of 1997. The 3-foot-high dam on Ge-be-on-e-quet Creek requires a lift-over. The dam on Pocket Creek is located at the beginning of the portage from Pocket Creek to Lac La Croix. If that dam continues to hold the water at a high level, the 15-rod portage to Pocket Lake may not be necessary. Try paddling right up through the narrow, shallow channel.

Campsites along this chain of lakes are generally small, most with only one good tent site, until you reach Pocket Lake. There you will find a beautiful campsite at the top of a large outcrop of ledge rock sloping up from the water on the west shore of Pocket Lake. It has plenty of space for three or four tents. Anglers may find walleyes, northern pike and smallmouth bass swimming nearby.

Day 5 (12 miles): Pocket Lake, p. 15 rods, **Pocket Creek**, p. 15 rods, **Lac La Croix**, p. 80 rods, **Bottle Lake, Bottle River, Iron Lake.** This is, by far, the easiest day of your trip so far, if a strong south wind is not a problem on Lac La Croix. It affords an opportunity to explore the fascinating southeast end of Lac La Croix while en route to Iron Lake. The short portage from Pocket Creek to Lac La Croix may vary from 15 to 20 rods, depending on the water level in the creek.

On the west shore of Canada's Irving Island, at two locations, there are fine displays of old Indian rock paintings—the largest displays of pictographs in the Quetico-Superior region. About a mile farther south, then, you will see Warrior Hill, also on the Canadian shoreline (8 miles from your Pocket Lake campsite). Legends suggest that this was once the testing ground for the bravery and strength of Ojibway braves who ran from the lake's edge to the summit of the rocky precipice.

The only challenging portage of the day (Bottle Portage) bypasses a 23-foot drop in the Bottle River by cutting across a large Canadian peninsula. The wide trail is well used but not well maintained, with muddy potholes throughout the path. You'll be heading uphill, but the climb isn't nearly as bothersome as the muddy path.

You may see or hear a few motorboats on the Canadian side of the border throughout this day. Guides from the Lac La Croix First Nation, an Ojibway community living on the north shore of Lac La Croix, use them. By agreement with the Canadian government, the guides are permitted to use motorboats up to 10 horsepower on 10 lakes each year from a list of 20 lakes in the western third of Quetico Provincial Park. Crooked, Bottle and Iron lakes are among those 20 lakes. Plan to camp in the quiet south end of Friday Bay.

There are several campsites on the US side of Iron Lake. Stake your claim to the first available site that you see at the west end of the lake. This is a popular destination for both anglers and sightseers.

Day 6 (12 miles): Iron Lake, p. 140 rods, **Crooked Lake** to **Friday Bay**. If you thought the previous day was easy, this one should also be a breeze. Your only portage is around beautiful Curtain Falls, which cascades a total of 29 feet from Crooked Lake to Iron Lake. It is, by far, the most spectacular waterfall in the western part of the BWCA Wilderness. You'll be approaching it from the bottom. The portage on the US side is not difficult, but steadily uphill. You may put in at the very brink of the falls, or about 100 feet farther into Crooked Lake. The choice is yours, but I recommend the second as the safest one during normal water conditions for a group that may not be strong enough to contend with the swift current at the top of the falls. Use your own judgment and be careful.

Day 7 (8 miles): Crooked Lake, p. 130 rods, **Papoose Creek, Papoose Lake, Papoose Creek, Chippewa Lake, Chippewa Creek,** p. 5 rods, **creek, Niki Lake,** p. 45 rods, **Wagosh Lake,** p. 320 rods, **Gun Lake,** p. 30 rods, **Gull Lake,** p. 260 rods, **Home Lake.** This is a quiet part of the BWCA Wilderness where you aren't likely to encounter many other people paddling on the tiny creeks and small lakes. All of the portages this day have surprisingly good paths, but there are a few challenging trail segments. The first half of the first portage is uphill, but not steep. At a junction near the end of the trail, bear left on a newer path that leads to a boggy landing on the upstream side of a beaver dam. The old landing is below the dam.

The creeks from Friday Bay to Niki Lake pass through tamarack swamps. Watch for pitcher plants along the boggy banks of the creeks. The 5-rod portage on the creek bypasses a beaver dam.

The 45-rod portage starts with a steep climb from the shore of Niki Lake, gaining nearly 70 feet in elevation over the first 30 rods. Then, after passing through a mud hole, the final 10 rods surmount another small hill before dropping down to the east end of Wagosh Lake.

The mile-long carry from Wagosh Lake to Gun Lake may be a pleasant surprise. Although it starts on a rather rocky path, the path gets better and better as it progresses south to Gun Lake. The first 50 rods are fairly level, but then the trail surmounts a large hill, gaining over 100 feet in as many rods. The last half of the trail is either level or sloping gently downhill, with an excellent gravel path that descends as many feet as it gained on the other side of the hill.

The short portage at the other end of Gun Lake (30 rods) has a good path until you reach the end. A beaver dam flooded the landing area on Gull Lake, and the put-in is now awkward, at best.

If you want to save the last long portage to Home Lake for tomorrow, you'll find a couple of nice campsites on the north shore of Gull Lake. During the busiest part of the summer, though, there will be competition for these sites. So claim one early. Then relax. You'll need your energy tomorrow.

Day 8 (5 miles): Home Lake, p. 48 rods, **Angleworm Lake,** p. 640 rods. Your final day of this route is the reverse of your first day. Unfortunately, the Angleworm portage isn't any easier heading this way. But at least you'll get the toughest part over with first this time.

Entry Point 77 — South Hegman Lake

SEASONAL PERMITS: 205

POPULARITY RANK: 32nd

DAILY QUOTA: 2

LOCATION: South Hegman Lake is located 10 miles almost due north of Ely. To drive there, follow the Echo Trail north from County Road 88 for 10.8 miles to a mile beyond the point at which the blacktop ends and gravel begins. Watch for the signed access road on the east (right) side of the Echo Trail, which loops in to the beginning of the South Hegman Lake portage.

DESCRIPTION: Small parking lots flank each side of the trailhead for the portage. Designed to accommodate about a dozen vehicles, the lot is sometimes overflowing with cars and trucks. From the parking lot an 80-rod portage leads east to the southwest corner of South Hegman Lake.

The Fenske Lake Campground is the closest public campground. Located along the Echo Trail just three miles away (toward Ely), it is a good place to spend the night before your canoe trip. A fee is charged.

The Hegman lakes (North and South) have been included in the BWCA Wilderness only since 1979. But they have long been favorites among weekend campers and day-trippers, as well as amateur historians in search of the most vivid display of Indian rock paintings in the entire Quetico-Superior region.

Don't let the statistics above fool you. South Hegman Lake is one of the most popular entry points along the Echo Trail. Most visitors, however, don't spend a night in the wilderness. They paddle to the pictographs, have lunch nearby and then leave the Wilderness. It is a wonderful day trip. Among all BWCAW entry points, South Hegman Lake ranks 3rd in the number of non-quota day-use permits issued each summer (2nd among canoeing entry points).

There is also high demand for the limited number of overnight permits available. South Hegman Lake ranked 14th among all entry points with quotas filled the greatest number of days in 1997. So don't wait to make your reservation. Without a reservation, your chances of getting a permit at the last minute are slim, especially if you plan to start your journey on a Friday, Saturday, Sunday or Monday. Motorboats are not allowed here.

A canoe trip from South Hegman Lake can be much more than a visit to the pictographs. This lovely entry point also provides access to the same remote, peaceful and rugged wilderness that is served by neighboring Angleworm Lake. While a day trip to the rock paintings is quite easy, a journey beyond them is a difficult task not recommended for weak or inexperienced canoeists. In addition to the routes described below, you can also access from South Hegman Lake the two routes suggested for the Angleworm Lake entry point.

ROUTE #77-1: The Angleworm Fairy Route

3 Days, 22 Miles, 13 Lakes, 3 Creeks, 15 Portages

DIFFICULTY: Challenging

FISHER MAPS: F-9 (F-17 optional)

INTRODUCTION: This is a terrific route for seasoned canoeists with only three days to spend in the Wilderness. From South Hegman Lake, you will first paddle northeast to Trease Lake, where a long portage leads farther north to Angleworm Lake. After continuing northeast to Gull Lake, your route then loops southeast through a chain of popular lakes leading to Mudro Lake. From there you will steer a westward course, exit the BWCA Wilderness and continue paddling through Picket Lake to the public landing at Nels Lake. The route ends 2 miles by road from your origin.

You may enjoy a variety of experiences along this short route, including a peaceful night in remote isolation, followed by another night on one of the most popular lakes in this part of the Boundary Waters. Small lakes, large lakes, tiny creeks and portages of all sizes all contribute to the appeal of this multifaceted loop. While most of the portages are quite easy and less than ¼ mile long, three trails exceed ½ mile in length, including one measuring 1½ miles long.

Anglers will have some good opportunities along this route to hook some game fish. With a good population of walleyes, northern pike, bluegills and smallmouth bass, Fourtown Lake has long been a popular destination for anglers. The same species are found in Fairy and Gun lakes, and most other lakes also contain walleyes and northern pike.

Since only 2 miles of road separate your starting and ending points, you'll have the option of either shuttling vehicles between boat landings or walking the final 2 miles back to your car at the South Hegman Lake parking lot. Either way, when you get to the west end of the Nels Lake access road, turn right and follow the Echo Trail 1.3 miles north to find the South Hegman Lake entry point.

Day 1 (7 miles): P. 80 rods, **South Hegman Lake**, p. 15 rods, **North Hegman Lake, creek, Trease Lake**, p. 480 rods, **Angleworm Lake**, p. 48 rods, **Home Lake.** Even if you have never carried a canoe before, that first ¼-mile portage should pose no problem. It has an excellent path that descends more than 80 feet. The charred stumps along the north (left) side of the trail are the results of a fire that burned 74 acres in May of 1996. The fire was intentionally ignited by the Forest Service to manage the forest. Near the end of the portage, you'll pass through a lovely stand of Norway pines. The final 2 rods of trail descend steeply to the shore of South Hegman Lake, with log steps to mitigate the treachery there.

The short carry between South Hegman and North Hegman lakes (15 rods) can be even shorter (5 rods) if the connecting creek is deep enough to float a canoe.

As you enter the creek that joins North Hegman and Trease lakes, you'll see steep cliffs on the west shoreline. Look closely about 8 feet above the waterline and you will see dark red symbols on the rock that were painted hundreds of years ago by unknown artists. This small display is one of the most vivid rock paintings found in the BWCA Wilderness. As you continue northbound through the shallow creek, also watch for pitcher plants growing in the bordering bog.

At the north end of Trease Lake, 3 rods to the right of a rock shelf that serves as a picnic site for day-trippers, you'll find the start of the longest portage on this route. After crossing over a small hill, the trail descends into a soft, wet spruce bog where it is difficult to maintain dry feet. Then a field of large boulders obstructs the path. Soon, however, the path improves as the trail climbs more than 100 feet to a high (and dry) rock ridge. A few rock cairns help mark the way along the bald parts of the ridge. About 400 rods north of Trease Lake, you'll come to a 3-way junction with the Angleworm Trail. The trail to your left leads west to the Angleworm parking lot at the Echo Trail. The east branch of the Angleworm Trail (for hikers) leads east (hard right), while the portage continues in a northeast direction. Just ¼ mile farther, watch for a short spur trail branching off to the right from the hiking trail. It leads down to the south end of Angleworm Lake.

If you've had enough for one day after that long portage, you'll find several good campsites on Angleworm Lake. There are 4 sites along the west shore of the lake accessible to backpackers. The nicest sites, however, are on the east shore of the lake. If you can make it a little farther, there is a nice campsite for canoeists on Home Lake. Another site for backpackers is in a lovely stand of tall pines just north of the lake, 20 rods west of the portage trail to Gull Lake.

Day 2 (8 miles): Home Lake, p. 260 rods, **Gull Lake**, p. 30 rods, **Gun Lake**, p. 50 rods, **Fairy Lake**, p. 15 rods, **Boot Lake**, p. 35 rods, **Fourtown Lake.** The long portage from Home Lake has a good path that starts out with a gradual climb for the first 70 rods, followed by a steeper descent for the next 60 rods. The last half of the trail is nearly level or gently undulating, ending at a rock outcrop on the west shore of Gull Lake. At 12 rods from Home Lake a trail spurs off to the left from the portage trail leading to the backpacker campsite. Stay to the right for the portage to Gull Lake. You will cross the Angleworm Trail 30 rods from Home Lake. There are some large, very old white pines along the portage, including one that must surely be over 300 years old.

The other four short portages are well used and, for the most part, easy. The landing for the 30-rod trail connecting Gull and Gun lakes, however, may be submerged, muddy and somewhat concealed if a beaver dam is still maintaining a high level on Gull Lake (as it was during the summer of 1998). The only poor path is found at the 50-rod portage, where rocks, roots and mud obstruct the path.

Find a campsite as early as possible on Fourtown Lake. There are several nice sites. This popular lake attracts many visitors throughout the summer. If you don't mind paddling 3 miles out of your way (round-trip), you'll probably find the most solitude at one of the nice campsites at the north end of the lake.

Day 3 (7 miles): Fourtown Lake, p. 10 rods, **Fourtown Creek**, p. 140 rods, **creek**, p. 30 rods, **Mudro Lake, Picket Creek**, p. 30 rods, **Picket Lake**, p. 20 rods, **Picket Creek**, p. 185 rods, **Nels Lake.** The three portages between Fourtown and Mudro lakes have rough, rocky paths that may be treacherous when wet. At the first portage, in low water, you may have to take out on the west (right) bank of Fourtown Creek 5 rods before the start of the 10-rod portage (which is on the east bank of the creek). The 140-rod trail climbs up along a high rock ridge on the west side of a steep ravine. Use caution! There are some slippery spots, especially when the ground is wet, and the rocky path sometimes skirts precariously close to the edge of the steep ravine. When the water level is low, you may have to add up to 10 more rods to the end of the 30-rod trail.

Watch out for submerged rocks in Picket Creek. It is quite shallow and rocky even when running full, especially where it enters Mudro Lake. When the water level is low in the creek, you may have to start the 30-rod carry to Picket Lake along the soft, grassy bank of the creek, 15-30 rods before the official start of the portage, which has a smooth, sandy and level path. At the end of that portage, the trail crosses a gravel road. The Chainsaw Sisters Saloon is on the north side of the portage, along with a private parking lot for visitors using the Mudro Lake entry point. Although this is a public portage, the land it crosses is private. You can shorten your trip by 3½ miles if you leave a car at this parking lot. It is 8¼ miles by road from the South Hegman Lake parking lot. After that point, you'll be outside the BWCA Wilderness, although it looks much the same along the final 3½ miles of the route to the Nels Lake landing.

The final portage is mostly level, but challenging. A log spans a small creek midway across the portage. It is quite slippery when wet, so use caution!

ROUTE #77-2: **The Pictograph Route**

5 Days, 49 Miles, 17 Lakes, 2 Rivers, 4 Creeks, 20 Portages

DIFFICULTY: Challenging

FISHER MAPS: F-9, F-10, F-17

INTRODUCTION: This interesting route leads to some of the most interesting and beautiful scenery in the BWCA Wilderness. From South Hegman Lake, you will first paddle northeast to Trease Lake, where a long portage leads farther north to Angleworm Lake. The route continues northeast through a chain of small lakes and tiny creeks leading to the Canadian border. From Friday Bay of Crooked Lake, then, you will paddle southeast to the mouth of the Basswood River. After portaging past three lovely waterfalls and several sets of rapids, you will then enter big Basswood Lake. From the southwest end of Jackfish Bay, the route then leads west to exit the BWCAW at Mudro Lake and terminate at the Nels Lake landing.

Along the way, you'll have splendid opportunities to view ancient Indian rock paintings at two different sites. You'll also experience several tiny creeks, two larger rivers, and picturesque lakes ranging in size from tiny to the largest in the BWCA Wilderness. While much of the route is quite popular with visitors, you'll also enjoy a part of the Wilderness that entertains very few paddlers, even during the busiest part of the summer season.

Although most groups of competent paddlers should have no problem completing this loop in five days, serious photographers and avid anglers should consider adding a sixth day.

Since only 2 miles of road separate your starting and ending points, you'll have the option of either shuttling vehicles between boat landings or walking the final 2 miles back to your car at the South Hegman Lake parking lot. Either way, when you get to the west end of the Nels Lake access road, turn right and follow the Echo Trail 1.3 miles north to find the South Hegman Lake entry point.

Day 1 (7 miles): P. 80 rods, **South Hegman Lake,** p. 15 rods, **North Hegman Lake, creek, Trease Lake,** p. 480 rods, **Angleworm Lake,** p. 48 rods, **Home Lake.** (See comments for Day 1, Route #77-1.)

Day 2 (8 miles): Home Lake, p. 260 rods, **Gull Lake,** p. 30 rods, **Gun Lake,** p. 320 rods, **Wagosh Lake,** p. 45 rods, **Niki Lake, creek,** p. 5 rods, **creek, Chippewa Lake, creek, Papoose Lake, Papoose Creek,** p. 130 rods, **Friday Bay of Crooked Lake.** (See comments for Day 2, paragraph 1, Route #77-1.) On this day you'll pass through another lovely region that entertains few visitors. The long portage leading north from the east end of Gun Lake is not nearly as bad as you might expect. It has an excellent gravel path that gradually ascends nearly 100 feet in elevation during the first 160 rods. It then descends for 110 rods before it levels out near the end. The path is rockier and rougher toward the Wagosh Lake end.

The next short portage (45 rods) first climbs up over a small hill for 10 rods to drop into a mud hole. The final 35 rods descend steeply to Niki Lake.

The 5-rod portage on the creek passes a beaver dam. The creeks from Niki Lake to Friday Bay pass through tamarack swamps. Watch for pitcher plants along the boggy banks of the creeks.

The final portage starts in a soft, muddy bog, from which a newer trail first skirts the edge of Papoose Creek to bypass a beaver dam. It then joins the original trail, which has a much better path that descends gradually to the south end of Friday Bay.

Claim the first good campsite you see in Friday Bay. Crooked Lake is a popular destination for anglers. Walleyes, northern pike, small-mouth bass and black crappies inhabit the lake.

Day 3 (13 miles): Crooked Lake. Without a single portage, this easy day of paddling will enable you to enjoy the many interesting bays

Lower Basswood Falls

of Crooked Lake and the historic sites along the Canadian border. Keep your compass handy. Crooked Lake is aptly named and quite confusing, especially in the east end. At least one eagle's nest is near the east end of the lake, and it is not unusual to see eagles soaring overhead. Table Rock, located just east of Wednesday Bay, is an historic campsite where many a Voyageur rested while en route from Lake Superior to Lake Athabasca. A fine display of Indian rock paintings may be seen on the cliffs along the US shore of the lake, about 1½ miles north of Lower Basswood Falls.

You may see or hear a few motorboats on the Canadian side of Crooked Lake. Guides from the Lac La Croix First Nation, an Ojibway community living on the north shore of Lac La Croix, use them. By agreement with the Canadian government, the guides are permitted to use motorboats up to 10 horsepower on 10 lakes each year from a list of 20 lakes in the western third of Quetico Provincial Park. Crooked is one of those lakes.

Try to get an early start this day and claim a campsite near Lower Basswood Falls as early in the day as possible. The Basswood River is a *very* popular destination. During the busy summer season, *all* of the campsites may be occupied by *early* afternoon.

Day 4 (10 miles): Crooked Lake, p. 43 rods, **Basswood River,** p. 32 rods, **river,** p. 30 rods, **river,** p. 340 rods, **Basswood Lake, Jackfish**

Bay. This is one of the most scenic parts of the entire BWCA Wilderness. Get an early start this day. Then take your time to explore the beautiful Basswood River, where three waterfalls and several more rapids attract photographers and anglers alike.

At the first three short portages, there are trails on both sides of the river. I prefer the trails on the Canadian side of the border at the first two portages and the US trail at the third portage. All have well-beaten paths. The easiest access to the first portage is also the farthest from the base of Lower Basswood Falls, at a small sandy landing on the Canadian shoreline. The trail passes through a campsite and leads to a good, smooth landing near the top of the waterfall. Exercise caution while launching in the swift current at the top of the falls, especially when the water level is high. The second trail goes around Wheelbarrow Falls, and the clay path may be muddy after rains. The third portage skirts past a small set of rapids. The path is a little rocky.

The longest and most challenging portage of the day passes Basswood Falls and several rapids and pools below the falls. The trail begins on the US shore and follows a pretty good path east for just over a mile. At several points along the trail, there are spur trails leading off to the left. Some lead to campsites; others lead to river access points between rapids. The safest, easiest and quickest way to bypass the whole area is to bear right at all intersections and walk the entire distance to Basswood Lake. But if you wish, you can take three or four shorter portages and contend with some swift water and/or rapids (depending on the water level). Beware dangerous currents! Many people have drowned in the Basswood River. That's why I recommend simply portaging around the whole area.

Jackfish Bay constitutes the westernmost end of huge Basswood Lake. Motorboats with 25-horsepower motors are permitted on the bay. They are not allowed, however, on the main part of Basswood Lake northeast of the Bay. The farther from Basswood Falls you paddle, the less competition there is for the campsites. If a southwest wind is blowing, however, you may want to claim one of the sites near the entrance to the Bay (about 13 miles from the route's end at Nels Lake). Then get an early start the next morning to cross the bay before the wind picks up.

Day 5 (11 miles): Jackfish Bay of Basswood Lake, **Range River,** p. 15 rods, **river,** p. 25 rods, **Sandpit Lake,** p. 80 rods, **Mudro Lake, Picket Creek,** p. 30 rods, **Picket Lake,** p. 20 rods, **Picket Creek,** p. 185 rods, **Nels Lake.** On your way up the Range River, you may see some old dock pilings and an abandoned boat access that was once used at Pete's Landing. A 3-foot-high beaver dam barricaded the river in 1998 just beyond the first portage. The 15-rod trail passes a small set of rapids, and you have two trail choices, one on each side of the river.

The next short portage (25 rods) extends 10 rods from the Range River to a junction with a long portage connecting Range and Sandpit lakes. At the junction, bear right and follow that excellent trail another 15 rods to the southeast end of Sandpit Lake.

The next portage (80 rods) climbs over a big hill. From the west end of Sandpit Lake, the trail gains nearly 85 feet in elevation during the first 40 rods, before descending more gradually to the east end of Mudro Lake. (Also see comments for Day 3, paragraphs 2-3 Route #77-1.)

Entry Points 22 & 23 — Mudro Lake

SEASONAL PERMITS: 984

POPULARITY RANK: 9th

DAILY QUOTA: 8

LOCATION: Mudro Lake is 8 airline miles north of Ely. From County Road 88, follow the Echo Trail 8¼ miles northwest to Forest Route 459. Just beyond the Fenske Lake Campground, watch for a sign on the right pointing to Mudro Lake and Fenske Lake Resort. Turn right onto F.R. 459 and follow this good, but narrow, gravel road 4.3 miles to a stop sign at a T intersection with Forest Route 457 (may not be marked). Turn left there and continue on a rougher, narrower gravel road for 1.1 more miles to the USFS drop-off spot on the left side of the road. Parking is not allowed at the drop-off area or along the road near there. However, 0.2 mile farther down the road is a private parking lot adjacent to the Mudro Lake access point at the Chainsaw Sisters Saloon. A daily parking fee is charged ($2.50 in 1998) that must be paid in advance. It is open daily from 8 am to 10 pm throughout the summer (in 1998). You can also buy cold pop and beer, snacks and T-shirts there. If someone else is not dropping you off, this is the most convenient place to park and start your trip. The portage to Mudro Lake starts alongside Picket Creek just north of the wooden bridge on the east (right) side of the road.

Mudro Lake affords relatively easy access to one of the most attractive and most popular parts of the BWCA Wilderness. One of the loveliest parts of the Canadian boundary lies just one long day's journey from this entry point. There the Basswood River cascades over three waterfalls and several more rapids en route from Basswood Lake to Crooked Lake. The border region is quite popular among anglers and sightseers alike. But Mudro Lake also provides access to the same quiet and

Chainsaw Sisters Saloon at the Mudro Lake entry point

secluded part of the Wilderness that lies south of the border and is served by the preceding three entry points. Regardless of your taste in canoe trips, you're bound to find a suitable route from Mudro Lake. That just might explain why this is such a popular entry point.

A reservation is nearly always necessary for the Mudro Lake entry point. Without one, your chances of getting a permit are slim at best. It is the most heavily used entry point in the far-western part of the BWCA Wilderness. It also ranked 3rd among *all* entry points with quotas filled the greatest number of days in 1997, when 80% of the available permits were issued to visitors that summer. With eight overnight groups allowed to enter here each day, wilderness solitude may be elusive in the immediate vicinity of Mudro Lake.

Mudro Lake is unlike most other entry points by virtue of the fact that it has been assigned two entry point numbers. Entry Point 22 is "restricted," which means that visitors with this permit may not camp on Horse Lake at any time during their visit. Entry Point 23, on the other hand, is *not* restricted, which means that visitors may camp anywhere they wish, including on Horse Lake. The quota is 2 groups per day for Entry Point 22 and 6 groups per day for Entry Point 23. Neither of the routes described below includes a night on Horse Lake, so either entry point will work. If you think you may add an extra day or two to your canoe trip, and there is a chance that you may want to camp on Horse Lake, be sure to request Entry Point 23. Nevertheless, you may want to avoid Horse Lake even if you *are* allowed to camp there. It is often difficult to find an available campsite on that popular lake.

The Fenske Lake Campground is the closest place to camp the night before your canoe trip. You'll pass it on the way to Mudro Lake, 8 miles north of County Road 88 on the Echo Trail. A fee is charged for camping there.

ROUTE #22-1: The Three Falls Loop

3 Days, 28 Miles, 5 Lakes, 3 Rivers, 2 Creeks, 18 Portages

DIFFICULTY: Challenging

FISHER MAPS: F-9, F-10

INTRODUCTION: This is a marvelous route for conditioned canoeists who want to experience a little bit of everything that the BWCAW can offer in just three short days. From the parking lot at Picket Creek, you will first proceed east through Mudro and Sandpit lakes to Jackfish Bay of big Basswood Lake. From the northwest corner of Basswood Lake, you'll turn west and follow the picturesque Basswood River downstream to Lower Basswood Falls. From there, you will paddle into the mouth of the Horse River and follow that scenic stream southwest to Horse and Fourtown lakes. Fourtown Creek will carry you south to Mudro Lake and then you'll return to your origin.

Along the route, you'll enjoy three waterfalls, numerous rapids, three lovely rivers, a couple of tiny creeks and lakes ranging in size from tiny to huge. Portages also range from tiny to huge, the longest (over a mile long) marking the midpoint of the route. Most of the portages are short and relatively easy. Only three exceed ¼ mile in length, but all three are challenging. Experienced voyageurs should have no problem completing the loop in just three days. But this is not an easy trip. Northwoods neophytes and avid anglers should probably add a fourth day to their itinerary. If there is a strong northeast wind on your first day, you may want to reverse the route. Jackfish Bay is no place to contend with a strong headwind.

Anglers will find walleyes inhabiting most of the lakes along this route. Northern pike and bluegills are also present in Fourtown and Horse lakes. You may find lake trout, walleyes, northern pike, bass and whitefish occupying the depths of big Basswood Lake.

Day 1 (10 miles): P. 26 rods, **Picket Creek, Mudro Lake,** p. 80 rods, **Sandpit Lake,** p. 25 rods, **Range River,** p. 15 rods, **river, Jackfish Bay of Basswood Lake.** The first portage from the road has a good, smooth, sandy path to the main creek access. If the water level is quite high, the portage may not be necessary. Simply launch your canoe into Picket Lake, paddle under the wooden bridge and proceed through the narrow, shallow creek. When the water level is quite low in the creek, however, you may have to extend the carry along the soft, grassy bank of the creek another 15-30 rods before you can find a place where the creek is deep enough to float a loaded canoe. When such is the case, watch out for submerged rocks throughout the course of the creek. It is quite shallow and rocky, for that matter, even when running full, especially where it enters Mudro Lake.

The next portage (80 rods) climbs over a big hill and drops steeply down to Sandpit Lake, 63 feet lower than Mudro Lake. Be glad you are going this way.

At the southeast end of Sandpit Lake, paddle past the first landing that you see and proceed to the very end of the lake, where the 25-rod portage begins. If you stop at the first landing, you will add 15 rods to the portage, and those rods are likely to be wet ones. The portage starts out for 15 rods on an excellent path that extends all the way to Range Lake on an old railroad bed. Watch for the turnoff (left) to the Range River after 15 rods.

A 3-foot-high beaver dam barricaded the river in 1998 just above the next portage (15 rods). Two trails bypass some rapids, one path on each side of the river. A short distance farther downstream, you may see some old dock pilings and an abandoned boat access that were once used at Pete's Landing.

Jackfish Bay constitutes the westernmost end of huge Basswood Lake. Motorboats with 25-horsepower motors are permitted on the bay. They are not allowed, however, on the main part of Basswood Lake northeast of the Bay. You will have access to more than a dozen campsites in the motor-free area just beyond the bay. Don't wait too long to claim one. The closer you get to Basswood Falls, the more competition there is for the campsites nearby.

Day 2 (7 miles): Basswood Lake, p. 340 rods, **Basswood River,** p. 30 rods, **river,** p. 32 rods, **river.** Get ready for some strenuous activity, beautiful scenery, and probably lots of people. That sums up the Basswood River experience. Keep your camera handy.

The first long hike ("Horse Portage") is around Basswood Falls and several rapids and pools below the falls. The trail begins on the US shore just above the falls and follows a pretty good path west for just over a mile. At several points along the trail, there are spur trails leading off to the right. Some lead to campsites; others lead to river access points between rapids. The safest, easiest and quickest way to pass through the whole area is to bear left at all intersections and walk the entire distance. But if you wish, you can take three or four shorter portages and contend with some swift water and/or rapids (depending on the water level). Beware dangerous currents! Many people have drowned in the Basswood River. That's why I recommend simply portaging around the whole area. The trail has a good, well-worn path over a gentle downhill grade. Take time along the way to view the scenic river, falls and rapids that you are passing.

At the next two short portages, there are trails on both sides of the river. I prefer the trail on the US side of the border at the 30-rod portage and the trail on Canadian side of the border at the 32-rod "Wheelbarrow Portage." Both have well-beaten paths. While the first is a little rocky, though, the second will be muddy after rains. The first portage skirts past a small set of rapids, while the second trail goes around Wheelbarrow Falls.

Claim your campsite near Lower Basswood Falls as early as possible (not later than mid-day). There are several excellent sites from which to choose. This is a very popular area where campsites are definitely at a premium. Then take time to explore the falls and rapids along the Basswood River. Afternoon is the best time to photograph the waterfalls. If you cannot find an open campsite above Lower Basswood Falls, portage around the falls and claim a site in the narrow southeast end of Crooked Lake (see Day 3, paragraph 2 below).

Day 3 (11 miles): Basswood River, Horse River, p. 75 rods, **river,** p. 50 rods, **river, rapids, river,** p. 50 rods, **river, rapids, river, rapids, river, Horse Lake,** p. 70 rods, **Horse River,** p. 15 rods, **river,** p. 10 rods, **river,** p. 5 rods, **Fourtown Lake,** p. 10 rods, **Fourtown Creek,** p. 140 rods, **creek,** p. 30 rods, **Mudro Lake, Picket Creek,** p. 26 rods. By any measure, this is a long day of travel, with 11 portages along the way. And if the water level is low, it will take even longer, with several additional rapids around which there are no portage trails.

Nevertheless, if Indian rock paintings interest you, 3 more miles of paddling and 2 more portages may be in order. Before heading south to the Horse River, then, first head north to Crooked Lake. Take the 43-rod portage around Lower Basswood Falls on the Canadian (right) side of the border, and then paddle 1½ miles north on Crooked Lake to the spectacular cliffs on the US (west) shoreline. You'll see an assortment of fascinating Indian rock paintings there that have intrigued paddling passersby for centuries. Use extreme caution while approaching the portage near the top of the falls. The current there is usually swift, especially when the water level is high. The best put-in spot is the farthest from the base of the falls. As you approach the river below the falls, bear right and walk through a Canadian campsite to a small sandy beach at the landing beyond. You can put in sooner (30-33 rods), but you'll have to launch your canoe at the base of a steep rock ledge. This is no problem when the water level is high, but it's quite awkward when the river is low.

There are three bona-fide portages on the Horse River. None is difficult. They all have pretty good, well-beaten paths. The first and longest (75 rods) may be muddy, though, after rains or early in the summer. The second (50 rods) climbs the steepest at the beginning. The third (50 rods) has an 18-rod boardwalk near the middle which crosses a grassy bog. Depending on the water level and beaver activity, there will also be from 3 to 6 other shallow, rocky rapids where it may be necessary to walk or line your canoe—one about midway between the two 50-rod portages, and the others between the last portage and Horse Lake. In 1998, when the river was extremely low, a beaver dam at the 3rd rapids above the last 50-rod portage required another 10-rod carry on the right (north) side of the river. The final rapids are in a very narrow channel—barely wide enough for a canoe—regardless of the water level.

Four more rocky rapids slow travel between Horse and Fourtown lakes. Near the end of the 70-rod portage, you can put in at a newer landing after 55 rods (left fork here), if you wish, or continue on to the old landing at the end of 70 rods.

The three portages between Fourtown and Mudro lakes have rough, rocky paths that may be treacherous when wet. At the first portage, in low water, you may have to take out on the west (right) bank of Fourtown Creek 5 rods before the start of the 10-rod portage (which is on the east bank of the creek). The 140-rod trail climbs up along a high rock ridge on the west side of a steep ravine. Use caution! There are some slippery spots, especially when the ground is wet. The rocky path sometimes skirts precariously close to the edge of the steep ravine. When the water level is low, you may have to add up to 10 more rods to the end of the 30-rod trail.

Route #22-2: The Crooked Border Loop

8 Days, 90 Miles, 27 Lakes, 7 Rivers, 5 Creeks, 43 Portages

DIFFICULTY: Challenging

FISHER MAPS: F-9, F-10, F-16, F-17

INTRODUCTION: This is a terrific route for experienced and strong canoe trippers with plenty of time to explore much of the lovely region between the Echo Trail and the Canadian border. From Mudro Lake, you will first paddle and portage your way north through a popular part of the BWCA Wilderness to Thunder Lake. Then you'll steer northwest from Beartrap Lake and follow the Beartrap River downstream to Sunday Lake. Sterling Creek will carry you west to a short chain of small lakes that entertains very few visitors. At Stuart Lake, you will steer northwest and follow the Dahlgren and Boulder rivers to Agnes Lake. The Oyster River will then carry you farther west to Oyster Lake. At that point, you will turn north and cross a chain of small lakes leading to Pocket Lake. That's when the easiest part of the journey begins. From the mouth of Pocket Creek, you'll enter Lac La Croix and paddle east to the Canadian border. After viewing a couple of historic sites there, you will follow the international boundary southeast through Bottle, Iron and Crooked lakes to the mouth of the Basswood River at Lower Basswood Falls. At that point, the route veers southwest, away from the Canadian border, and follows the Horse River to Horse Lake. Finally, a southbound course from there leads you across Tin Can Mike and Sandpit lakes, back to your origin at Mudro Lake.

Along the way, you will be entertained by three spectacular waterfalls, two large displays of prehistoric Indian rock paintings, and scenery that includes large and small lakes, picturesque rivers and tiny creeks. The label of "challenging" for this route is well deserved, but only because the first two days of the expedition are downright rugged. Twenty of the 43 portages are encountered during the first two days. The rest of the loop ranges from less challenging to downright easy. The rugged beginning, however, makes the loop unsuitable for weak or inexperienced canoeists to do in 8 days. They should consider adding a couple of days or shortening the loop.

Pulling through a shallow spot in the Horse River

Although the international border lakes and the immediate vicinity of Fourtown Lake are well traveled, you should feel a degree of isolation throughout much of the rest of the route. On the second day, in particular, you will pass through the Sundial Lake Primitive Management Area (see Chapter 1). Portages are not maintained by the Forest Service between Beartrap Lake and Stuart Lake, and camping is not permitted there without a special permit. Wildfire consumed 4,750 acres of forest in that PMA in 1996.

If you're behind schedule after the second day, or if 8 days in the Wilderness is just too long for your summer vacation, a couple of good shortcuts are possible. You could eliminate 2 days of travel by heading directly to Iron Lake from Stuart Lake (see comments for Day 2, Route #19-2). Or you could take a longer route to Iron Lake via the Dahlgren River to Lac La Croix, then east through Bottle Lake. Either way, though, you'll still have two rugged days at the beginning of this route.

This probably isn't the kind of route that most dedicated anglers would consider. If you have enough energy left at the end of each day to cast a line, however, you'll find plenty of game fish in the lakes along this route. Walleyes, northern pike, smallmouth bass, black crappies and even lake trout may be found in the water beneath your canoe. Some of the best fishing in the BWCAW is found along the Canadian border, from Lac La Croix to the Basswood River.

Warning: *When water levels are low, one of the streams on this route may be too shallow for navigation of a loaded canoe. Sterling Creek is capa-*

ble of nearly drying up by late summer or during a dry year. When it does, you could alter your route by continuing down the Beartrap River to Iron Lake, bypassing Sterling Creek altogether.

Day 1 (11 miles): P. 26 rods, **Picket Creek, Mudro Lake,** p. 30 rods, **Fourtown Creek,** p. 140 rods, **creek,** p. 10 rods, **Fourtown Lake,** p. 35 rods, **Boot Lake,** p. 15 rods, **Fairy Lake,** p. 50 rods, **Gun Lake,** p. 30 rods, **Gull Lake,** p. 40 rods, **Mudhole Lake,** p. 60 rods, **Thunder Lake.** With 10 portages on the very first day of your canoe trip, this is certainly not an easy start. Fortunately, only one is long enough to create much of a challenge. The rest are simply good leg-stretchers and most have pretty good paths. The three portages between Mudro and Fourtown lakes, however, have rough and rocky paths that may be treacherous when wet. When the water level is low, you may have to add 10 more rods to the beginning of the 30-rod trail. The 140-rod trail climbs up along a high rock ridge on the west side of a steep ravine. Use caution! There are some slippery spots, especially when wet. The rocky path sometimes skirts precariously close to the edge of the steep ravine. In low water, you may have to extend the 10-rod portage by 5 more rods, after crossing the creek, to find a place in the creek deep enough to float a loaded canoe.

Travel is quicker from Fourtown Lake onward. The 50-rod trail, though, is plagued with rocks, roots and mud. There is a log "bridge" over one of the boggy spots. A big beaver dam on Gull Lake (1998) resulted in high water that makes the landings wet and muddy at both the 30-rod and 40-rod trails in and out of Gull Lake.

Although the traffic northwest of Fourtown Lake is somewhat less than that in the immediate Horse-Fourtown area, there is still considerable competition for the few campsites on these lakes. Get an early start this day and claim your site as soon as possible.

Day 2 (11 miles): **Thunder Lake,** p. 5 rods, **Beartrap Lake,** p. 200 rods, **Beartrap River,** p. 65 rods, **river,** p. 20 rods, **river, Sunday Lake,** p. 17 rods, **Beartrap River, Sterling Creek,** p. 160 rods, **creek,** p. 8 rods, **Sterling Lake,** p. 148 rods, **Bibon Lake,** p. 10 rods, **Nibin Lake,** p. 180 rods, **Stuart Lake.** (See comments for Day 2, Route #20-1.)

Day 3 (10 miles): **Stuart Lake,** p. 118 rods, **Dahlgren River,** p. 140 rods, **Boulder River, Lac La Croix,** p. 65 rods, **Boulder River,** p. 24 rods, **Agnes Lake.** (See comments for Day 3, Route #20-2.)

Day 4 (11 miles): **Agnes Lake,** p. 180 rods, **Oyster River,** p.60 rods, **Oyster Lake,** p. 65 rods, **Rocky Lake,** p. 85 rods, **Green Lake,** p. 120 rods, **Ge-be-on-e-quet Lake,** p. 23 rods, **Ge-be-on-e-quet Creek, Pocket Creek,** p. 15 rods, **Pocket Lake.** (See comments for Day 4, Route #20-2.)

Day 5 (12 miles): Pocket Lake, p. 15 rods, **Pocket Creek,** p. 15 rods, **Lac La Croix,** p. 80 rods, **Bottle Lake, Bottle River, Iron Lake.** (See comments for Day 5, Route #20-2.)

Day 6 (11 miles): Iron Lake, p. 140 rods, **Crooked Lake** to **Friday Bay.** (See comments for Day 6, Route #20-2.)

Day 7 (13 miles): Crooked Lake. (See comments for Day 3, Route #77-2.)

Day 8 (12 miles): Crooked Lake, p. 42 rods, **Basswood River, Horse River,** p. 75 rods, **river,** p. 50 rods, **river, rapids, river,** p. 50 rods, **river, rapids, river, rapids, river, Horse Lake,** p. 90 rods, **Tin Can Mike Lake,** p. 160 rods, **Sandpit Lake,** p. 80 rods, **Mudro Lake, Picket Creek,** p. 26 rods. (See comments for Day 3, Route #22-1, paragraphs 2-3.) The long portages to and from Tin Can Mike Lake have excellent paths that are well worn. The 90-rod trail passes over a very low hill. The 160-rod trail is virtually flat, with a 10-rod boardwalk across a boggy section near the beginning. The rest of the portage follows the path of an old railroad bed that once served logging operations in the area. Thus you can save your energy for the 80-rod portage, which gains nearly 85 feet in elevation during the first 40 rods before it descends more gradually to the east end of Mudro Lake.

|5

Entry from the **Fernberg Road**

The North-Central Area

THE FERNBERG ROAD IS PROBABLY KNOWN BY MORE VISITORS TO THE
BWCA Wilderness than any other highway. Four of the ten most popular entry points for the entire Wilderness are served by this road,
including Moose Lake and Lake One, the two most heavily used points
of access. The Fernberg Road also serves three other canoeing entry
points included in this guide.

To get there, simply follow State Highway 169 northeast from Ely,
past the International Wolf Center, through the small town of Winton
and across the Lake County line. This highway becomes the Fernberg
Road, an extension of Highway 169 into Lake County.

The road surface is blacktop all the way to its end at the Lake One
landing, about 20 miles east of Ely. It is a good, smooth road with relatively few sharp curves but numerous hills after the first few miles.
Some locals who are familiar with the road drive it quite fast, so
beware.

Ely is the town that serves visiting canoeists en route to the entry
points along Fernberg Road. The place to pick up your permit is at the
International Wolf Center (see paragraphs 2 and 3 in the introduction
to Chapter 3).

Entry Point 24—Fall Lake

SEASONAL PERMITS: 1,384

POPULARITY RANK: 5th

DAILY QUOTA: 14

LOCATION: Fall Lake is located about 3 miles northeast of Ely. To get to the public boat landing, follow the Fernberg Road for 5 miles from the International Wolf Center to Forest Route 551 (the "Fall Lake Road"). Turn left there and drive one mile north on that good blacktop road to the road's end at the Fall Lake Campground. The boat landing and a large parking lot are located adjacent to the campground.

DESCRIPTION: The Fall Lake Campground is, of course, a very convenient place to spend the night before your canoe trip. It is the largest campground on Superior National Forest, and it has a nice sandy beach that is popular among local swimmers. A fee is charged to camp there.

Located so close to Ely and accessible by such good roads, Fall Lake is by far the most convenient entry point for the BWCA Wilderness. Most of Fall Lake lies outside the Boundary Waters, where there are no restrictions on the use of motorboats. Along with several resorts and many private cabins and lake homes, some local outfitters also have bases on this lake. Only the northeast third of the lake is contained within the Wilderness boundary, where motorboats may not exceed 25 horsepower.

Fall Lake is also one of the most popular entry points for the Boundary Waters Canoe Area Wilderness—much busier than the statistics above might indicate. That is due in part to the fact that motorboats are permitted to enter the wilderness here. A designated motor route leads north to Basswood Lake, which is arguably the most popular and most productive fishing lake in the Ely area. About 20% of the overnight permits issued in 1997 went to motorists. But over 1,500 day-use motor permits were also issued. About 30% of those groups were restricted to Fall Lake; the rest were allowed to enter Basswood Lake.

In spite of its popularity, Fall Lake usually has available permits. Less than ⅔ of the available overnight permits are issued each summer. So, if you avoid starting on one of the busiest days of the week, you should have no problem acquiring a permit.

Although Fall Lake, itself, may have little appeal to the wilderness enthusiast, it does provide easy access to big, beautiful Basswood Lake, the enticing Basswood River, and a degree of wilderness solitude beyond. If you can tolerate the wakes of passing motorboats and the potential for strong, frustrating winds on Basswood Lake, you will surely find a worthwhile trip from Fall Lake. (See Entry Point 26—Wood Lake for other route ideas in this area.)

ROUTE # 24-1: The Basswood Lake Route
            3 Days, 36 Miles, 6 Lakes, 3 Portages

DIFFICULTY: Easier

FISHER MAPS: F-10

INTRODUCTION: This is a good route choice for a group of competent paddlers who prefer to avoid portages. It's also the easiest way to access Basswood Falls and the lovely river into which it cascades. From Fall Lake, you will first head north to enter the southwest end of big Basswood Lake at Pipestone Bay. From there, you will paddle without a single portage across the vast expanse of Basswood Lake to its east end at Inlet Bay. A short portage will then carry you south to Sucker Lake, the first in a chain of lakes leading southwest to Moose Lake. You will end your canoe trip at the Moose Lake landing, 15 miles by road from your origin.

Unless wind is a problem, this is one of the easiest routes you can take in the BWCA Wilderness. At trip's end you will have crossed only three portages, all of them easy trails. The vast majority of your time will be spent paddling along the historic Canadian border on the largest lake in the BWCA Wilderness, where strong winds are a constant threat and motorboats are permitted (except in the north-central part of the lake). If menacing winds are forecast, consider a different route. Basswood Lake is no place to be during a gale.

Throughout most of the route, anglers will find smallmouth bass, northern pike and walleyes in the depths below them. The largest northern pike ever caught in Minnesota (45 lbs. 12 oz.) was pulled from Basswood Lake. Lake trout also reside in parts of the lake. Since motorboats are permitted throughout much of the route, you should not expect silence and solitude. But the scenery is lovely, the campsites are plentiful, and the fishing is usually excellent.

Of course, you must leave a car at the Moose Lake landing, or make prior arrangements to be picked up there. It's a long walk from Moose Lake back to the Fall Lake Campground.

Day 1 (12 miles): Fall Lake, p. 80 rods, **Newton Lake,** p. 90 rods, **Pipestone Bay, Jackfish Bay, Basswood Lake.** Beware the effects of a strong north wind. It could slow your progress considerably right from the start, and it could also be quite treacherous on Pipestone Bay.

Both portages this day are virtual "highways," in terms of both trail quality and traffic quantity. Both trails have smooth paths that are 6 to 8 feet wide—smooth enough for portage wheels to transport motorboats and loaded canoes from lake to lake. The first trail bypasses Newton Falls, which is actually a long set of rapids that drop about 8 feet from Fall Lake to Newton Lake. There are two landings for the 90-rod portage about 10 rods apart. The two trails join together after about 10 rods of walking, so it matters not which one you choose. The westernmost trail has the widest and smoothest path and is the choice of those using portage wheels. Toward the end of the portage, it is a very scenic trail with a panoramic view across Pipestone Falls, some rapids and the narrow end of Pipestone Bay.

On a nice day, you may see as many day-tripping anglers and sightseers as overnight visitors heading to Pipestone Bay. A narrow trail that starts just west of the main (westernmost) portage trail skirts close to Pipestone Falls and leads to a good vantage point at the base of the falls. Use this trail to take photos, but use the good 90-rod path to portage your gear. It's much easier and safer.

Motorboats that don't exceed 25 horsepower are permitted on Pipestone Bay and Jackfish Bay. For a peaceful evening, plan to camp at one of the many campsites located just northeast of Jackfish Bay, where motorboats are prohibited.

Day 2 (13 miles): Basswood Lake. Because of the ever-present threat of wind on Basswood Lake, plan to get an early start this day. A strong head wind is always a retarding menace, but also beware the strong *tail* wind. When starting across a wide-open expanse of water with a strong wind at your back, the lake ahead of you may appear relatively calm and quite safe. As you proceed farther and farther out from the lee side of a sheltering shoreline, however, you will find that the waves grow higher and higher. Suddenly you may find your canoe in rougher water than you can handle, resulting in either a swamped or a capsized canoe. Wind can be either a friend or a foe, depending on how much respect you have for it and how much good judgment you demonstrate in its presence. It is always best to paddle close to the shoreline of a large lake. Not only is it safer, it is also far more interesting. That's where the wildlife resides.

For a pleasant diversion from a long day of paddling, consider a morning side trip to Basswood Falls at the source of the Basswood River, before paddling east along the Canadian border. "Horse Portage" bypasses Basswood Falls and several rapids and pools below the falls. The trail begins on the US shore (left side) just above the falls and follows a pretty good path west for just over a mile. At several points along the trail, there are spur trails leading off to the right. Some lead to campsites; others lead to river access points between rapids. Stow your canoe out of the way at the beginning of the portage. Then take time to explore this scenic area on foot. Your legs will appreciate the exercise.

For a 13-mile day, plan to camp on the south shore of Basswood Lake, just south of Norway Point, which separates Little Merriam Bay from Bayley Bay. Motorboats are once again permitted in this part of the lake on the US side of the international border. You may also see or hear a few motorboats on the Canadian side of the border throughout this day. Guides from the Lac La Croix First Nation, an Ojibway community on the north shore of Lac La Croix, use them. By agreement with the Canadian government, the guides are permitted to use motorboats up to 10 horsepower on 10 lakes each year from a list of 20 lakes in the western third of Quetico Provincial Park. Basswood Lake is among those 20 lakes.

Day 3 (11 miles): Basswood Lake, Bayley Bay, Inlet Bay, p. 20 rods, **Sucker Lake, Newfound Lake, Moose Lake.** If you haven't seen many other people during the first two days, consider yourself lucky. But your luck will surely end this day as you approach Moose Lake, the busiest of all BWCAW entry points. The chain of lakes from Moose to the Canadian border is a *very* popular route for paddlers heading northeast along the border lakes, for anglers en route to Basswood Lake, and for canoeists entering Canada's Quetico Provincial Park.

The only portage on this day has a good, uphill path on the Canadian side of the border. "Prairie Portage" is the location of a Canadian ranger station where paddlers en route to Quetico Provincial Park must check in to pick up their permits. Don't linger on this portage. It can be quite congested at times. A "truck portage" on the US side of the border transports motorboats between Basswood and Sucker lakes.

Route # 24-2: The Four Falls Route

5 Days, 48 Miles, 15 Lakes, 1 River, 4 Creeks, 19 Portages

Difficulty: Challenging

Fisher Maps: F-9, F-10, F-17

Introduction: This excellent route should appeal to just about anyone—angler, photographer, explorer, amateur historian, rookie or seasoned veteran of BWCAW trips. From Fall Lake, you will first head north to enter the southwest end of Basswood Lake at Pipestone Bay. From there, you will paddle the full length of Pipestone Bay and across the northeast corner of Jackfish Bay to the Canadian border at the northwest corner of big Basswood Lake. The scenic Basswood River will then transport you west, past three lovely waterfalls and several rapids, to the southeast corner of Crooked Lake. After pausing to view some ancient Indian pictographs, you will continue paddling along the Canadian border to Friday Bay of Crooked Lake. From that point, you will steer south to enter a region of tranquil lakes and tiny creeks that lead to popular Fourtown Lake. Continuing southbound to Mudro Lake, you will then exit the BWCA Wilderness via Picket Creek and head west to the public landing at Nels Lake. That is where this route ends, about 18 miles by road from its origin at Fall Lake.

This fascinating route leads to some of the most interesting and beautiful scenery in BWCA Wilderness. Along the way, you'll experience waterfalls and rapids, tiny creeks, large and small lakes, Indian rock paintings, and some of the best fish habitat in the entire Boundary Waters. While much of the route is quite popular with visitors, you'll also enjoy a part of the Wilderness that entertains relatively few paddlers, even during the busiest part of the summer season.

You will likely see and hear motorboats during the first day of your trip. Motors that do not exceed 25 horsepower are permitted on Fall and Newton lakes and on Pipestone and Jackfish bays of Basswood Lake. Guides from the Lac La Croix First Nation may also use 10-horsepower motorboats on the Canadian side of Basswood and Crooked lakes. The rest of the route is strictly for paddlers.

Pictographs on the Basswood River Cliffs

Northern pike and walleyes inhabit much of the water along this route. Anglers may also find smallmouth bass and black crappies in Basswood, Crooked and Fourtown lakes. In fact, all three lakes are considered by many to be among the best fishing lakes in the Boundary Waters.

Although most groups of competent paddlers should have no problem completing the route in five days, serious photographers, avid anglers, and weak or inexperienced parties should consider adding a sixth day. Furthermore, if you have an extra day to spare and you don't mind backtracking much of the first day's route, you could make this trip into a complete loop and avoid having to shuttle vehicles between starting and ending points. From Mudro Lake, steer east, instead of west, to enter the southwest end of Jackfish Bay (see comments for Day 1, Route #22-1). Spend your fifth night on Jackfish Bay and then return to Fall Lake via Pipestone Bay and Newton Lake.

Day 1 (11 miles): **Fall Lake,** p. 80 rods, **Newton Lake,** p. 90 rods, **Pipestone Bay, Jackfish Bay, Basswood Lake.** (See comments for Day 1, Route #24-1.)

Day 2 (7 miles): **Basswood Lake,** p. 340 rods, **Basswood River,** p. 30 rods, **river,** p. 32 rods, **river,** p. 43 rods, **Crooked Lake.** (See comments for Day 2 and Day 3, paragraph 2, Route #22-1.)

Day 3 (13 miles): **Crooked Lake** to **Friday Bay.** (See comments for Day 3, Route #77-2, paragraphs 1 and 2.)

Day 4 (8 miles): **Crooked Lake,** p. 130 rods, **Papoose Creek, Papoose Lake, Papoose Creek, Chippewa Lake, Chippewa Creek,** p. 5 rods, **creek, Niki Lake,** p. 45 rods, **Wagosh Lake,** p. 320 rods, **Gun Lake,** p. 50 rods, **Fairy Lake,** p. 15 rods, **Boot Lake.** (See comments for Day 7, Route #20-2, paragraphs 1-4.) Rocks, roots and mud obstruct the path of the 50-rod portage to Fairy Lake. There is a log "bridge" over one of the boggy spots. The final short portage has a good path.

Don't delay in claiming your campsite on Boot Lake, which receives a good deal of traffic from Fourtown Lake. The first site you'll come to sits high on a rock outcrop across from a scenic cliff.

Day 5 (9 miles): **Boot Lake,** p. 35 rods, **Fourtown Lake,** p. 10 rods, **Fourtown Creek,** p. 140 rods, **creek,** p. 30 rods, **Mudro Lake, Picket Creek,** p. 30 rods, **Picket Lake,** p. 20 rods, **Picket Creek,** p. 185 rods, **Nels Lake.** (See comments for Day 3, Route #77-1.)

Entry Point 25—Moose Lake

SEASONAL PERMITS: 3,060

POPULARITY RANK: 1st

DAILY QUOTA: 27

LOCATION: Moose Lake is15 airline miles northeast of Ely, a scant 3 miles south of the Canadian border. To get to the public access, drive east on the Fernberg Road for 16 miles from the International Wolf Center. Turn left onto Forest Route 438 (the "Moose Lake Road"). Follow that good blacktop road for nearly 3 miles north to the public landing and large parking area at the road's end.

DESCRIPTION: The Fall Lake Campground is a good place to spend the night prior to your canoe trip (see Entry Point 24: Location). Some outfitters on Moose Lake also offer bunkhouse accommodations for canoeists.

Moose Lake is, by far, the busiest entry point for the BWCA Wilderness. *More overnight travel permits are issued for Moose Lake each summer than for the 40 least popular entry points—combined.* The statistics above, however, tell only part of the story. Many private cabins and several resorts and outfitters are located in the southwest half of the 5-mile-long lake, which lies outside the BWCAW. The entry point is popular among both paddlers and motorboat operators. Motorboat use is restricted to 25 horsepower on Moose (the northeast half that lies in the BWCAW), Newfound, Sucker and Basswood lakes. While only 15% of the overnight camping permits were issued to motorists in 1997, there were over *2,000 day-use motor permits* also issued that summer. Most of the motor permits (72%) were issued to anglers heading for big Basswood Lake on the Canadian border, which is arguably the most popular and productive fishing lake in the Boundary Waters Canoe Area Wilderness.

In addition to providing easy access to the BWCAW, Moose Lake is also the quickest link to Quetico Provincial Park in Ontario. The Prairie Portage Ranger Station, located at the portage between Sucker and Basswood lakes (about 7 miles from the Moose Lake landing), is one of the most popular entry points for that Canadian park. Those paddlers are not reflected in the numbers mentioned above (if they don't camp in the BWCAW).

Nevertheless, if you can see past the noise and congestion on Moose Lake, you'll see a lovely chain of lakes that leads you to some of the most beautiful, interesting and peaceful lakes and streams in the Wilderness. Don't expect total solitude anywhere on either of the routes suggested below between Memorial Day and Labor Day. If sharing "your" lakes with other nature lovers doesn't bother you, however, you'll surely find these routes to be delightful. Furthermore, 25-30% of the overnight permits available for this popular entry point are *not* used each summer. So if you avoid starting on one of the busiest days of the week, you can probably get a permit. (See Entry Point 26 for other route ideas in this area.)

ROUTE # 25-1:   The Isle of Pines Loop

3 Days, 27 Miles, 11 Lakes, 1 River, 9 Portages

DIFFICULTY: Easier

FISHER MAPS: F-10, F-11

INTRODUCTION: This short loop leads you to the former homestead site of the last human inhabitant of the Boundary Waters Canoe Area Wilderness. From the Moose Lake landing, you will paddle northeast on the Moose chain of lakes to the Canadian border at the north end of Sucker Lake. You'll continue in a northeast direction along the international boundary to the southwest end of Knife Lake. Then, after paddling past Isle of Pines, you will steer southwest to cross Vera, Ensign and Splash lakes. Finally, from the east end of Newfound Lake, you will backtrack to the Moose Lake landing.

If you're looking for a quick and easy escape into seclusion, this is not the route to choose. But it offers a good introduction to wilderness canoeing on a blend of large and small lakes and the scenic Knife River. Portages are, for the most part, short and quite easy. There are two notable exceptions, however—one each on the second and third days. All along this busy route, campsites are at a premium. Don't wait too late each day to claim yours.

Throughout the loop, anglers will find walleyes, northern pike and smallmouth bass. There are also lake trout in Knife Lake for those who have the time and inclination to search for them. Although deer and moose are seldom seen along the route, the same is not true for black bears. Be sure to hang your food up in the air at night and during the day when you are away from camp. This is generally true for any heavily used part of the Wilderness.

Day 1 (10 miles): Moose Lake, Newfound Lake, Sucker Lake, Birch Lake. With no portages, this day is short and easy. Resist the temptation to continue traveling beyond Birch Lake. There is only one campsite on the US side of the Canadian border between Birch and Knife lakes. With 5 portages along that same stretch, however, it makes a long day of travel from Moose Lake all the way to Knife Lake. So relax. Claim a campsite near the east end of Birch Lake as early as possible, while there are still unoccupied sites. Although much of the traffic from Moose Lake heads east to Ensign Lake or northwest to Basswood Lake, a good deal of it continues along the Canadian border toward Knife Lake. Campsites are at a premium most of the time.

If you would like to shorten the paddling distance by a mile and stretch your legs on a short, easy portage, consider taking the 5-rod portage from the east end of Sucker Lake to Birch Lake. In addition, if you prefer to get off the busy border route for a night of solitude, you might consider portaging 100 rods south from Birch Lake to spend a night on Frog Lake. Of course, that means you'll have to start the next morning with the same 100-rod carry. You must decide whether solitude is worth the extra effort.

Day 2 (6 miles): Birch Lake, p. 48 rods, **Carp Lake,** p. 25 rods, **Melon Lake,** p. 15 rods, **Seed Lake,** p. 15 rods, **Knife River,** p. 75 rods, **Knife Lake,** p. 200 rods, **Vera Lake.** If the water level is high enough (but not too high) and you don't mind wet feet, you could eliminate all of the portages along the Knife River by walking your canoe up the series of gentle rapids around which the portages pass. Only on one occasion must you lift your canoe and gear—around a low falls. Use caution, though! Visibility in rapids is restricted, and there may be sharp rocks or deep holes between the rocks. On a warm, sunny day when the river is not too swift, however, it's a refreshing way to avoid four portages.

About a mile east of "Big Knife Portage" (75 rods), in a cluster of 3 small islands in Knife Lake, is the site of the BWCAW's last permanent resident. Dorothy Molter sold homemade rootbeer to canoeing passersby for nearly half a century. She called her home Isle of Pines. She passed away in December 1986. Two of her log cabins were then moved, log by log, to Ely and reconstructed as a memorial to her near the International Wolf Center.

The 200-rod portage from Knife to Vera Lake is a tough one—one of only two portages that challenge the "easier" rating for this route. It ascends steeply at the beginning, eventually to an elevation of nearly 120 feet above Knife Lake, before descending nearly that much to the east end of Vera Lake. Because of this difficult trail, canoe traffic on Vera is much lighter than on either Knife Lake or Ensign Lake. Nevertheless, don't delay in claiming your campsite. There is a nice one on the north shore soon after the portage.

Day 3 (11 miles): Vera Lake, p. 150 rods, **Ensign Lake,** p. 5 rods, **Splash Lake,** p. 30 rods, **Newfound Lake, Moose Lake.** The only challenging portage on the last day of this route is your first one—challenging in *two* ways. First, it climbs over a large hill, gaining nearly 100 feet in elevation during the first 65 rods. Second, *finding* the correct portage may be a challenge. As you paddle toward the west end of Vera Lake, you will first see a trail that starts just west of a campsite on the *east* side of a creek draining a bog into Vera Lake. That's a winter portage and not the one you want. Paddle past it to the very end of the lake, on the *west* side of the creek, where the correct portage for canoeists begins. Unlike the winter portage, this trail is high and dry, climbing to a rocky ridge inhabited by scrub oaks and maple trees. It then descends fairly steeply to the shore of Ensign Lake.

After you rejoin Newfound Lake, you will be backtracking the final 5 miles to your origin at the Moose Lake landing.

ROUTE # 25-2:	**The Scenic Lakes Loop**
	6 Days, 62 Miles, 25 Lakes, 4 Ponds, 1 River, 1 Creek, 28 Portages
DIFFICULTY:	Challenging
FISHER MAPS:	F-10, F-11, F-19
INTRODUCTION:	This route is a good choice for anyone in search of outstanding scenery. From the Moose Lake landing, you will paddle northeast on the Moose chain of lakes to the Canadian border at the north end of Sucker Lake. From there you'll continue in a northeast direction along the international boundary to Knife and Ottertrack lakes. The route then veers away from the Canadian border and loops back toward the southwest to

enter one of the loveliest parts of the entire BWCA Wilderness. From Ester Lake southwest to Kekekabic Lake, you will enjoy cliff-lined lakes, excellent campsites and a scenic waterfall. Then you'll follow a chain of smaller lakes that parallels the border from Kekekabic Lake to popular Ensign Lake, before returning to your origin at the Moose Lake landing.

Virtually every inch of this route is quite popular with wilderness visitors. As long as you stay on the main route, you are likely to see other people, especially during the busiest summer season. Nevertheless, if campsite solitude is important to your group, you can usually find it by simply veering off course each afternoon to make one short portage out of your way to camp on a lake that is not on any main route. Or seek campsites in back bays of such larger lakes as Knife and Kekekabic. Even on popular routes, solitude is available for those who seek it and who are willing to exert a little more effort than the average visitor is.

If winds are out of the south or west (both common), you should make good time traveling along the Canadian border to Ottertrack Lake. There are only 8 portages during the first 3 days of this loop. Of course, that leaves 20 carries for the last 3 days. But only two of them are longer than 100 rods (both near the end of the route) and none is very difficult.

Strong paddlers who don't care about fishing could probably complete this loop in just 5 days. For many folks, however, 7 or 8 days would be appropriate, allowing 1 or 2 layover days to explore the lakes and cliffs along the way.

Anglers will find walleyes, northern pike and smallmouth bass in much of the water on this route. Lake trout also inhabit Knife, Ottertrack and Kekekabic lakes, as well as most of the beautiful, clear, smaller lakes sandwiched between Ottertrack Lake and the South Arm of Knife Lake. If fishing is your "thing," by all means you should enjoy this outstanding wilderness journey.

Day 1 (10 miles): Moose Lake, Newfound Lake, Sucker Lake, Birch Lake. (See comments for Day 1, Route #25-1.)

Day 2 (12 miles): Birch Lake, p. 48 rods, **Carp Lake,** p. 25 rods, **Melon Lake,** p. 15 rods, **Seed Lake,** p. 15 rods, **Knife River,** p. 75 rods, **Knife Lake.** (See comments for Day 2, paragraphs 1 and 2, Route #25-1.) Where the South Arm of Knife Lake joins the main part of the lake, at the westernmost end of the long island that separates the lake, is Thunder Point. There you'll find a ¼-mile trail that leads to an overlook. A hike to the top is rewarded by a fabulous panorama of the Canadian border country from 150 feet above the lake.

Although the southwest end of Knife Lake is sometimes "crowded" with campers, vacant campsites should appear as you approach Little Knife Portage into Ottertrack Lake. If not, there are 4 campsites just beyond the short portage. Or, if you prefer to get off the "beaten path" to camp in a more secluded location, consider a detour to one of the two campsites on Amoeber Lake. The uphill 20-rod portage from Knife Lake is quite easy.

Note: If you are behind schedule already, you can shorten this loop by one full day's travel if you camp on Amoeber Lake and then skip Day 3 entirely. If you do this, however, you'll miss the prettiest part of the loop, and one of the loveliest parts of the entire BWCA Wilderness.

Day 3 (10 miles): Knife Lake, p. 5 rods, **Ottertrack Lake,** p. 80 rods, **Ester Lake, creek, Hanson Lake,** p. 110 rods, **Cherry Lake.** Ottertrack Lake is long, narrow and lined with bluffs and a rocky shore. While paddling northeast, watch for a plaque cemented to the base of a cliff on the Canadian shoreline, about ½ mile before the lake splits into two arms. The plaque commemorates "Ben Ambrose 1896-1982." Benny was a prospector who sought gold for more than 60 years in this area. His homestead once occupied the property across the lake, on the US shore.

The 80-rod portage, which gains about 65 feet in elevation from Ottertrack Lake to Ester Lake, will accelerate your heart. But the main challenge of the day comes on the 110-rod trail. It climbs steeply up from Hanson Lake, surmounts a 100-foot hill, and then descends more gradually to the northeast end of Cherry Lake. The shallow creek connecting Ester and Hanson lakes may have a beaver dam across it that requires a quick lift-over.

You'll find a wonderful campsite at the narrows on Cherry Lake. It faces the northeast end of the lake, which is adorned on the north by some breathtaking cliffs. This is one of the nicest campsites you could ever hope to find, with plenty of good tent sites for a larger group. If it's already occupied, however, the other campsite on Cherry Lake is also a pretty good one.

Day 4 (9 miles): Cherry Lake, p. 11 rods, **Topaz Lake,** p. 20 rods, **Amoeber Lake,** p. 75 rods, **Knife Lake,** p. 50 rods, **South Arm of Knife Lake,** p. 25 rods, **Eddy Lake,** p. 22 rods, **Kekekabic Pond,** p. 3 rods, **pond,** p. 27 rods, **pond,** p. 18 rods, **pond,** p. 3 rods, **Kekekabic Lake.** With 10 portages this day, it might appear as too much for an average group of paddlers. But none of the portages is difficult and the longest is less than ¼ mile. That 75-rod portage, however, does have a gradual incline for the first 45 rods, followed by a steeper descent to Knife Lake

One of the tranquil Kekekabic Ponds

at the north end of the small, secluded bay (about ⅕ mile northwest of where the 1998 Fisher map shows it ends).

You'll want to get an early start in order to claim a good campsite on Kekekabic Lake. Along the way, at the 25-rod portage between Knife and Eddie lakes, take time to enjoy the scenic waterfall on the connecting stream. The best view of the lower falls can be found by paddling past the beginning of the portage to the creek's outlet and then hiking up the trail on the *east* side of the creek. The short portage there gains 75 feet in elevation. Take a deep breath before starting out.

The last five portages connecting Eddy and Kekekabic lakes via the Kekekabic Ponds are also uphill, but none is difficult. The first 3-rod carry may be eliminated altogether when the water level is high enough to walk or line your canoe through the shallow stream connecting the two ponds. When such is the case, the next portage may be shortened to only 16 rods. After completing the 18-rod portage, hike back a few rods to view the lovely waterfall and rapids that parallel the trail.

Enjoy your paddle across beautiful Kekekabic Lake. The east end, with its many majestic rock cliffs and pine-covered hills, is magnificent. The best campsites are on the north shore of the lake, including a few large enough for three or four large tents.

If you feel like stretching your legs at the end of this long day, you can access the famed Kekekabic Trail on the south shore of Kekekabic Lake, about a mile from the east end of the lake. It starts at an old USFS ranger cabin (not clearly visible from the lake) and leads 190 rods uphill to the site of the former Kekekabic lookout tower, 425 feet above the lake.

Day 5 (10 miles): Kekekabic Lake, p. 80 rods, **Pickle Lake,** p. 25 rods, **Spoon Lake,** p. 20 rods, **Dix Lake,** p. 30 rods, **Skoota Lake,** p. 180 rods, **Missionary Lake,** p. 35 rods, **Trader Lake,** p. 80 rods, **Vera Lake.** Although there are fewer portages than on the previous day, this day may be more tiring, since the trails are longer. All have pretty good paths. The longest (180 rods) is mostly level to gently sloping; but it has one short, steep incline and two short, steep declines. Because Vera Lake is isolated by longer portages from all directions, it offers a good, peaceful place to spend your final night in the Wilderness. If all the sites are occupied, you can continue on to Ensign Lake, where you will find many more good campsites. You will also find many more people, however, on that popular fishing lake.

Day 6 (11 miles): Vera Lake, p. 150 rods, **Ensign Lake,** p. 5 rods, **Splash Lake,** p. 30 rods, **Newfound Lake, Moose Lake.** (See comments for Day 3, Route #25-1.)

Entry Point 26—Wood Lake

SEASONAL PERMITS: 204

POPULARITY RANK: 33rd

DAILY QUOTA: 2

LOCATION: The portage to Wood Lake is located on the north (left) side of the Fernberg Road, 12 miles from the International Wolf Center in Ely. A large parking lot adjacent to the trailhead will accommodate as many as 30 vehicles.

DESCRIPTION: The Fall Lake Campground is a good place to spend the night before your trip—the only public campground along the Fernberg Road (see Entry Point 24: Location).

For the wilderness canoeist in search of good fishing on popular Basswood Lake, this quiet entry point offers a good alternative to one of the busy motor-designated lakes nearby. With a quota of only two groups per day and the prohibition of motorboats, Wood Lake affords a much more peaceful wilderness entry than does either Moose Lake to the east or Fall Lake to the west. The entry point does entertain some day-use visitors, but those folks generally go no farther than Wood Lake itself. Only ⅔ of the available permits are actually used each summer.

The only drawback to starting a canoe trip here is the initial half-mile-plus portage from the Fernberg Road. But fortunately the trail descends about 90 feet on a good path to Wood Lake. Soon after the beginning, there is a boardwalk across a wet area. The portage trail receives a fair amount of use, often by day-use visitors from nearby resorts and Ely area residences. The north end of the portage lies outside the BWCAW, and you may see canoes stored there, as well as some sunken boats that were abandoned along the creek that drains into Wood Lake. The lake is bordered by an extensive stand of paper birch trees, more attractive at its north end where there are some rocky ledges and small cliffs.

ROUTE # 26-1: The Wood Wind Route

2 Days, 16 Miles, 6 Lakes, 3 Creeks, 6 Portages

DIFFICULTY: Challenging

FISHER MAPS: F-10

INTRODUCTION: This route is a good choice for anyone who wants to access the good fishing opportunities on Basswood Lake, while avoiding most of the motorboat traffic that is common on both Fall and Moose lakes. From Wood Lake, you will head north through Hula and Good lakes to Hoist Bay of Basswood Lake. Then you'll paddle northeast along the shore of big Basswood Lake to Wind Bay. From there, two long portages will carry you to Wind and Moose lakes. The route ends at the Moose Lake landing, 7 miles by road from the Wood Lake parking lot.

Although this is not a particularly busy route, don't expect to totally escape from other people along it. Motorboats are not permitted on Wood, Hula, Good or Wind lakes, but they *are* allowed on Basswood and Moose lakes. Basswood Lake attracts many visitors throughout the summer, so don't delay in claiming a campsite.

Completing this route in 2 days doesn't leave much time for fishing. If angling is your #1 priority, consider adding a third day. That would also allow you to camp both nights on quiet lakes where motorboats are not permitted—Good Lake and Wind Lake—with nearly a full day of fishing on Basswood Lake in between. Basswood Lake has virtually every type of fish to be found in the BWCA Wilderness, including walleyes, northern pike, smallmouth bass, black crappies, bluegills and lake trout. The largest northern pike ever caught in Minnesota (45 lbs. 12 oz.) was pulled from Basswood Lake. Good and Wind lakes also have large populations of northern pike.

Day 1 (9 miles): P. 180 rods, **creek, Wood Lake,** p. 40 rods, **Hula Lake,** p. 150 rods, **Good Lake,** p. 2 rods, **Good Creek, Hoist Bay, Basswood Lake.** Between Wood Lake and Hoist Bay of Basswood Lake, the portages receive light use and may be somewhat overgrown during the latter part of the summer. The second portage (40 rods) may be muddy at both ends, but should be dry in the middle. The longest trail (150 rods) is uphill at the beginning, but more downhill toward the end, and it has a path plagued with rocks, roots and mud. During dry spells, you may have difficulty crossing shallow Hula Lake and navigating Good Creek. Late in the summer, the creek may be so choked

Paddling across Wood Lake

with lily pads, reeds and other aquatic vegetation that navigation may be nearly impossible.

Motorboats that don't exceed 25 horsepower are permitted in this part of Basswood Lake, including Hoist and Wind bays. You may also see or hear a few motorboats on the Canadian side of the border. Guides from the Lac La Croix First Nation, an Ojibway community living on the north shore of Lac La Croix, use them. By agreement with the Canadian government, the guides are permitted to use motorboats up to 10 horsepower on 10 lakes each year from a list of 20 lakes in the western third of Quetico Provincial Park. Basswood Lake is among those 20 lakes.

For a 9-mile day, look for a campsite in the vicinity of Norway Island, northwest of the entrance to Wind Bay. That's about ¾ mile from the Canadian border.

Day 2 (7 miles): Basswood Lake, Wind Bay, p. 175 rods, **creek, Wind Lake,** p. 175 rods, **Moose Lake.** Prepare yourself for a couple of exhausting portages this day, especially the first one. During mid-to-late summer, weeds in the small bay may obscure the landing for the first portage. The trail begins on a very rocky path for the first 40 rods, crosses a creek, and then ascends over 100 feet in elevation during the next 90 rods. The trail then descends 20 rods to the first access to the creek. When the water level is too low there, due to a beaver dam upstream (as it was in 1998), however, you'll have to continue on a trail that skirts the edge of the creek for another 25 rods to a more suitable landing. When the entire creek is too low for navigation, you may have to continue walking all the way to the northwest end of Wind Lake.

The second long portage has a good, well-worn path that probably carries more day-tripping anglers than overnight campers. The trail gradually ascends about 80 feet during the first 80 rods from the east end of Wind Lake. Over the final 40 rods, the trail drops nearly 90 feet en route to the north shore of Moose Lake.

ROUTE # 26-2: The Good Horse Loop

5 Days, 50 Miles, 6 Lakes, 3 Rivers, 2 Creeks, 19 Portages

DIFFICULTY: Challenging

FISHER MAPS: F-10

INTRODUCTION: This route is a good combination of huge and small lakes, tiny creeks and impressive rivers. From Wood Lake, you will head north through Hula and Good lakes to Hoist Bay of Basswood Lake. Then you'll paddle north to cross the main part of the biggest lake in the BWCA Wilderness. From the northwest corner of Basswood Lake, the Basswood River will transport you west to the mouth of the Horse River. That lovely river will then carry you southwest to Horse Lake. From the south end of Horse Lake, you will cross two smaller lakes and then follow the Range River to the west end of Basswood Lake. After paddling across Jackfish, Pipestone, Back and Hoist bays, you will return to Wood Lake via Good and Hula lakes.

This route will lead you to two of the loveliest rivers in the Boundary Waters, where you'll see three spectacular waterfalls and numerous rapids. If time permits, you may also visit a fascinating display of Indian rock paintings. You may never find total seclusion along this popular route, but the scenery is worth sharing.

If fishing is your "thing," you'll have plenty of opportunities to catch (and release) all types of fish, including walleyes, northern pike, smallmouth bass, black crappies, and even lake trout. Basswood Lake, in particular, is considered one of the best fishing lakes in the

Wilderness. And you'll be spending a good deal of your time on that huge lake.

For that reason, beware strong winds. If the weather forecast includes gale warnings, you would be wise to avoid Basswood Lake altogether. It is no place to be in a canoe when the wind is strong and the waves are running high.

Day 1 (11 miles): P. 180 rods, **creek, Wood Lake,** p. 40 rods, **Hula Lake,** p. 150 rods, **Good Lake,** p. 2 rods, **Good Creek, Hoist Bay, Basswood Lake.** (See comments for Day 1, Route #26-1.) For an 11-mile day, plan to camp on the north side of Washington Island. Motorboats are not permitted on the US side of Basswood Lake north of the island.

Day 2 (10 miles): Basswood Lake, p. 340 rods, **Basswood River,** p. 30 rods, **river.** Because of the ever-present threat of wind on Basswood Lake, plan to get an early start this day. A strong head wind is always a retarding menace, but also beware the strong *tail* wind. When starting across a wide-open expanse of water with a strong wind at your back, the lake ahead of you may appear relatively calm and quite safe. As you proceed farther and farther out from the lee side of a sheltering shoreline, however, you will find that the waves grow higher and higher. Suddenly you may find your canoe in rougher water than you can handle, resulting in either a swamped or a capsized canoe. Wind can be either a friend or a foe, depending on how much respect you have for it and how much good judgment you demonstrate

On the Wood Lake portage

Good Creek

in its presence. It is always best to paddle close to the shoreline of a large lake. Not only is it safer, it is also far more interesting. That's where the wildlife resides. (Also, see comments for Day 2, paragraphs 1-3, Route #22-1.)

Plan to camp in the calm 1-mile stretch of the river above Wheelbarrow Falls, where you'll find several good campsites from which to choose. This is a very popular destination, so try to claim your campsite as early in the day as possible. During the busy summer months, *all* of the campsites along the Basswood River may be occupied by early afternoon.

Day 3 (9 miles): Basswood River, p. 32 rods, **river, Horse River,** p. 75 rods, **river,** p. 50 rods, **river, rapids, river,** p. 50 rods, **river, rapids, river, rapids, river, Horse Lake,** p. 90 rods, **Tin Can Mike Lake.** (See comments for Day 3, paragraphs 2-3, Route #22-1.) The last portage has an excellent path that passes over a low hill between Horse and Tin Can Mike lakes.

As on the previous day, don't wait too late to claim a campsite. The region around Horse Lake is extremely popular and quite easily accessible from the Mudro Lake entry point.

Day 4 (12 miles): Tin Can Mike Lake, p. 160 rods, **Sandpit Lake,** p. 25 rods, **Range River,** p. 15 rods, **river, Jackfish Bay, Pipestone Bay,** p. 70 rods, **Back Bay of Basswood Lake.** The 160-rod trail is quite easy—virtually flat, with a 10-rod boardwalk across a boggy section near the beginning. The rest of the portage follows the path of an old railroad bed that once served logging operations in the area.

At the southeast end of Sandpit Lake, paddle past the first landing that you see and proceed to the very end of the lake where the 25-rod portage begins. If you stop at the first landing, you will add 15 rods to the portage, and those rods are likely to be wet ones. The portage starts out for 15 rods on an excellent path that extends all the way to Range Lake on an old railroad bed. Watch for the turnoff (left) to the Range River after 15 rods.

A 3-foot-high beaver dam barricaded the river in 1998 just above the next portage (15 rods). Two trails bypass some rapids, one path on each side of the river. A short distance farther downstream, you may see some old dock pilings and an abandoned boat access that were once used at Pete's Landing.

Boats with no more than 25-horsepower motors are permitted on all three of the Basswood Lake bays that you'll be crossing this day. The 70-rod trail that connects Pipestone and Back bays is another easy portage that passes over a low rise in the land that separates the two bays.

Day 5 (8 miles): Back Bay, Hoist Bay, Good Creek, p. 2 rods, **Good Lake,** p. 150 rods, **Hula Lake,** p. 40 rods, **Wood Lake, creek,** p. 180 rods. Most of this day should look familiar.

Entry Points 27 & 28—Snowbank Lake

SEASONAL PERMITS: 1000

POPULARITY RANK: 8th

DAILY QUOTA: 9

LOCATION: Snowbank Lake is located about 20 miles northeast of Ely, 3 miles south of the Canadian border. To get to the public access, drive east on the Fernberg Road for 18 miles from the International Wolf Center. Turn left onto the Snowbank Lake Road and proceed (carefully) on this narrow, winding gravel road for about 4 miles to the public landing. En route, you will pass at least 4 private roads. At each of these intersections, bear to the right and stay on the main road to its end. It provides access to the southeast corner of Snowbank Lake.

DESCRIPTION: The Fall Lake Campground is a good place to spend the night before your trip—the only public campground along the Fernberg Road (see Entry Point 24: Location).

Snowbank Lake is a popular entry point, but not nearly as busy as neighboring Moose Lake to the west or Lake One to the east. There are two active resorts on the south shore and a third on the east shore that is accessible only by water. Anglers base themselves at these resorts and fish during the days on Snowbank and its neighboring lakes. Snowbank is one of the few deep lakes (150' deep) in the Ely area inhabited by lake trout for which there is direct road access. It also contains walleyes, smallmouth bass, northern pike and some largemouth bass.

The southwest part of the lake lying outside the BWCAW has no horsepower restrictions. Motorboats that do not exceed 25 horsepower are permitted in the wilderness part of this large lake. Only 43 overnight permits and 342 day-use motor permits were issued to motorboat visitors in 1997—$\frac{1}{2}$ of the motor use on Moose Lake. Furthermore (unlike the Moose Lake entry point), if you travel beyond Snowbank Lake itself, you will leave all motor traffic behind.

Like the Mudro Lake entry point, Snowbank Lake is unusual because it was assigned two different entry point numbers. Permits issued for Entry Point #28 are restricted for use only on Snowbank Lake. Entry Point #27 has no restrictions and is intended for paddlers who will be traveling beyond Snowbank Lake. It is, therefore, the appropriate entry point for the routes described in this book. The quotas are 8 for Entry Point #27 and 1 for Entry Point #28.

About ¾ of the available overnight permits for Entry Point #27 were issued in 1997. Furthermore, Snowbank Lake ranked 15th among all BWCAW entry points with quotas filled the greatest number of days. So don't delay in making your reservation if your heart is set on a canoe trip from this entry point, especially if you plan to start on a Friday, Saturday, Sunday or Monday.

A seeker of wilderness solitude may not find as much peace and quiet as desired in the immediate vicinity of this beautiful, big lake. But the routes leading away from Snowbank Lake should appeal to most paddlers in search of a high-quality wilderness experience. They provide access to the heart of the Boundary Waters for anyone with the time and energy it takes to ply the waters and tackle the portages in this fascinating region.

ROUTE # 27-1: The Disappointment Loop

3 Days, 18 Miles, 11 Lakes, 12 Portages

DIFFICULTY: Easier

FISHER MAPS: F-11

INTRODUCTION: This route is a good introduction to canoeing in the BWCA Wilderness. The little loop will take you through the chain of Snowbank's eastern neighbor lakes. From the public landing, you will paddle 4 miles across big Snowbank Lake to its northeast corner. Two short portages and a small pond will lead you to Boot Lake, and then the longest portage of the route will transport you farther north to popular Ensign Lake. From the east end of that long lake, you will then steer a southwestward course through a chain of small lakes leading to Disappointment Lake. From the southwest end of that lovely lake, you will then portage to Parent Lake and then again to Snowbank Lake. A short paddle across the southeast corner of Snowbank Lake will return you to the public landing.

There is a good deal of variety on this short loop, from tiny, shallow lakes like Jitterbug to the wide-open expanse and depth (140 feet) of Snowbank Lake. Although portages are frequent, only the trail from Boot Lake to Ensign Lake is long enough to challenge the "easier" rating on this route. Except for Snowbank Lake, the loop is restricted to paddlers.

Spread over 3 full days, this route should be easy enough for just about any group of canoeists. And there should be plenty of time to fish along the way. Ensign Lake is a popular destination for anglers in search of walleyes, northern pike and smallmouth bass. Disappointment Lake, too, is certainly not disappointing for most anglers. It contains good populations of walleyes, smallmouth bass, northern pike and largemouth bass. Add a fourth day to your trip, and you could also have time to hike the Old Pines Trail (see Day 2 below).

Water levels should not be a serious factor for this route, but low water can alter the complexion of the smaller lakes between Ensign and Disappointment. Stumps and rocks protrude from the bottom of Cattyman Lake, and the landing on the portage from Jitterbug to Ahsub Lake may extend for several more rods out into the marshy lake.

At such times, in fact, Jitterbug Lake is scarcely more than a foot deep at any point. Wind may be more of a factor on this route, especially on the first day when crossing Snowbank Lake. If there is a gale wind out of the west, you may want to reverse this route to save Snowbank for the final day.

Day 1 (6 miles): Snowbank Lake, p. 50 rods, **pond,** p. 30 rods, **Boot Lake,** p. 220 rods, **Ensign Lake.** Because of the ever-present threat of wind on Snowbank Lake, plan to get an early start this day. A strong head wind is always a retarding menace, and a strong cross wind creates waves that can tip your canoe. But also beware the strong *tail* wind. When starting across a wide-open expanse of water with a strong wind at your

Casting a line into a calm
Disappointment Lake

back, the lake ahead of you may appear relatively calm and quite safe. As you proceed farther and farther out from the lee side of a sheltering shoreline, however, you will find that the waves grow higher and higher. Suddenly you may find your canoe in rougher water than you can handle, resulting in either a swamped or a capsized canoe. Wind can be either a friend or a foe, depending on how much respect you have for it and how much good judgment you demonstrate in its presence. It is always best to paddle close to the shoreline of a large lake. Not only is it safer, it is also far more interesting. That's where the wildlife resides.

The three portages this day are generally downhill, descending a total of 80 feet from Snowbank to Ensign Lake, but there are a couple of climbs on the long trail to Ensign Lake.

There are many good campsites on Ensign Lake, but there is also a great deal of demand for them. During the busiest summer season, vacant sites could be hard to find. Try to claim yours as early in the afternoon as possible.

Day 2 (7 miles): Ensign Lake, p. 53 rods, **Ashigan Lake,** p. 105 rods, **Gibson Lake,** p. 25 rods, **Cattyman Lake,** p. 10 rods, **Adventure Lake,** p. 40 rods, **Jitterbug Lake,** p. 15 rods, **Ahsub Lake,** p. 25 rods, **Disappointment Lake.** On the portages this day, you'll be climbing most of the way from Ensign Lake to Ahsub Lake, gaining over 150 feet on the 248 rods of trails. The next portage is a gradual climb all the way from Ensign to Ashigan Lake, gaining 56 feet along the way. The greatest gain is on the longest portage—a gradual climb over a 75-foot-high hill between Ashigan and Gibson lakes.

At the next portage (25 rods), you'll find a scenic little waterfall on the creek draining Cattyman into Gibson Lake. If the day is warm, a cooling hydro-massage in the cascading stream might be in order.

When the water level is high enough, you may be able to paddle through the shallow channel connecting Cattyman and Adventure lakes, thus eliminating the 10-rod portage.

Though not as popular and busy as Ensign Lake, Disappointment Lake does entertain many visitors. Once again, claim your campsite as early as possible. If you still have energy at the end of the day, and the sun is still high in the sky, you could go for a hike. You can access the Old Pines Trail at a campsite near the center of the lake on its east shore. The trail makes a 10-mile loop through the region just east of Disappointment Lake. It passes through a virgin stand of impressive pines, some of which are thought to be more than 300 years old.

Day 3 (5 miles): Disappointment Lake, p. 85 rods, **Parent Lake,** p. 80 rods, **Snowbank Lake.** The two quarter-mile portages this day are not difficult. If you prefer a more direct route back to civilization, you can also portage 140 rods directly from Disappointment Lake to Snowbank Lake. The trail gradually climbs a few feet and then descends about 70 feet to the shore of Snowbank Lake. It starts at the same place where the 85-rod trail begins. In fact, if you're not careful, you may unwittingly take the longer portage when you meant to take the trail to Parent Lake.

If you have anglers in your party that still have ambition, take time crossing Parent Lake. It's known as a good source for both walleyes and northern pike.

ROUTE # 27-2: The Lake Trout Loop

7 Days, 60 Miles, 39 Lakes, 1 Creek, 48 Portages

DIFFICULTY: Challenging

FISHER MAPS: F-11, F-12

INTRODUCTION: This high-quality wilderness route is a good choice for an experienced group of strong paddlers that wants to penetrate the remote interior part of the BWCAW. From Snowbank Lake, the route first leads northeast through Disappointment Lake and a chain of smaller lakes to Ima Lake. You will then paddle southeast through Hatchet Creek to Thomas and Fraser lakes. From Fraser Lake you will continue eastbound to enter an interior portion of the BWCA Wilderness that is not visited by many other canoeists. A series of tiny lakes and long portages will lead you eventually to popular Little Saganaga Lake. At the north end of Little Sag you will steer a northwest course across big Gabimichigami Lake and past a lovely series of pools and rapids that drain into ever-popular Ogishkemuncie Lake. Through a chain of small lakes and tiny ponds you will continue moving westward to enter the east end of impressive, cliff-lined Kekekabic Lake. Then you'll head north, across Pickle, Spoon and Bonnie lakes, to Knife Lake on the Canadian border. You will follow this long, clear border lake southwest to its end and beyond it to Vera and Ensign lakes. After three more portages to the south, you will find yourself back on familiar Snowbank Lake. Four miles of paddling across this big lake will return you to your origin at the public landing on the south shore.

Although this route starts and ends on a motor-designated lake, motors are prohibited from the rest of this loop. Your third day will take you through the most remote interior portion of the entire BWCAW, where you will see only dedicated wilderness canoeists like yourself—if you see anyone else at all. Attractive scenery characterizes most of the route, and the part of the route between Little Saganaga Lake and Kekekabic Lake is truly exceptional.

If you are an angler in search of lake trout, you will have a golden opportunity to catch them on this trip. This species is known to inhabit Snowbank, Thomas, Fraser, Little Saganaga, Gabimichigami, Ogishkemuncie, Kekekabic and Knife lakes. You will also find northern pike and walleyes in many of the lakes along this interesting route.

Day 1 (8 miles): Snowbank Lake, p. 80 rods, **Parent Lake,** p. 85 rods, **Disappointment Lake,** p. 25 rods, **Ahsub Lake,** p. 15 rods, **Jitterbug Lake,** p. 40 rods, **Adventure Lake,** p. 10 rods, **Cattyman Lake,** p. 55 rods, **Jordan Lake.** Although five of these portages are uphill, none is difficult. When the water level is high enough, you may be able to paddle through the channel connecting Adventure and Cattyman lakes, eliminating the 10-rod portage.

If time permits, you might enjoy a short side trip to the north end of Cattyman Lake. At the 25-rod portage there you'll find a scenic little waterfall on the creek draining into Gibson Lake. If the day is warm, a cooling hydro-massage in the cascading stream might be in order. But don't delay too long in claiming your campsite on Jordan Lake. You'll be camping on a popular route where sites are usually in great demand.

Day 2 (10 miles): Jordan Lake, p. 5 rods, **Ima Lake,** p. 50 rods, **Thomas Creek, Hatchet Lake,** p. 10 rods, **Thomas Creek,** p. 10 rods, **creek,** p. 10 rods, **Thomas Pond,** p. 5 rods, **Thomas Lake, creek, Fraser Lake,** p. 65 rods, **Sagus Lake.** Access to the 50-rod portage is quite limited at the rocky landing on Ima Lake. With heavy canoeing traffic in this area, you may have to wait in line for your turn to cross the portage. Don't crowd the party in front of you. Hopefully, the group behind you won't crowd you.

Under normal water conditions, you can probably pull your canoe up through the first two shallow rapids in the creek between Hatchet and Thomas lakes, eliminating two 10-rod portages. The third 10-rod trail crosses the famed Kekekabic Trail, a 40-mile footpath that connects the Fernberg Road with the Gunflint Trail.

Elton Lake

At the northeast end of Fraser Lake, you'll witness the site of a forest fire that burned over a thousand acres in 1976. Charred pillars from the former 100-year-old pine forest still tower above the surrounding new growth (also visible on the north shore of Sagus Lake). The 65-rod portage from the east end of Fraser Lake has an excellent path that gradually ascends to a ridge overlooking a rather scenic large bog and pond to the north. It is an easy portage. If you prefer two shorter trails (11 rods and 22 rods), however, you could take an alternate route to Sagus Lake via Shepo Lake.

Day 3 (7 miles): Sagus Lake, p. 42 rods, **Roe Lake,** p. 65 rods, **Cap Lake,** p. 200 rods, **Ledge Lake,** p. 160 rods, **Vee Lake,** p. 80 rods, **Fee Lake,** p. 40 rods, **Hoe Lake,** p. 100 rods, **Makwa Lake,** p. 55 rods, **Elton Lake.** You will surely look back on this day as the roughest of the whole trip. Ten portages total 742 rods. If you need two trips to get all of your gear across every portage, that translates into nearly 7 miles of walking this day. Few people penetrate this remote part of the BWCAW. For the first time along this route, you should sense a feeling of true wilderness solitude. You may also experience portages that are brushed over and obviously receive much less use than those crossed on the previous days. Nevertheless, most have surprisingly good paths underneath the brush.

The portages to and from Roe Lake have good, dry paths that climb over low hills. At the east end of Roe Lake, contrary to the way it appears on the map, you must paddle about 40 rods into a small creek before you will see the portage landing on the north (left) side of the creek. The creek's outlet is hard to see amidst the boggy shoreline. You will find it at the easternmost end of the shallow lake.

There are three portage landings near the southeast end of Cap Lake. The first two that you will see on the *south* shore lead to Boulder Lake. The landing for the trail to Ledge Lake is nearby on the *north* side of the eastern tip of the lake. The portage has a good path that skirts the edge of a swamp and gradually ascends 82 feet from Cap to Ledge Lake. There is just one wet spot near the middle. If you are traveling here near the end of July or in early August, you will surely see a plethora of blueberries along the path.

There are a couple of nice campsites resting atop rocky outcrops along the east shore of Elton Lake. If they are already occupied, proceed to Little Saganaga Lake, where there are many more sites from which to choose.

Day 4 (9 miles): Elton Lake, p. 19 rods, **creek,** p. 19 rods, **Little Saganaga Lake,** p. 30 rods, **Rattle Lake,** p. 25 rods, **Gabimichigami Lake,** p. 15 rods, **Agamok Lake,** p. 100 rods, **Mueller Lake,** p. 100 rods, **Ogishkemuncie Lake.** This area is one of the most beautiful parts of canoe country—from island-studded Little Saganaga Lake, to the wide-open expanse of Gabimichigami Lake, to the sheltered little pools and rapids between Mueller and Agamok lakes.

At the 15-rod portage from Gabimichigami to Agamok Lake, there are actually two paths from which to choose. Both are short, virtually flat, and not difficult. The one on the right is muddier and more grassy than the left alternative. The left choice is rockier, but a bit shorter. Take your pick.

Use caution paddling through pretty, little Agamok Lake. At the narrow parts of the lake, it is very shallow. There are rocks lurking just below the surface to grab your canoe.

The next 100-rod portage bypasses Mueller Falls and a scenic series of pools and rapids that drain from Agamok to Mueller Lake. The quickest way through is the one long portage. But you can also divide the stretch into three or four short carries, separated by brief paddles on small pools between the rapids (see the sketch on page 178). Regardless of your choice, start your portage at the same good landing on Agamok Lake. You can bypass the first two rapids and the small pool in between by veering off the main portage trail 35 rods from the beginning. If you stay on the long portage, you will encounter a couple of hills with two steep descents as well as a couple of wet spots bridged by logs. It's not the easiest of portages, but at least it's mostly downhill traveling in this direction. To view Mueller Falls, watch for the inter-section of the Kekekabic Trail about midway across the portage. The

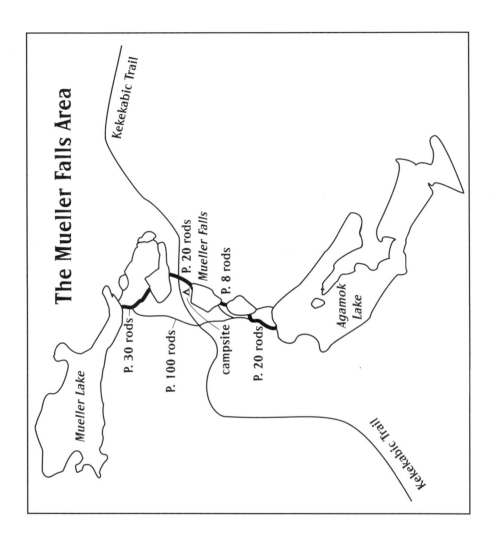

The Mueller Falls Area

Kekekabic Trail

Mueller Lake

P. 30 rods

P. 100 rods

P. 20 rods

Mueller Falls

P. 8 rods

campsite

P. 20 rods

Agamok Lake

Kekekabic Trail

Kekekabic Trail leads east (right) 45 rods to a good wooden bridge that spans the stream and affords a great view of the falls. A campsite for backpackers is nearby.

At the west end of Mueller Lake, another 100-rod portage first climbs for 18 rods, then descends steeply for 19 rods. It then levels off for the rest of the way to Ogishkemuncie Lake (with one more short descent).

Ogishkemuncie is a very popular lake. In spite of numerous campsites there, it is best not to wait too late to claim one. They are in great demand. Those who arrive late in the day may be disappointed to find no vacancies.

Day 5 (8 miles): Ogishkemuncie Lake, p. 15 rods, **Annie Lake,** p. 15 rods, **Jenny Lake,** p. 15 rods, **Eddy Lake,** p. 22 rods, **Kekekabic Pond,** p. 3 rods, **pond,** p. 27 rods, **pond,** p. 18 rods, **pond,** p. 3 rods, **Kekekabic Lake,** p. 80 rods, **Pickle Lake,** p. 25 rods, **Spoon Lake.** On this day, you will witness one of the prettiest lakes in the BWCA Wilderness—big Kekekabic Lake. To get there, however, you must first cross eight short portages. All are well used, and most are quite easy. Beware the trail between Jenny and Eddy lakes, however. It bypasses rather scenic rapids in a narrow gorge populated with tall cedar trees. The path is rocky and treacherous where it descends steeply toward Eddy Lake. It's better to make two trips on this one, even if you normally take all your gear in just one trip.

All five portages connecting Eddy and Kekekabic lakes via the Kekekabic Ponds are uphill, but none is too difficult. The first 3-rod carry may be eliminated altogether when the water level is high enough to walk or line your canoe through the shallow creek that connects the two ponds. When such is the case, the next portage may be shortened to just 16 rods. After completing the 18-rod portage, hike back a few rods to view the lovely waterfall and rapids that parallel the trail.

Kekekabic Lake is nothing less than spectacular when you enter it from the ponds. As you emerge from the narrow east end, majestic bluffs tower above your canoe, and along the distant south shoreline pine-covered hills rise 400 feet above the lake. Ahead of you lie over four miles of scenic lakeshore—most impressive after the chain of little ponds from which you came.

Day 6 (7 miles): Spoon Lake, p. 25 rods, **Bonnie Lake,** p. 33 rods, **Knife Lake,** p. 200 rods, **Vera Lake.** With only three portages, this will be one of the easiest days of the route, although the 200-rod portage is a challenge. Where the South Arm of Knife Lake joins the main part of the lake, at the westernmost end of the long island that divides the lake, is Thunder Point. There you'll find a ¼-mile trail that leads to an overlook. A hike to the top is rewarded by a fabulous panorama of the Canadian border country from 150 feet above the lake.

About a mile from the southwest end of Knife Lake, in a cluster of 3 small islands, is the site of the BWCAW's last permanent resident. Dorothy Molter sold homemade rootbeer to canoeing passersby for nearly half a century. She called her home Isle of Pines. She passed away in December 1986. Two of her log cabins were then moved, log by log, to Ely and reconstructed as a memorial to her near the International Wolf Center.

The 200-rod portage from Knife to Vera Lake is the only real challenge of the day. It ascends steeply at the beginning, eventually to an elevation of nearly 120 feet above Knife Lake, before descending nearly that much to the east end of Vera Lake. Canoe traffic on Vera Lake is much lighter than on either Knife Lake or Ensign Lake. Nevertheless, don't delay in claiming your campsite. There is a nice one on the north shore soon after the portage.

Day 7 (9 miles): Vera Lake, p. 150 rods, **Ensign Lake,** p. 220 rods, **Boot Lake,** p. 30 rods, **pond,** p. 50 rods, **Snowbank Lake.** The most challenging portage on the last day of this route is your first one—challenging in *two* ways. First, it climbs over a large hill, gaining nearly 100 feet in elevation during the first 65 rods. Second, *finding* the correct portage may be a challenge. As you paddle toward the west end of Vera Lake, you may first see a trail that starts just west of a campsite on the *east* side of a creek draining a bog into Vera Lake. That's a winter portage and not the one you want. Paddle past it to the very end of the lake, on the *west* side of the creek, where the correct portage for canoeists begins. Unlike the winter portage, this trail is high and dry, climbing to a rocky ridge inhabited by scrub oaks and maple trees. It then descends fairly steeply to the shore of Ensign Lake.

Be wary of strong winds blowing across Snowbank Lake. This huge, open body of water can be treacherous for canoes. If a storm is approaching, you will be wise to hug the shoreline or, better yet, to wait it out at one of the campsites in the north end of the lake.

Entry Point 29—North Kawishiwi River

SEASONAL PERMITS: 108

POPULARITY RANK: 40th

DAILY QUOTA: 1

LOCATION: The Kawishiwi River starts at Kawishiwi Lake, 33 airline miles southeast of Ely. It zigzags west across numerous lakes, ponds and pools, and through countless rapids en route to its ultimate destination at Basswood Lake on the Canadian border, 90 miles from its source. About 3 miles west of Lake One, the river splits into two forks. From there, the North Kawishiwi River flows almost straight west to Farm Lake, while the South Kawishiwi River first heads southwest to Birch Lake and then veers north to rejoin the North branch at Farm Lake. The landmass bordered by the 2 branches of the river is referred to as the Kawishiwi Triangle.

The North Kawishiwi River roughly parallels the Fernberg Road, about 2-3 miles south of the road. Access to the river is by way of a long portage from Triangle Lake, which lies south of Ojibway Lake, about 13 miles east of Ely. From the International Wolf Center, drive 14 miles east on the Fernberg Road to the Ojibway Lake public access road. This is ¼ mile beyond the "Ojibway Lake Summer Homes" road (right) and the Tofte Lake access road (left). Turn right and proceed south on this good gravel road ½ mile to the public landing at the northwest corner of Ojibway Lake. A small parking lot nearby accommodates day-use visitors. Farther away from the landing is a larger parking lot for overnight visitors.

DESCRIPTION: The Fall Lake Campground is a good place to spend the night before your trip—the only public campground along the Fernberg Road (see Entry Point 24: Location).

The North Kawishiwi River entry point is accessible by crossing two lakes that lie entirely outside the BWCA Wilderness. Ojibway is a crystal clear, lovely lake that is dotted with private cabins and lake homes along its east and north shorelines. It harbors good populations of lake trout and smallmouth bass—one of only a few lake trout lakes in the Ely area that have direct road access. Consequently, it receives a fair amount of day-use during the fishing season, along with its neighbor to the south, Triangle Lake. A well-maintained 10-rod "roller portage" joins the two lakes. A path of rolling pins allows boaters to easily slide their boats from one lake to the other. While motorboats are permitted on Ojibway and Triangle lakes, they are not allowed to enter the Wilderness here.

This entry point ranks relatively low in popularity. With a daily quota of only one, however, you should make your reservation early to get a permit, especially if your trip will start on a Friday, Saturday, Sunday or Monday. The North Kawishiwi River ranked 11th among all BWCAW entry points with quotas filled the greatest number of days during the summer of 1997.

Like the Farm Lake Entry Point to the west and the South Kawishiwi River Entry Point to the south, Ojibway Lake provides access to the "Kawishiwi Triangle" region. In this attractive area you can usually find good fishing, excellent campsites and surprisingly little human congestion, in spite of the easy access. The North Kawishiwi River Entry Point is the most difficult of the three. The 190-rod portage from the south end of Triangle Lake to the river discourages most would-be visitors from entering the BWCAW here.

ROUTE # 29-1: **The Kawishiwi Triangle Loop**

2 Days, 20 Miles, 3 Lakes, 2 Rivers, 12 Portages

DIFFICULTY: Challenging

FISHER MAPS: F-31

INTRODUCTION: This route is a good introduction to the BWCAW for competent paddlers with no aversion to portaging. The short weekend loop will take you south from Ojibway Lake to the Kawishiwi River. On the first day, you will follow the South Kawishiwi River southwest to camp on either Clear Lake or Eskwagama Lake. From there, you'll portage north to the North Kawishiwi River and then follow it back to the junction of the two river branches. From that point, you must backtrack to your origin on the north shore of Ojibway Lake.

A misty morning on the Kawishiwi River

This corner of the Wilderness receives relatively light overnight use during all but the very busiest parts of the summer. You could take the loop in a counterclockwise direction if you preferred the longest portage of the route (210 rods) to be downhill. But then you would have three long portages on the first day instead of just one. A clockwise loop is recommended to make your first day easier.

Anglers will find walleyes and northern pike throughout this route, as well as smallmouth bass in Triangle and Ojibway lakes. If you choose to spend your night alone on Eskwagama Lake, where there is only one campsite, you'll find northern pike inhabiting that shallow lake. Clear Lake offers better fishing opportunities for walleyes and northern pike, but you will probably have to share it with other parties. It has five campsites, four of which are along the north shore.

Day 1 (10 miles): Ojibway Lake, p. 10 rods, **Triangle Lake**, p. 190 rods, **Kawishiwi River, South Kawishiwi River**, p. 12 rods, **river**, p. 18 rods, **river**, p. 28 rods, **river, rapids, river**, p. 70 rods, **Clear Lake**. At the first portage, you won't have to unload your gear. Simply slide it onto the rollers and push it up the slight incline to Triangle Lake, which is about 4 feet higher than Ojibway Lake. Save your strength for the next portage, where you will surely need it. It has a very rocky, rooty path and is likely to be muddy, especially near the beginning of the trail. It gradually ascends about 50 feet during the first 60 rods, then descends about 85 feet (rather steeply in a couple of places) to the grassy shore of the Kawishiwi River.

On your way down the South Kawishiwi River, if the water level is suitable, you'll have an opportunity to avoid all three portages by walking, lining or running your canoe down the shallow rapids instead of portaging around them. *Be very careful, though!* If you have any doubts about your safety (and *certainly* if you have no experience in whitewater), use the portages. That's why they are there. A small island in the river divides the final rapids. There is no portage there. The deepest channel is on the west (left) side of the island. Indeed, when the water level is quite low, that is the *only* unobstructed channel.

Clear is a serene and pretty little lake that has several campsites, most along the north shore. Anglers will find walleyes, northern pike, crappies and bluegills in the shallow water. If you prefer more solitude than you might find on Clear Lake, the one campsite on Eskwagama Lake offers a good alternative. But it requires more effort. Instead of just one 70-rod portage to Clear Lake, you must portage 85 rods to Eskwagama Lake and then 100 rods to Clear Lake. Neither of the portages is difficult. After committing to that additional effort, however, you may find that the campsite on Eskwagama Lake is already occupied. It's a gamble.

Day 2 (10 miles): Clear Lake, p. 160 rods, **North Kawishiwi River,** p. 10 rods, **river,** p. 18 rods, **river,** p. 210 rods, **river, Kawishiwi River,** p. 190 rods, **Triangle Lake,** p. 10 rods, **Ojibway Lake.** With three long portages, this is a much more challenging day than the first. The first is the easiest of the three. After a short climb at the beginning, the trail then levels off until the final 50 rods, where it drops about 80 feet to the North Kawishiwi River. There is a mud hole with logs across it about 40 rods from Clear Lake. You may be able to walk or line your canoe up through the first two short sets of rapids to avoid the 10-rod and 18-rod portages. Save your energy for the longest portage of the route. The 210-rod portage is mostly uphill, gaining nearly 100 feet elevation during the first 140 rods. It has a good but rocky path with a couple of short boardwalks across boggy ground.

On the 190-rod portage back to Triangle Lake, if you didn't notice the fairly steep drop near the end of the trail (heading south), you will surely notice the short climb near the beginning of the trek north. The remainder of the route should look familiar.

ROUTE # 29-2: The Bald Eagle Loop

4 Days, 30 Miles, 13 Lakes, 1 River, 2 Creeks, 24 Portages

DIFFICULTY: Challenging

FISHER MAPS: F-3, F-4, F-10

INTRODUCTION: This interesting and varied route is a good choice for anyone who wants to experience large and small lakes, a couple of tiny creeks, and a substantial part of the lovely Kawishiwi River. From Ojibway Lake, you will first head south to the Kawishiwi River. You will continue paddling southwest down the South Kawishiwi River. Then, after portaging to Little Gabbro Lake, you will veer toward the southeast and paddle across Gabbro and Bald Eagle lakes. From the east shore of Bald Eagle you will portage north to negotiate a chain of lakes, creeks and portages leading to the "numbered lakes." From Lake One, you will rejoin the Kawishiwi River and follow it west back to the Triangle Lake portage. Finally, you will backtrack to your origin at Ojibway Lake.

Though much of this route receives light to moderate use, parts of it do attract many visitors. The loop crosses several notable fishing lakes and penetrates a region known for its moose population. Walleyes and northern pike inhabit most of the water along the route. Gabbro and Bald Eagle lakes are particularly popular with early summer anglers, when the walleyes are easiest to catch. Lakes One and Two are nearly always popular, attracting both anglers and non-anglers alike. If you are looking for solitude at night, you should probably avoid camping on any of those lakes. Elsewhere, you will probably encounter relatively few other people.

Day 1 (8 miles): Ojibway Lake, p. 10 rods, **Triangle Lake,** p. 190 rods, **Kawishiwi River, South Kawishiwi River,** p. 12 rods, **river,** p. 18 rods, **river,** p. 28 rods, **river.** (See comments for Day 1, paragraphs 1 and 2, Route #29-1.) You will find several nice campsites just before the portage to Little Gabbro Lake.

Day 2 (8 miles): South Kawishiwi River, p. 122 rods, **Little Gabbro Lake, Gabbro Lake,** p. 5 rods, **Bald Eagle Lake,** p. 190 rods, **Gull Creek,** p. 40 rods, **Gull Lake,** p. 50 rods, **Pietro Lake.** The two longest portages this day are mostly uphill, but they are well maintained and not too difficult. The 122-rod trail gains over 55 feet in elevation during the first 60 rods. The 190-rod portage out of Bald Eagle Lake ascends to 125 feet above the lake before dropping steeply near the end of the trail.

You may have to paddle against some swift current in the narrows between Little Gabbro and Gabbro lakes. It's really not enough drop to label it a set of "rapids" but, depending on the water level, it may require some extra paddling effort.

Along the north shore of Little Gabbro Lake and the northwest shore of Gabbro Lake, you may see the charred evidence of a forest fire. During the dry June of 1995, the Gabbro Lake Fire burned nearly 4,000 acres of forest across the region just north of Gabbro Lake and east of the South Kawishiwi River.

Several campsites await you along the north shore of Pietro Lake. Anglers will find average fishing opportunities for northern pike there.

Day 3 (5 miles): Pietro Lake, p. 65 rods, **Camdre Lake,** p. 125 rods, **Clearwater Lake,** p. 240 rods, **pond,** p. 40 rods, **Rock Island Lake, creek,** p. 40 rods, **creek, Lake Two.** The only notable uphill trek of the day is at your first portage, where the trail gains about 80 feet elevation before dropping 30 feet to the southwest corner of Camdre Lake. The 125-rod portage, on the other hand, is mostly downhill. The 240-rod trail from Clearwater Lake has a rather steep uphill section at the beginning, but it soon levels off and then gradually slopes down to the unnamed pond. There may be some wet and muddy spots on the path.

In the creek connecting Rock Island Lake and Lake Two, if the water level is not extremely low, avoid the temptation to start the portage at the first landing you see. It will add about 20 rods to your carry on a trail that is not well maintained and may be plagued with windfalls. It should be used only when the creek is too low from that point to the start of the 40-rod portage, which also begins on the right side of the creek. If the water level is high enough, in fact, you may be able to eliminate all but the last 5 rods of the 40-rod portage.

This is a short day of travel for one good reason. Lake Two is one of the busier lakes in the Boundary Waters. If you don't claim a camp-site there early in the afternoon, you may not find a vacant site. If you prefer a night of solitude, you might want to stop at Rock Island Lake, where there is an unofficial campsite. To camp there, however, you must get *prior authorization* from the USFS to spend a night in the Weasel Lake Primitive Management Area (see Chapter 1), which includes Rock Island Lake. The nice, but undeveloped, campsite is located at the southeast end of the lake, away from the main line of traffic.

Day 4 (9 miles): Lake Two, p. 40 rods, **pond,** p. 30 rods, **Lake One,** p. 41 rods, **Confusion Lake,** p. 25 rods, **Kawishiwi River,** p. 20 rods, **river,** p. 40 rods, **river,** p. 8 rods, **river,** p. 190 rods, **Triangle Lake,** p. 10 rods, **Ojibway Lake.** If you find yourself running behind sched-ule, or in case of emergency, you can access the Fernberg Road at a pub-lic landing on the north end of Lake One. There is also a resort nearby. But you won't see either one of them if you access the Kawishiwi River by way of Confusion Lake, as suggested.

You'll be paddling on a very pretty part of the Kawishiwi River this day. Confusion Lake is also as attractive as it is confusing. The only portage that you might be able to eliminate by walking, lining or running your canoe down the rapids is at the 20-rod trail along the Kawishiwi River (but only if you are absolutely sure that you know what you are doing). Don't ever be tempted to bypass the 40-rod and 8-rod portages by walking or running the corresponding rapids. There is a small waterfall at the shorter portage, and the current is far too swift and the drop is too great at the longer trail. These rapids are not navigable at any time, regardless of the water level.

On the 190-rod portage back to Triangle Lake, if you didn't notice the fairly steep drop near the end of the trail (heading south), you will surely notice the short climb near the beginning of the trek north. The remainder of the route should look familiar.

Entry Point 30—Lake One

SEASONAL PERMITS: 2,168

POPULARITY RANK: 2nd

DAILY QUOTA: 18

LOCATION: Lake One lies 17 miles by air straight east of Ely. To get there from the International Wolf Center, follow the Fernberg Road for 19 miles to its end. A large parking lot is adjacent to the nice public landing.

DESCRIPTION: Camping is prohibited at the landing. The Fall Lake Campground is a good place to spend the night before your trip—the only public campground along the Fernberg Road (see Entry Point 24: Location).

This is one of the most popular entry points in the Boundary Waters Canoe Area, both by overnight visitors and by day-trippers. In fact, among all canoeing entry points, it ranks #1 for the number of day-use permits and #2 for the number of overnight permits issued each summer. Although a resort is on the north shore of Lake One, motorboats are not permitted on the lake. So, in spite of its popularity, Lake One remains a quiet way into the BWCA.

With 18 permits allowed for Lake One visitors each day, it might appear that an advance reservation would not be necessary. Wrong. Lake One ranks high (11th in 1997) among entry points filled the greatest number of days. About 80% of its permits are issued each summer. So make your reservation early, especially if you are planning to start your trip on Friday, Saturday, Sunday or Monday.

After your canoe trip begins, it won't take long to discover why Lake One and the region beyond it are so popular. You'll encounter beautiful scenery. Moose are abundant in this region, too. Don't leave home without plenty of film and a good compass. Lake One may be confusing even to an experienced map-reader. (See Route #31-1 for another route suggestion. This easy route could simply be reversed by starting at Lake One and ending at Farm Lake.)

ROUTE # 30-1: The Clearwater Turtle Loop

3 Days, 26 Miles, 8 Lakes, 1 River, 1 Creek, 15 Portages

DIFFICULTY: Challenging

FISHER MAPS: F-3, F-4, F-31 (or McKenzie Map #18)

INTRODUCTION: This little loop will first take you southeast across Lake One and Lake Two. Then you will portage off of this busy route and head south into a part of the BWCAW that receives lighter traffic. After crossing Rock Island, Clearwater and Turtle lakes, you will portage back into a more popular area. From Bald Eagle Lake you will paddle northwest across Gabbro and Little Gabbro lakes. Then the lovely pools and rapids of the South Kawishiwi River will lead you back to the public landing on Lake One.

Motorboats are prohibited throughout this route, but canoeing traffic may be heavy at the beginning. Most of the loop, however, receives only moderate visitation. Anglers are attracted to the walleyes, northern pike, bass and pan fish that inhabit much of the water along the course.

Day 1 (8 miles): Lake One, p. 30 rods, **pond,** p. 40 rods, **Lake Two, creek,** p. 40 rods, **creek, Rock Island Lake,** p. 40 rods, **pond,** p. 240 rods, **Clearwater Lake.** If you can find your way across Lake One, guiding through the remainder of this route will be easy. Lake One, with its many islands and irregular bays, offers a sporty challenge to the map-reader right from the beginning. From the landing, first bear left and then right, as you pass through a very narrow channel en route to the main body of the lake—a channel that you won't actually see until you are nearly upon it. Just beyond that channel is Kawishiwi Lodge on the north shore of Lake One. This resort is unique in the Ely area because motorboats are not permitted on the lake in front of it. If confused by the many islands in Lake One, use your compass and your common sense. Remember that the real world doesn't always look as you think it should based on your interpretation of the map.

Watch carefully for the portage connecting Lake Two and Rock Island Lake. After paddling into the shallow creek about 20 rods, you'll find the beginning of the portage on the east (left) side. After walking 40 rods, watch for the steep drop back down to the creek on your right. The trail continues from that point another 20 rods to a wider and deeper part of the creek, to use when the water level is too low at the first access. But this part of the trail is not as well maintained as the first 40 rods. It also doesn't get as much use, so windfalls may obstruct the path. If the water level is high enough (in early spring and during rainy summers), you may be able to put back into the creek after a portage of only 5 rods.

As you approach the southwest end of Rock Island Lake, watch carefully for the portage that starts on the boggy shoreline on the southeast (left) side of the outlet creek. It is very difficult to see until you are right there. The final, long portage to Clearwater Lake is relatively level most of the way, but downhill at the end, where a nice sandy beach greets you.

Clearwater Lake is aptly named. You will find several nice campsites along its north shore. Anglers should find northern pike in the cool, clear water.

Day 2 (9 miles): Clearwater Lake, p. 200 rods, **Turtle Lake,** p. 186 rods, **Bald Eagle Lake, rapids, Gabbro Lake, Little Gabbro Lake,** p. 122 rods, **South Kawishiwi River.** Your first long portage is nearly level and nothing to worry about, although there is a bog at the end of the trail. Your "reward" for this long hike is a very unattractive scene. The forest along the east shoreline of Turtle Lake sustained considerable damage from a windstorm. All three campsites were in the path of the storm and were littered by windfalls. The reward for anglers, however, is much more appealing. Turtle Lake is known to harbor big northern pike.

The second portage this day is a challenge. It climbs steeply during the first 30 rods from Turtle Lake before descending gradually to the northwest tip of Bald Eagle Lake.

The short, swift rapids between Bald Eagle and Gabbro lakes can usually be easily run in your canoe. If you are not comfortable running the rapids, however, you could portage 5 rods across the northwest end of the rocky island around which the rapids pass.

Along the northwest shore of Gabbro Lake and the north shore of Little Gabbro Lake, you may see the charred evidence of a forest fire. During the dry June of 1995, the Gabbro Lake Fire burned nearly 4,000 acres of forest across the region just north of Gabbro Lake and east of the South Kawishiwi River.

Your final carry of the day is on a good downhill path from Little Gabbro Lake to the South Kawishiwi River. At the top of the rapids there, just north of the portage landing, you may see the remnants of an old, deteriorated logging dam and sluice used by loggers in the early 1900's. It is barely visible in high water, but quite noticeable when the water is low. You'll find several nice campsites just beyond the final portage.

Day 3 (9 miles): **South Kawishiwi River,** p. 28 rods, **river,** p. 18 rods, **river,** p. 12 rods, **river,** p. 8 rods, **river,** p. 40 rods, **river,** p. 20 rods, **river,** p. 19 rods, **Lake One.** You will be paddling upstream this day, but the current is seldom noticeable in the quiet pools between rapids. Most of the portages this day are quite easy and all are well maintained. The two longest trails (28 rods and 40 rods), however, do pass over small but steep hills. With normal water conditions, you could eliminate four of the portages by walking or lining your canoe up the shallow rapids. The only two that must be portaged are the 8-rod and 40-rod trails. Make certain that your final carry is on the 19-rod path to Lake One. It is an easy mistake to take the 25-rod portage to Confusion Lake instead. Continue paddling past the first portage landing that you see on the right, around a small island to the correct portage landing at the northeast end of the tiny bay.

ROUTE # 30-2: **The Adams Boulder Route**

5 Days, 52 Miles, 27 Lakes, 1 River, 2 Creeks, 32 Portages

DIFFICULTY: Challenging

FISHER MAPS: F-11, F-31

INTRODUCTION: This interesting route is a fine choice for anyone who wants to taste a little bit of everything the BWCA Wilderness has to offer—large and small lakes, a lovely river, tiny creeks, portages of varied lengths, and even access to a couple of hiking trails. The route penetrates the remote interior portion of the Boundary Waters where motor-boats are not allowed and where few canoeists travel. From Lake One, you will first paddle southeast through the popular "numbered lakes" to the island-studded bays of beautiful Lake Insula. From the northeast end of Insula, you will continue traveling in a northeast direction on the Kawishiwi River. Then you'll steer north and cross a chain of lakes leading to Boulder Lake, your farthest point east. After a long portage north to Cap Lake, you will then steer back toward the west to cross Fraser, Thomas and Ima lakes. From Ima, the route leads southwest through the tiny lakes leading to Disappointment, Parent and Snowbank lakes. Your canoe trip will end at the public landing at the south end of Snowbank Lake, 5 miles by road from the origin at Lake One. Unless you made prior arrangements to have a vehicle waiting, your trip will end with a 5-mile hike.

All along this route, fishing is usually good for walleyes and northern pike. Lake trout are also found in Fraser, Thomas, Ima and Snowbank lakes. If there are hikers in your group, they will also have opportunities to trek on the famed Kekekabic Trail or to explore the Old Pines Loop during a layover side trip.

The route, as described herein, is recommended for strong and seasoned paddlers with no aversion to portages. Five days are needed for experienced groups. Six days would be much better for parties prone to fishing or for a group that would like to layover one day and hike on either the Kekekabic Trail or the Old Pines Trail. A good short-cut is available for those who need it. It bypasses the most remote interior part of the route by heading straight north from Lake Insula to Kiana and Thomas lakes. Spread over five full days, this alternate route would qualify for an "easier" rating. Regardless of which route you choose, you'll surely enjoy the scenery and variety in this part of the Wilderness.

Day 1 (10 miles): Lake One, p. 30 rods, **pond**, p. 40 rods, **Lake Two, Lake Three, Lake Four,** p. 25 rods, **Kawishiwi River,** p. 25 rods, **river,** p. 10 rods, **river, Hudson Lake.** (See comments for Day 1, paragraph 1, Route #30-1.) All of the portages this day are quite easy on well-maintained and well-traveled paths. You will surely see many other paddlers, but most of them go no farther than the numbered lakes. In spite of the traffic, moose are commonly seen throughout the area. Look for them in the shallow bays and creek inlets along the shoreline.

Day 2 (12 miles): Hudson Lake, p. 105 rods, **Lake Insula,** p. 18 rods, **Kawishiwi River, Alice Lake,** p. 20 rods, **Kawishiwi River,** p. 90 rods, **river.** Lake Insula may be confusing even to an experienced map-reader, particularly in the southwest end of the lake. Use your compass, if necessary, to follow a general heading, instead of trying to account for every little island you see.

The portages should be no problem again this day. After completing the final portage, if you steer south, away from the main course of the river, you'll find a small display of Indian rock paintings along the west shore of the bay, about ½ mile from the portage. Several campsites are nearby.

Campsite on Lake Insula

If you are behind schedule at the end of this day and have only five days available for this trip, you should consider the alternate route mentioned in the introduction. Spend your second night on Lake Insula. Then head north on Day 3 through Kiana Lake to Thomas Lake. There you will rejoin the main route that is described in Day 4 below.

Day 3 (9 miles): Kawishiwi River, p. 20 rods, **river, River Lake, river,** p. 22 rods, **Trapline Lake,** p. 30 rods, **Beaver Lake,** p. 90 rods, **Adams Lake, Boulder Creek,** p. 10 rods, **creek,** p. 15 rods, **creek, Boulder Lake.** You will surely see fewer people after you veer north from the Kawishiwi River into an area characterized by scenic lakes and some interesting portages. How easy this day is will depend, in large part, on the water levels. All of the portages have good paths, but you'll be hiking generally uphill throughout the day. Immediately after the 22-rod portage, there were a couple of small beaver dams across a creek that required lift-overs in 1998.

The 90-rod portage from Beaver Lake has an excellent path that gradually ascends to Adams Lake. It is a rather scenic trail that passes through a narrow gorge with steep rock slopes. Along Boulder Creek there may be a couple of beaver dams that require lift-overs in addition to the two short portages. When the creek is nearly dry, as it was during the summer of 1998, it might be necessary to portage nearly all of the way from Beaver Lake to Boulder Lake—a total distance of nearly 150 rods—by walking along the soft, grassy bank of the creek.

Boulder and Adams are both pretty lakes, with rock outcrops along their shores. There are several very nice campsites, including a large site in a cedar grove on the island in the middle of Boulder Lake.

Day 4 (11 miles): Boulder Lake, p. 220 rods, **Cap Lake,** p. 65 rods, **Roe Lake,** p. 42 rods, **Sagus Lake,** p. 65 rods, **Fraser Lake, creek, Thomas Lake,** p. 5 rods, **Thomas Pond,** p. 10 rods, **Thomas Creek,** p. 10 rods, **creek,** p. 10 rods, **Hatchet Lake, Thomas Creek,** p. 50 rods, **Ima Lake.** The only difficult portage this day is the first long trail from Boulder Lake. Not only is it exhausting, it is also confusing because of intersecting trails along the way. (See the sketch on opposite page for a visual illustration of this area.) The trail starts on a good path that gradually climbs during the first 25 rods and then continues on a level-to-gently-sloping path for 95 more rods until it reaches an unnamed creek (it looks like a narrow lake on the Fisher map). For the next 15 rods, the trail skirts the edge of the grassy creek bog on a rocky, winding path, until it crosses the creek on rocks and boulders. On the north side of the creek is the first intersection. The path that heads north up a steep incline is *not* the shortest route to Cap Lake. It joins the Cap-to-Ledge lakes portage. Instead of that trail, you should continue along the north edge of the grassy creek bog and meadow for 55 more rods to another intersection. At that point, the best trail to Cap Lake veers northwest, away from the creek valley, and passes over a low ridge toward the east tip of Cap Lake.

At the north end of Sagus Lake and along the northeast shore of Fraser Lake, you'll witness the site of a forest fire that burned over a thousand acres in 1976. Charred pillars from the former 100-year-old pine forest still tower above the surrounding new growth. The 65-rod portage from Sagus Lake to the east end of Fraser Lake has an excellent path that gradually descends along a ridge overlooking a rather scenic bog and pond to the north. It is an easy portage. If you prefer two shorter trails (22 rods and 11 rods), however, you could take an alternate route to Fraser Lake via Shepo Lake.

The first 10-rod portage along Thomas Creek crosses the famed Kekekabic Trail, a 40-mile footpath that connects the Fernberg Road with the Gunflint Trail. If the water level is not too low, walking or lining your canoe down the shallow rapids may eliminate the second and third 10-rod portages.

Access to Ima Lake at the 50-rod portage is quite limited at the rocky landing on Ima Lake. With heavy canoeing traffic in this area, you may encounter congestion there. Don't take any longer than absolutely necessary to complete the portage and launch your canoe onto the lake. Then claim your campsite while there is still one available on this very popular lake.

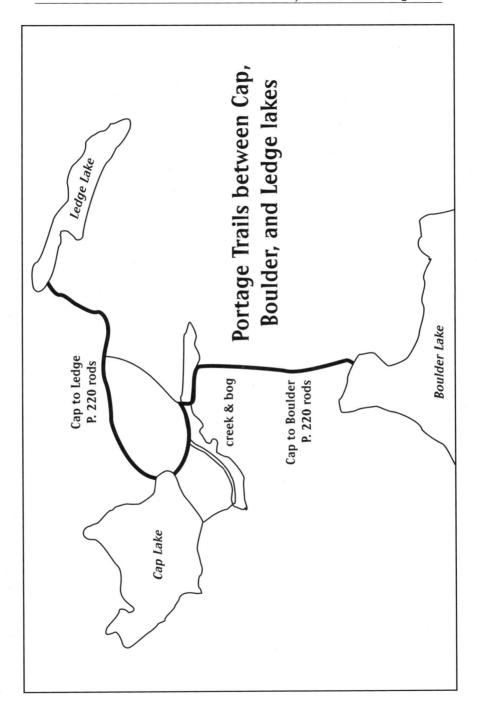

Portage Trails between Cap, Boulder, and Ledge lakes

Ledge Lake

Cap to Ledge
P. 220 rods

creek & bog

Cap Lake

Cap to Boulder
P. 220 rods

Boulder Lake

Day 5 (10 miles): Ima Lake, p. 5 rods, Jordan Lake, p. 55 rods, Cattyman Lake, p. 10 rods, Adventure Lake, p. 40 rods, Jitterbug Lake, p. 15 rods, Ahsub Lake, p. 25 rods, Disappointment Lake, p. 85 rods, Parent Lake, p. 80 rods, Snowbank Lake. All of these portages are well maintained, well traveled and not difficult. When the water level is high enough, you may be able to eliminate the 10-rod portage between Cattyman and Adventure lakes by paddling through the interconnecting channel.

If you have an extra day to spare and there are hikers in your group, Disappointment Lake is good place to lay over. You can access the Old Pines Trail at a campsite near the center of the lake on its east shore. The trail makes a 10-mile loop through the region just east of Disappointment Lake. It passes through a virgin stand of impressive pines, some of which are thought to be more than 300 years old.

The last two quarter-mile portages this day are not difficult. If you prefer a more direct route back to civilization, however, you can portage 140 rods directly from Disappointment Lake to Snowbank Lake. The trail gradually climbs a few feet and then descends about 70 feet to the shore of Snowbank Lake. It starts at the same place where the 85-rod trail begins. In fact, if you're not careful, you may unwittingly take the longer portage when you meant to take the trail to Parent Lake.

If you have anglers in your party that still have ambition, take time crossing Parent Lake. It's known as a good source for both walleyes and northern pike.

Entry Point 31—Farm Lake

SEASONAL PERMITS: 328

POPULARITY RANK: 25th

DAILY QUOTA: 3

LOCATION: Farm Lake is located about 5 airline miles straight east of Ely. From the International Wolf Center, drive 1 mile east on State Highway 169 to its intersection with County Road 58 (Kawishiwi Trail). Turn right and follow this good blacktop county road (which soon becomes Lake County Road 16) for a total distance of 4¼ miles from Highway 169 to the USFS access road on the left. Turn left there and proceed north on the gravel access road for 0.2 mile to the boat landing. A large parking lot that will accommodate up to 16 vehicles is located about a hundred yards away, and an outhouse is near the landing.

DESCRIPTION: The Fall Lake Campground is a good place to spend the night before your trip. It is reached via the Fall Lake Road, which meets the Fernberg Road 5 miles east of the International Wolf Center (past the turnoff to Farm Lake). A fee is charged to camp there.

Farm Lake, which lies entirely outside of the BWCA Wilderness, provides access to the wilderness at both South Farm Lake and the North Kawishiwi River. Motorboats are allowed on Farm and South Farm lakes, but they are not allowed on the North Kawishiwi River, where the routes in this book lead. Several resorts, numerous private cabins and a summer boys' camp occupy Farm Lake's shoreline. The lake is often buzzing with motorboats. But don't let all the traffic on Farm Lake discourage you. You'll be heading for the North Kawishiwi River where a good deal of solitude and relative isolation can be enjoyed within easy access from Farm Lake.

Over ⅔ of the available overnight permits are issued each summer. A reservation is advisable if your trip will start on Friday, Saturday, Sunday or Monday. If you avoid starting on one of the busiest days of the week, however, you should have no problem acquiring a permit for this entry point. Regardless, you may see some daytime use of this entry point, which ranks high for daytime use among all BWCA entry points.

ROUTE # 31-1: The North Kawishiwi River Route

2 Days, 15-17 Miles, 2-3 Lakes, 2 Rivers, 8-9 Portages

DIFFICULTY: Easier

FISHER MAPS: F3, F-31 (or McKenzie Map #18)

INTRODUCTION: This easy route takes you through the lovely scenery between Farm Lake and Lake One. From Farm Lake, you will paddle into the mouth of the North Kawishiwi River and follow that branch east to its junction with the South Kawishiwi River. From there you will continue on the Kawishiwi River northeast to the Lake One landing at the end of the Fernberg Road. The route has two alternative endings. You may either portage directly from the river to Lake One for a 15-mile route, or you may take a detour through Confusion Lake and the main part of Lake One for a 17-mile route.

Regardless of the final miles that you choose, you'll have a delightful trip along the scenic Kawishiwi River, with numerous rapids and a small waterfall to view along the way. Were it not for one long portage along the North Kawishiwi River, this would be a *very* easy route. But that long trail may be a challenge to weak or inexperienced trippers. Serious anglers might want to add an extra day to allow time to fish below each of the rapids in the river, where there are usually plenty of walleyes and northern pike for the catching.

After leaving Farm Lake, motorboats are not permitted on the rest of the route. Although there is easy access to the North Kawishiwi River region from three entry points, much of the traffic is for day-use only. This lovely area seldom feels congested. Nevertheless, you won't want to wait too late in the day to claim a good campsite. The sites do tend to fill up during the busier parts of the summer.

This route terminates at the end of the Fernberg Road, 22½ miles by road from the Farm Lake landing. Make arrangements before depar-

North Kawishiwi River

ture to have a vehicle waiting for you at the Lake One Landing (see Entry Point 30, Location).

Day 1 (9 miles): Farm Lake, North Kawishiwi River, p. 10 rods, **river,** p. 10 rods, **river,** p. 18 rods, **river,** p. 210 rods, **river.** When the water level is high on Farm Lake (which is part of a large reservoir regulated by a dam), it may not be necessary to take the first 10-rod portage. Simply paddle through the shallow channel in the river. You may also be able to walk or line your canoe up the next two short rapids to avoid the corresponding portages there. The first and only real challenge comes at the 210-rod portage. It is mostly uphill, gaining nearly 100 feet elevation during the first 140 rods. It has a good but rocky path with a couple of short boardwalks across boggy ground.

Find your campsite as soon as possible after completing the long portage for a 9-mile day of travel. There are also several good sites near the junction of the North and South Kawishiwi River branches, about a mile farther up the river.

Day 2 (8 miles): North Kawishiwi River, Kawishiwi River, p. 8 rods, **river,** p. 40 rods, **river,** p. 20 rods, **river,** p. 25 rods, **Confusion Lake,** p. 41 rods, **Lake One.** You'll be paddling on a very pretty part of the Kawishiwi River this day. Confusion Lake is also as attractive as it is confusing. The only portage that you might be able to eliminate by walking or lining your canoe through the rapids is at the 20-rod trail. Don't be tempted to bypass any of the other rapids. The gradient is too great and the current is far too swift. There is a small, scenic waterfall at the 8-rod portage.

If you prefer to shorten the route by a couple of miles, you'll have that opportunity after the 20-rod portage. Instead of portaging 25 rods to Confusion Lake, you may portage 19 rods directly to Lake One. Simply paddle past the first portage landing that you see on the right (to Confusion Lake), around a small island, to the next portage landing at the northeast end of the tiny bay.

ROUTE # 31-2: The Kawishiwi Knife Route

8 Days, 87 Miles, 28 Lakes, 3 Rivers, 1 creek, 34 Portages

DIFFICULTY: Challenging

FISHER MAPS: F3, F-4, F-10, F-11

INTRODUCTION: This interesting route will take you across a fascinating variety of lakes and rivers to penetrate the heart of the BWCA Wilderness. From Farm Lake you will paddle east up the North Kawishiwi River to its junction with the South Kawishiwi River. From there, you will continue following the Kawishiwi River northeast to the "numbered lakes." From the east end of Lake Four, the route continues eastbound through Hudson Lake to Lake Insula. You'll then steer a northeast course across Kiana, Thomas and Fraser lakes to Kekekabic Lake. After paddling and portaging north to the Canadian border, you will begin a westbound journey from Knife Lake down the Knife River ultimately to Basswood Lake. A full day of paddling without a single portage will take you to the northwest corner of that awesome lake. Finally, after viewing Basswood Falls, you will turn south and paddle across Pipestone Bay and Newton Lake en route to Fall Lake. Your trip will end at the Fall Lake Campground, 9½ miles by road from your origin at Farm Lake.

This route is a wonderful choice for anyone who likes variety on a canoe trip. From tiny lakes that barely show up on the map to the second largest lake in the Boundary Waters, variety is what you will get. The first three days follow the flowage of the Kawishiwi River, with its quiet pools, rushing rapids and many short portages to spice up the days. The last three days will be on "big water" with only three easy carries along the way. The middle two days are perhaps the most physically challenging, but perhaps also the most rewarding, as you explore the remote interior part of the Wilderness.

Only three of the 34 portages exceed 100 rods in length. Only one is longer than 200 rods, and you'll get that over with on your first day out. You'll be averaging over 6 carries each day during the first five days, but only one per day during the final three days. Weak or inexperienced parties should consider adding an extra day. Or they could shorten the route by ending it at Moose Lake instead of Fall Lake, by veering southwest from Sucker Lake (see Day 6 below) and skipping Basswood Lake entirely. This also serves as a good "escape route" in case of gale-force wind across Basswood Lake.

Anglers will find all types of fish along the route. Walleyes and northern pike inhabit many of the lakes and rivers. Smallmouth bass also lurk beneath the surface of the Canadian border lakes. The patient angler may find lake trout in several lakes, including Thomas, Kekekabic, Knife and Basswood. If fishing is an important part of your trip, definitely spread this route over more than 8 days, or shorten it by ending at Moose Lake.

Day 1 (10 miles): Farm Lake, North Kawishiwi River, p. 10 rods, **river,** p. 10 rods, **river,** p. 18 rods, **river,** p, 210 rods, **river.** (See comments for Day 1, Route #31-1.) Plan to camp near the junction of the North and South Kawishiwi River branches.

Day 2 (10 miles): North Kawishiwi River, Kawishiwi River, p. 8 rods, **river,** p. 40 rods, **river,** p. 20 rods, **river,** p. 25 rods, **Confusion Lake,** p. 41 rods, **Lake One,** p. 30 rods, **pond,** p. 40 rods, **Lake Two, Lake Three, Lake Four.** (See comments for Day 2, paragraph 1, Route #31-1.) All of the portages this day are quite easy on well-maintained and well-traveled paths. You will surely see many other paddlers after entering the "numbered lakes." In spite of the traffic, moose are relatively common in the region east of Lake One. Look for them in the shallow bays and creek inlets along the shoreline, especially at dawn and dusk.

There are several campsites near the east end of Lake Four. For the most privacy, paddle off the beaten path to one of the sites in the narrowest part of the lake leading to Bridge Lake. Then, after setting up your camp, cast a line for one of the many northern pike that lurk in the shallow water nearby.

Day 3 (12 miles): Lake Four, p. 25 rods, **Kawishiwi River,** p. 25 rods, **river,** p. 10 rods, **river, Hudson Lake,** p. 105 rods, **Lake Insula,** p. 170 rods, **Kiana Lake.** Lake Insula may be confusing even to an experienced map-reader, particularly in the southwest end of the lake. Use your compass, if necessary, to follow a general heading, instead of trying to account for every little island you see. ·

The portages should be no problem again this day. Even the final long trail is not difficult. It gradually ascends for the first 50 rods. It then levels out for much of the way and finally descends over the last 25 rods to the south end of Kiana Lake, for a net gain in elevation of 56 feet.

If the two campsites in the north end of Kiana Lake are occupied, don't worry. It's only a short downhill carry to Thomas Lake, where there are several nice campsites in its southwest end. In fact, if there are avid anglers in your group, they may prefer a night on Thomas Lake, which harbors lake trout, walleyes and northern pike. Northern pike is the only type of game fish in Kiana Lake.

Day 4 (10 miles): Kiana Lake, p. 25 rods, **Thomas Lake, creek, Fraser Lake,** p. 15 rods, **Gerund Lake,** p. 30 rods, **Ahmakose Lake,** p. 90 rods, **Wisini Lake,** p. 10 rods, **Strup Lake,** p. 85 rods, **Kekekabic Lake.** This day, you will experience some ups and downs as you visit a variety of lakes—down from Kiana to Thomas Lake, up from Fraser to Wisini Lake, and then down again from Wisini to Kekekabic Lake. The steepest climb you'll encounter is at the short portage connecting Gerund and Ahmakose lakes (30 rods), where the rocky path is deeply eroded. The trail is a streambed during heavy rains and the spring runoff. Look up to see an osprey nest near the start of the next portage on the north shore of Ahmakose Lake. It was an active nest in 1998. The trail (90 rods) passes over a small hill on a good path. The final portage passes through a lovely aspen forest on an excellent path that drops over 110 feet to the south end of Kekekabic Lake.

In the area from the northeast shore of Fraser Lake to the southeast shore of Wisini Lake, you'll witness the site of a forest fire that burned over a thousand acres in 1976. Charred pillars from the former 100-year-old pine forest still tower above the surrounding new growth.

There are several campsites in the northwest corner of Kekekabic Lake. Unfortunately, the prettiest part of the lake is the eastern half, which is bordered by some spectacular rock cliffs and pine-covered hills that tower as much as 400 feet above the water. If time permits, a side trip might be in order. Better yet, this is a good place to spend a layover day.

Day 5 (11 miles): Kekekabic Lake, p. 80 rods, **Pickle Lake,** p. 25 rods, **Spoon Lake,** p. 25 rods, **Bonnie Lake,** p. 33 rods, **Knife Lake,** p. 75 rods, **Knife River,** p. 15 rods, **Seed Lake,** p. 15 rods, **Melon Lake,** p. 25 rods, **Carp Lake,** p. 48 rods, **Birch Lake.** The portages this day are nothing to worry about. All nine are generally downhill, dropping a total of 156 feet from Kekekabic Lake to Birch Lake. The well-used paths are well maintained and easy to negotiate.

Where the South Arm of Knife Lake joins the main part of the lake, at the westernmost end of the long island that divides the lake, is Thunder Point. There you'll find a ¼-mile trail that leads to an overlook. A hike to the top is rewarded by a fabulous panorama of the Canadian border country from 150 feet above the lake.

About a mile from the southwest end of Knife Lake, in a cluster of three small islands, is the site of the BWCAW's last permanent resident. Dorothy Molter sold homemade rootbeer to canoeing passersby for nearly half a century. She called her home Isle of Pines. She passed away in December 1986. Two of her log cabins were then moved, log by log, to Ely and reconstructed as a memorial to her near the International Wolf Center.

If the water level is high enough (but not too high), you could eliminate all of the portages along the Knife River by running, lining or walking your canoe down the series of gentle rapids around which the portages pass. Only on one occasion must you lift your canoe and gear—around a low falls. Use caution, though! Never run rapids with which you are not 100% comfortable. Walking or lining your canoe may be more prudent. But visibility in rapids is restricted, and there may be sharp rocks or deep holes between the rocks. The *most* prudent way to negotiate rapids is to portage around them.

You'll find several campsites near the middle of Birch Lake on the US (south) side. Don't wait too late to claim yours for the night. Birch is part of a popular route that starts at Moose Lake, the busiest entry point in the entire BWCA Wilderness.

Day 6 (12 miles): Birch Lake, Sucker Lake, p. 20 rods, **Inlet Bay, Bayley Bay, Basswood Lake.** The rest of this route is a "piece of cake," unless strong winds are blowing across big Basswood Lake. You are likely to see more people this day than any other day of your canoe trip. The chain of lakes from Moose to the Canadian border is a *very* popular route for paddlers heading northeast along the border lakes, for anglers en route to Basswood Lake, and for canoeists entering Canada's Quetico Provincial Park. They all converge at Sucker Lake.

The only portage on this day has a good, downhill path on the Canadian side of the border. "Prairie Portage" is the location for a Canadian ranger station where paddlers en route to Quetico Provincial Park must check in to pick up their permits. Don't linger on this portage. It can be quite congested at times. A "truck portage" on the US side of the border transports motorboats between Sucker and Basswood lakes.

Because of the ever-present threat of wind on Basswood Lake, plan to get an early start this day. A strong head wind is always a retarding menace, but also beware the strong *tail* wind. When starting across a wide-open expanse of water with a strong wind at your back, the lake ahead of you may appear relatively calm and quite safe. As you proceed farther and farther out from the lee side of a sheltering shoreline, however, you will find that the waves grow higher and higher. Suddenly you may find your canoe in rougher water than you can handle, resulting in either a swamped or a capsized canoe. Wind can be either a friend or a foe, depending on how much respect you have for it and how much good judgment you demonstrate in its presence. It is always best to paddle close to the shoreline of a large lake. Not only is it safer, it is also far more interesting. That's where the wildlife resides.

Motorboats that don't exceed 25 horsepower are permitted on Sucker Lake and in the south part of Basswood Lake on the US side of the international border. You may also see or hear a few motorboats on the Canadian side of the border. Guides from the Lac La Croix First Nation, an Ojibway community living on the north shore of Lac La Croix, use them. By agreement with the Canadian government, the guides are permitted to use motorboats up to 10 horsepower on 10 lakes each year from a list of 20 lakes in the western third of Quetico Provincial Park. Basswood Lake is among those 20 lakes.

For a 12-mile day, plan to camp on the quieter north side of Washington Island. Motorboats are not permitted on the US side of Basswood Lake north of the island.

Day 7 (12 miles): Basswood Lake, Jackfish Bay, Pipestone Bay. You won't have a single portage this day, just a long day of paddling on the second largest lake in the BWCA Wilderness.

For a pleasant diversion from the routine of paddling, consider a side trip to Basswood Falls at the source of the Basswood River. "Horse Portage" bypasses Basswood Falls and several rapids and pools below the falls. The trail begins on the US shore (left side) just above the falls and follows a pretty good path west for just over a mile. At several points along the trail, there are spur trails leading off to the right. Some lead to campsites; others lead to river access points between rapids. Stow your canoe out of the way at the beginning of the portage. Then take time to explore this scenic area on foot. Your legs will appreciate the exercise.

Plan to camp at the north end of Pipestone Bay near Lewis Narrows for a 12-mile day of paddling. You'll be back in a part of Basswood Lake where motorboats are permitted. If you prefer to camp in a quieter part of the lake, claim a site near the Canadian border before taking your side trip to Basswood Falls. This is a very popular destination and the campsites closest to the falls fill up early each day. Of course, if you camp near the falls, that means your final day will cover more than 10 miles.

Day 8 (10 miles): Pipestone Bay, p. 90 rods, **Newton Lake,** p. 80 rods, **Fall Lake.** Both portages this day are virtual "highways," in terms of both trail quality and traffic quantity. Both trails have smooth paths that are 6 to 8 feet wide—smooth enough for portage wheels to transport motorboats and loaded canoes from lake to lake. Near the south end of the 90-rod portage, the trail splits into two paths that end about 10 rods apart. Either one works, but the westernmost trail has the widest and smoothest path and is the choice of those using portage wheels. After completing the portage, take time to view Pipestone Falls, near the south end of the trail. A narrow, rocky trail skirts close to the stream and leads to a good vantage point at the base of the falls.

The second portage bypasses Newton Falls, which is actually a long set of rapids that drop about 8 feet from Fall Lake to Newton Lake. This route ends at the Fall Lake Campground, where there is a good boat landing. Your car should be waiting in the large parking lot nearby.

|6

Entry from State Highway 1

The South-Central Area

SEVEN ENTRY POINTS ARE ACCESSIBLE FROM STATE HIGHWAY 1 SOUTHEAST of Ely. Only two—the South Kawishiwi River and Little Gabbro Lake— are easily accessible. The other five require extensive backwoods driving on gravel county roads and forest routes through the heart of Superior National Forest. As a group, these entry points are probably the least familiar to paddlers from outside the Ely area. Most visitors seem to be attracted to routes that lead north to the Canadian border region. The southernmost routes served by these entry points are often overlooked. With low quotas at all of these entry points, the south-central area should never feel crowded.

Ely is the closest commercial center to these entry points (see paragraphs 2 and 3 in the introduction to Chapter 3). You may pick up your permit at the International Wolf Center in Ely. If you are driving up from the North Shore and have no reason to stop in Ely before your trip, however, you may pick up your permit at the Isabella Work Station. It is located adjacent to Highway 1, 1 mile west of "downtown" Isabella and 35 miles southeast of Ely. When making your permit reservation, be sure to designate at which location you wish to pick up your permit. If you'll need last-minute provisions, don't count on picking them up in Isabella. There really is no "downtown" there. In fact, there really is no town at all. Scattered along Highway 1 are a few gas pumps, a couple of bars and two cafes. If you need groceries, be sure to stop in Finland on your northbound journey from Lake Superior.

To get to these entry points from Ely, simply follow State Highway 1 southeast from Ely. It is a winding, often hilly, blacktop road that must be driven slowly. The highway was resurfaced in 1997 from Ely to the South Kawishiwi River bridge (10½ miles) and much of the next 8 miles was resurfaced in 1999. Keep a watchful eye for logging trucks, which are abundant in this area.

The South Kawishiwi River and Gabbro Lake entry points are close to the highway. The other five entry points are reached via the "Tomahawk Road," which spurs off of Highway 1 at a point 18¾ miles from the Chamber of Commerce building in Ely (which is ½ mile west of the International Wolf Center at the intersection of Highways 1 and 169). The Tomahawk Road is a good, mostly straight, USFS-maintained gravel road that connects Highway 1 with the site of a former logging camp near the south shore of Isabella Lake. Unimproved one-lane spur roads lead north from the Tomahawk Road to provide access to the Snake River, the Little Isabella River, and the Bog Lake entry points. The Island River and Isabella Lake entry points are at the end of the Tomahawk Road.

Entry Point 32—South Kawishiwi River

SEASONAL PERMITS: 225

POPULARITY RANK: 30th

DAILY QUOTA: 2

LOCATION: The Kawishiwi River starts at Kawishiwi Lake, 33 miles southeast of Ely. It zigzags west across numerous lakes, ponds and pools, and through countless rapids en route to its ultimate destination at Basswood Lake on the Canadian border, 90 miles from its source. About 3 miles west of Lake One, the river splits into two forks. From there, the North Kawishiwi River flows almost straight west to Farm Lake, while the South Kawishiwi River first heads southwest to Birch Lake and then veers north to rejoin the north branch at Farm Lake. The landmass bordered by the two branches of the river is referred to as the Kawishiwi Triangle.

Public access to the South Kawishiwi River is located 8 airline miles southeast of Ely. From the Chamber of Commerce building, drive 10¾ miles southeast on Highway 1 to the South Kawishiwi River Campground, ¼ mile past the bridge across the river. Enter the campground (left) and proceed ⅓ mile to the boat landing, just west of the log pavilion. A parking lot is about 100 yards south of the boat landing, across from the swimming beach. Outhouses are next to the parking lot. Do NOT park in the small lot adjacent to the pavilion. That is for day-use visitors using the pavilion and picnic grounds. Cars parked there overnight are ticketed.

An alternate access provides a quicker and more direct route to the Boundary Waters by way of a portage from the Spruce Road. To get there, continue driving past the campground on Highway 1 for ¼ mile to its intersection with County Road 230 (a.k.a. "Spruce Road" and Forest Route 181). Turn left there and drive 4 miles northeast on this good gravel road to the "Filson Creek" sign at the portage to the South Kawishiwi River, 1.7 miles past the turnoff to Voyageur Outward Bound School (left). A small parking lot in front of the trailhead will accommodate 4-5 vehicles. About 100 yards farther down the road is a larger overflow parking space that will hold 6-8 more vehicles. The 140-rod portage from the road to the river is rough and rocky in places, rooty in others, and it could be muddy in spring or after rains. After a short 15-rod ascent, however, the trail slopes gradually downhill most of the way to the river. A 5-rod boardwalk crosses a wet spot near the end of the trail. By using this access, you will eliminate four miles of paddling and four shorter portages. You will also bypass a lovely section of the river, however. So I suggest putting in at the campground, unless you are in a hurry to enter the BWCA Wilderness.

DESCRIPTION: The South Kawishiwi River Campground is a convenient place to spend the night before your canoe trip. A fee is charged to camp there.

The South Kawishiwi River is a shallow, wide, rocky-bottomed series of pools and rapids. Red pine, balsam fir, white cedar and spruce trees populate its shoreline. Walleyes and northern pike inhabit its depths. Good campsites are found all along its course, wherever a rocky outcropping exists. Under normal water conditions, many of the portages en route may be avoided by walking, lining or running your canoe through the accompanying whitewater. The portages are more desirable, however, when the water is low, the day is cool, or you feel anything less than 100% confident about your ability to negotiate the swift current. Never take chances in rapids. The portages are there for your safety.

The first 4 miles of the river upstream from the campground lie outside of the BWCA Wilderness. Motorboats are permitted there, but they are seldom seen beyond the first set of rapids. Private homes and cabins dot the shoreline along the first 1½ miles of the river, and the Voyageur Outward Bound School sits beside the first set of rapids.

Like the Farm Lake Entry Point to the north and the North Kawishiwi River Entry Point to the northeast, the South Kawishiwi River provides access to the "Kawishiwi Triangle" region. In this attractive area you can usually find good fishing, excellent campsites and surprisingly little human congestion, in spite of the easy access. The South Kawishiwi River Entry Point is the easiest of the three. There are no long or difficult portages to discourage would-be visitors from entering the BWCAW here.

If your heart is set on entering this part of the wilderness, make your reservation early. The quota is filled 80% of the time. The South Kawishiwi River ranked 6th among all BWCAW entry points filled the greatest number of days in 1997. In spite of that fact, it almost never feels "crowded" in this riparian wilderness area, and there are usually plenty of campsites to accommodate the two groups that are allowed to enter the Wilderness here each day. Motorboats are not permitted.

If you want a longer route than either of those suggested below, consider adding the last seven days of Route #31-2 to the first two days of Route #32-1. That makes a challenging 9-day route that ends at the Fall Lake Campground, 17 miles by road from your origin at the South Kawishiwi River Campground.

ROUTE # 32-1: **The Split River Route**

3 Days, 22 Miles, 2 Lakes, 2 Rivers, 15 Portages

DIFFICULTY: Challenging

FISHER MAPS: F3, F-4 (or McKenzie Map #18)

INTRODUCTION: This interesting route will take you through the middle of the scenic Kawishiwi Triangle region. From the campground, you will first paddle up the South Kawishiwi River. Then you will portage through Clear Lake to the North Kawishiwi River and follow that stream east to its junction with the south branch of the river. For the first time, then, you will paddle downstream on the South Kawishiwi River until you reach the portage to Little Gabbro Lake. From Little Gabbro, you will portage out of the Boundary Waters and end this canoe trip at a parking lot 6½ miles by road from your origin.

Motorboats are prohibited from all but the first 4 miles of this route. If the water level is appropriate and your whitewater skills are sufficient, you may have an excellent opportunity to shoot through several small rapids, as well as to walk or line your canoe up several more. A strong group of competent paddlers could complete this route is just two days. Stretching it over three full days, however, allows you time to appreciate the natural beauty that surrounds you. It also affords good opportunities for anglers to fish below many alluring rapids for the walleyes and northern pike that feed there.

If you have only two days for this trip, you could start your journey at the Filson Creek portage (see Location above) to bypass the first four short portages and eliminate about 4 miles of paddling. Camp along the North Kawishiwi River, just past the 210-rod portage. It's only 1.7 miles by road between the two parking lots at Little Gabbro Lake and Filson Creek—close enough to walk if you don't want to shuttle vehicles before departure.

Day 1 (7 miles): South Kawishiwi River, p. 33 rods, **river,** p. 26 rods, **river,** p. 25 rods, **river,** p. 62 rods, **river,** p. 5 rods, **river.** You could probably avoid all of the portages this day by walking or lining your canoe up the accompanying rapids, if the water is deep enough and the current is not too swift. Use caution, as always. The most difficult to walk is the first set of rapids, where there is the greatest drop. There you may see some canoes or kayaks lined up on the river, awaiting turns to run these Class II rapids. Voyageur Outward Bound School uses this set of rapids to train its students in whitewater skills.

The second portage may be muddy or even under a few inches of water in early spring or after prolonged periods of heavy rain. Just downstream from the start of the 62-rod portage you'll paddle under a steel bridge that carries snowmobilers over the river on the Tomahawk Trail. The 62-rod trail could be split into two shorter portages around two short rapids. The first would then be 13 rods and the second 23 rods, with 26 rods of paddling between them. It is quicker to simply take the 62-rod portage, which has an excellent path and no steep inclines. After that portage (or rapids), you'll be in the BWCA Wilderness.

There are three campsites within a mile of the Clear Lake portage. Although this is *usually* not a congested part of the Wilderness, try to claim your campsite as early as possible.

Day 2 (8 miles): South Kawishiwi River, p. 70 rods, **Clear Lake,** p. 160 rods, **North Kawishiwi River,** p. 10 rods, **river,** p. 18 rods, **river,** p. 210 rods, **river.** With two long portages, this is a much more challenging day than the first. The first long carry (160 rods) is the easier of the two. After a short climb at the beginning, the trail then levels off until the final 50 rods, where it drops about 80 feet to the North Kawishiwi River. You may be able to walk or line your canoe up through the first two short sets of rapids to avoid the 10-rod and 18-rod portages. Save your energy for the longest portage of the route. The 210-rod portage is mostly uphill, gaining nearly 100 feet elevation during the first 140 rods. It has a good, but rocky path with a couple of short boardwalks across boggy ground.

There are two very nice campsites near the junction of the North and South Kawishiwi River branches. Don't delay in claiming your site. This area is accessible to visitors from four other entry points, and the routes converge at this river intersection.

Day 3 (7 miles): North Kawishiwi River, South Kawishiwi River, p. 12 rods, **river,** p. 18 rods, **river,** p. 28 rods, **river,** p. 122 rods, **Little Gabbro Lake,** p. 200 rods. You'll be paddling downstream on the South Kawishiwi River this day—your first opportunity to run some rapids. Use caution, and don't even consider bypassing the portages unless you know what you're doing in whitewater.

The last two portages are long and mostly uphill. The 122-rod trail gains about 55 feet elevation in as many rods, before leveling off and then descending to the shore of Little Gabbro Lake. It has an excellent path.

The final portage starts on the *west* shore of Little Gabbro Lake, just north of the entrance to the weedy southwest bay. Older maps may show a former portage that started on the east side of that bay. Don't take that old trail. The correct portage starts out on a grassy mudflat. It has a rocky and rooty path that climbs rather steeply for the first 20 rods. After about 80 rods, the undulating trail merges with the smooth, wide path of an old forest road that eventually leads to a large parking lot where your car should be waiting.

ROUTE # 32-2: The Clear Confusion Loop

5 Days, 43 Miles, 10 Lakes, 2 Rivers, 1 Creek, 28 Portages

DIFFICULTY: Challenging

FISHER MAPS: F3, F-4, F-31 (or McKenzie Map #18)

INTRODUCTION: This interesting route will take you through one of the busiest parts of the BWCAW, as well as through parts of the Wilderness that entertain relatively few visitors. From the campground, you will first paddle up the South Kawishiwi River. Then you will portage through Clear Lake to the North Kawishiwi River and follow that stream east to its junction with the south branch of the river. From there, you will continue following the Kawishiwi River northeast to lakes One and Two. From Lake Two, you will then portage southward and cross a chain of more peaceful lakes leading to Bald Eagle Lake. At that point, the route veers toward the northwest, where you'll cross Gabbro and Little Gabbro lakes. From the northwest corner of Little Gabbro Lake, you will portage back to the South Kawishiwi River and paddle downstream to your origin at the campground.

Although you may see numerous other people in the vicinity of the "numbered lakes," and again on Bald Eagle and Gabbro lakes, the rest of the route should be relatively quiet. Gentle rapids, quiet pools, large, open lakes and generally good fishing all combine to make this route a very good one. Anglers should find walleyes and northern pike in much of the water along the route. Serious anglers may want to add a sixth day to shorten the amount of travel required each day. Motorboats are permitted only on the first (and last) 4 miles of the South Kawishiwi River.

If your time is limited to just four days, you could end this route at the Little Gabbro Lake parking lot, 6½ miles from your origin at the campground (see comments for Day 3, paragraph 3, Route #32-1).

Day 1 (7 miles): South Kawishiwi River, p. 33 rods, **river,** p. 26 rods, **river,** p. 25 rods, **river,** p. 62 rods, **river,** p. 5 rods, **river.** (See comments for Day 1, Route #32-1.)

Day 2 (8 miles): South Kawishiwi River, p. 70 rods, **Clear Lake,** p. 160 rods, **North Kawishiwi River,** p. 10 rods, **river,** p. 18 rods, **river,** p. 210 rods, **river.** (See comments for Day 2, Route #32-1.)

Day 3 (10 miles): North Kawishiwi River, Kawishiwi River, p. 8 rods, **river,** p. 40 rods, **river,** p. 20 rods, **river,** p. 25 rods, **Confusion Lake,** p. 41 rods, **Lake One,** p. 30 rods, **pond,** p. 40 rods, **Lake Two, creek,** p. 40 rods, **creek, Rock Island Lake,** p. 40 rods, **pond,** p. 240 rods, **Clearwater Lake.** (See comments for Day 2, paragraph 1, Route #31-1, and comments for Day 1, paragraphs 2 and 3, Route #30-1.)

Day 4 (9 miles): Clearwater Lake, p. 200 rods, **Turtle Lake,** p. 186 rods, **Bald Eagle Lake, rapids, Gabbro Lake, Little Gabbro Lake,** p. 122 rods, **South Kawishiwi River.** (See comments for Day 2, Route #30-1.)

Day 5 (9 miles): South Kawishiwi River, rapids, river, p. 5 rods, **river,** p. 62 rods, **river,** p. 25 rods, **river,** p. 26 rods, **river,** p. 33 rods, **river.** On your way down the South Kawishiwi River, if the water level is suitable, you'll have an opportunity to avoid all five portages by walking, lining or running your canoe down the shallow rapids instead of portaging around them. *Be very careful, though!* If you have any doubts about your safety (and *certainly* if you have no experience in whitewater), use the portages. That's why they are there. A small island in the river divides the first rapids. There is no portage there. The deepest channel is on the west (left) side of the island. Indeed, when the water level is quite low, that is the *only* unobstructed channel.

There is an alternate route back to the campground that eliminates about 4 miles of paddling but adds 168 more rods of portaging. A 285-rod portage leads straight west from Little Gabbro Lake to Bruin Lake, and then a 10-rod trail connects Bruin Lake with the South

Kawishiwi River. Depending on your portaging efficiency versus your paddling speed, this shortcut may or may not save you time. It is a good choice, however, when there is a strong south wind blowing up the Kawishiwi River. The long trail passes over several small hills. It doesn't get as much use as most of the portages in this area, but it has a good, generally dry path.

Kawishiwi River

Entry Point 33—Little Gabbro Lake

SEASONAL PERMITS: 254

POPULARITY RANK: 29th

DAILY QUOTA: 2

LOCATION: Little Gabbro Lake lies 10 miles southeast of Ely as the goose flies. From the Chamber of Commerce Building in Ely, drive 11 miles to the Spruce Road (Lake County 230), about ½-mile past the South Kawishiwi River bridge. Turn left there and continue on this good gravel road for 5.1 miles to the "Gabbro Access" road junction. Along the way, you'll pass the turnoff to the Voyageur Outward Bound School (left at 2.3 miles) and the Filson Creek parking lot for the South Kawishiwi River entry point (left at 4.0 miles). After crossing Filson Creek, County Road 230 becomes Forest Route 181. Turn left onto the Gabbro Access road and continue another 0.6 mile to the road's end. Although it's less than 17 miles from town, allow at least 35 minutes for the drive from Ely to this entry point.

DESCRIPTION: You can unload your gear at the end of the turn-around loop. A large parking lot nearby will accommodate at least 25 cars. From the end of the turn-around loop a 200-rod portage leads north to Little Gabbro Lake. For the first 120 rods the trail follows the smooth, undulating path of an old forest road, more downhill than uphill. For the next 80 rods it climbs over a large hill on a newer footpath that is quite rocky and rooty. The final 30 rods descend rather steeply down to the lake. Overall, it's a good, dry portage. At one low spot in the trail and again near the shore of Little Gabbro Lake, however, the trail may be wet and muddy at times.

215

The South Kawishiwi River Campground, located midway between the bridge and the Spruce Road turnoff, is a fine place to spend the night before your canoe trip. There are 32 campsites, well water and a small swimming beach. A fee is charged.

Although Little Gabbro Lake ranks only 29th in popularity among all BWCAW entry points, permits are very hard to come by. Make your reservation early. The daily quota here is filled over 90% of the time, which distinguishes this lovely entry point as #1 among all entry points with quotas filled the greatest number of days each summer. Motorboats are not allowed to enter the wilderness here. Although the region served by this entry point is seldom crowded, it does entertain a good number of visitors each summer. It is not unusual to see day-time visitors along with the campers.

The popularity of this entry point is due, in large part, to its use by anglers. Little Gabbro Lake affords quick access to two lakes with excellent reputations for fishing. Gabbro and Bald Eagle lakes, just east of Little Gabbro Lake, are known for their good populations of walleyes and northern pike. This entry point also provides access to the central part of the lovely Kawishiwi Triangle region, where rocky shorelines, nice campsites and ample wildlife are found. It's a nice destination for wilderness neophytes who want a fairly easy route, but without the crowds associated with the more popular entry points along the Fernberg Road.

See Route #32-1 for a 3-day trip suggestion in this area. You could reverse that route by starting at Little Gabbro Lake and ending at the South Kawishiwi River Campground, 6½ miles by road from your origin. On the other hand, if you want a longer route than either of those suggested below, consider adding the last seven days of Route #31-2 to the first day of Route #33-2. That makes a challenging eight-day route that ends at the Fall Lake Campground, 23 miles by road from your origin.

ROUTE # 33-1: The Clear Bruin Loop
2 Days, 11 Miles, 4 Lakes, 1 River, 9 Portages

DIFFICULTY: Challenging

FISHER MAPS: F3

INTRODUCTION: This short loop is a good choice for a typical weekend outing in the BWCA Wilderness. You'll experience a variety of portages, three small lakes and the central part of the South Kawishiwi River with its rushing rapids. From Little Gabbro Lake, you will portage north to the South Kawishiwi River and then again to Clear Lake. After a night on that lovely lake, you will return to the river via Eskwagama Lake. A short portage will lead you to Bruin Lake, and then the longest carry of the journey will return you to Little Gabbro Lake.

To a group of seasoned wilderness trippers, this must surely be considered an "easier" route. Strong paddlers would have no problem completing the loop in just one day. To less experienced paddlers and to those who struggle on portages, however, it would be misleading to label this route as anything but "challenging." Four of the 11 portages exceed 100 rods in length and three of those exceed 200 rods. That's a challenge to most folks. Spread over two days, there should be plenty of time to fish for the walleyes and northern pike found throughout the route. (You can make the route easier by ending it at the Filson Creek parking lot. See Day 2 below.)

Day 1 (5 miles): P. 200 rods, **Little Gabbro Lake,** p. 122 rods, **South Kawishiwi River, rapids, river,** p. 70 rods, **Clear Lake.** The 122-rod portage begins just upstream (west bank) from the site of an old, now nearly indistinguishable logging dam. It has a good, well-beaten path that descends much of the way to the river below. Soon after launching onto the river, you will encounter a set of rapids divided by a small island. There is no portage, but you should have no problem running the rapids there. The deepest channel is on the west (left) side of the island. Indeed, when the water level is quite low, that is the *only* unobstructed channel.

Clear is a serene and pretty little lake that has several campsites, most along the north shore of the lake. Anglers will find walleyes, northern pike, crappies and bluegills in the shallow water. If you prefer more solitude than you might find on Clear Lake, continue on to Eskwagama Lake, where there is just one campsite. After committing to that additional effort, however, you may find the campsite there is already occupied. It's a gamble.

Day 2 (6 miles): **Clear Lake,** p. 100 rods, **Eskwagama Lake,** p. 85 rods, **South Kawishiwi River,** p. 5 rods, **river,** p. 10 rods, **Bruin Lake,** p. 285 rods, **Little Gabbro Lake,** p. 200 rods. Neither of the portages to or from Eskwagama Lake is difficult, but the trail is boggy at the end of the 100-rod trail. When the water level is high on the river, you can probably eliminate the 5-rod portage by running through the short rapids there. When the water is low, however, a rock ledge will grab your canoe, so watch out.

The longest portage of this route (285 rods) passes over several small hills. It doesn't get as much use as most of the portages in this area, but it has a pretty good, generally dry path.

An alternate end to this route will eliminate the two longest portages. Instead of looping back from the South Kawishiwi River to Little Gabbro Lake via Bruin Lake, you may portage from the river directly out of the BWCA Wilderness to the Filson Creek parking lot. The 140-rod portage from the river to the road is rough and rocky in places, rooty in others, and it could be muddy in spring or after rains. A 5-rod boardwalk crosses a wet spot near the beginning of the trail. The trail then slopes gradually uphill most of the way, before descending the final 15 rods to the parking lot.

ROUTE # 33-2:	**The Clearwater Gull Loop**
	4 Days, 29 Miles, 11 Lakes, 1 River, 2 Creeks, 21 Portages
DIFFICULTY:	Challenging
FISHER MAPS:	F3, F-4, F-31 (or McKenzie Map #18)
INTRODUCTION:	This interesting and varied route is a good choice for anyone who wants to experience large and small lakes, a couple of tiny creeks, and a lovely river with many rushing rapids. From Little Gabbro Lake, you will first portage north to the Kawishiwi River and then paddle down that stream to the "numbered lakes." Then, after a night on Lake Two, you will steer southeast across a chain of less frequently visited lakes leading to Bald Eagle Lake. From there, the route heads northwest across Gabbro Lake and back to Little Gabbro Lake.

Though much of this route receives light to moderate use, parts of it do attract many visitors. The loop crosses several notable fishing lakes and penetrates a region known for its moose population. Walleyes and northern pike inhabit most of the water along the route, and some pan fish may also be found along the way. Gabbro and Bald Eagle lakes are particularly popular with early summer anglers, when the walleyes are easiest to catch. Lakes One and Two are nearly always popular, attracting both anglers and non-anglers alike. If you are looking for solitude at night, you should probably avoid camping on any of those lakes. Elsewhere, you will probably encounter relatively few people.

Though most groups should have no problem completing this loop in just four days, avid anglers and inexperienced paddlers should consider adding a fifth day. With 15 of the 21 portages measuring less than 100 rods, this route might deserve an "easier" rating if spread over more than 4 days. All of the trails are well used and well maintained, and none is particularly tough.

Day 1 (7 miles): P. 200 rods, **Little Gabbro Lake,** p. 122 rods, **South Kawishiwi River,** p. 28 rods, **river,** p. 18 rods, **river,** p. 12 rods, **Kawishiwi River.** The 122-rod portage begins just upstream (west bank) from the site of an old, now nearly indistinguishable logging dam. It has a good path that descends much of the way to the river below. After reaching the South Kawishiwi River, you will be paddling upstream this day, but the current is seldom noticeable in the quiet pools between rapids. All of the portages along the river are quite easy. The longest trail (28 rods), however, does pass over a small but steep hill. With normal water conditions, you could eliminate all three of the portages by walking or lining your canoe up the shallow rapids.

Plan to camp near the confluence of the North and South Kawishiwi River branches, just beyond the final portage. There are some very nice campsites in that area, including a couple in the north branch of the river.

Day 2 (6 miles): **Kawishiwi River,** p. 8 rods, **river,** p. 40 rods, **river,** p. 20 rods, **river,** p. 19 rods, **Lake One,** p. 30 rods, **pond,** p. 40 rods, **Lake Two.** You'll be paddling on a very pretty part of the Kawishiwi River this day. Confusion Lake is also as attractive as it is confusing. The only portage that you might be able to eliminate by walking or lining your canoe through the rapids is at the 20-rod trail. Don't be tempted to bypass any of the other portages. The gradient is too great and the current is far too swift in the rapids. There is a small, scenic waterfall at the 8-rod portage.

This is a short day of travel for one good reason. Lake Two is one of the busier lakes in the Boundary Waters. If you don't claim a campsite there early in the afternoon, you may not find a vacant site. If you prefer a night of solitude, you might want to continue on to Rock Island Lake, where there is an unofficial campsite. To camp there, however, you must get *prior authorization* from the USFS to spend a night in the Weasel Lake Primitive Management Area (see Chapter 1), which includes Rock Island Lake. The nice, but undeveloped, campsite is located at the southeast end of the lake, away from the main line of traffic.

Day 3 (7 miles): **Lake Two, creek,** p. 40 rods, **creek, Rock Island Lake,** p. 40 rods, **pond,** p. 240 rods, **Clearwater Lake,** p. 125 rods, **Camdre Lake,** p. 65 rods, **Pietro Lake,** p. 50 rods, **Gull Lake.** Watch carefully for the portage connecting Lake Two and Rock Island Lake. After paddling into the shallow creek about 20 rods, you'll find the beginning of the portage on the east (left) side. After walking 40 rods, watch for the steep drop back down to the creek on your right. The trail continues from that point another 20 rods to a wider and deeper part of the creek, to use when the water level is too low at the first access. But this part of the trail is not as well maintained as the first 40 rods. It also doesn't get as much use, so windfalls may obstruct the path. If the water level is high enough (in early spring and during rainy summers), you may be able to put back into the creek after a portage of only 5 rods.

As you approach the southwest end of Rock Island Lake, watch carefully for the portage that starts on the boggy shoreline on the southeast (left) side of the outlet creek. It is very difficult to see until you are right there. The final, long portage to Clearwater Lake is relatively level most of the way, but downhill at the end, where a nice sandy beach greets you.

The portage leading south from Clearwater Lake climbs steadily for the first 80 rods, gaining nearly 80 feet in elevation, then descends to the northeast corner of Camdre Lake. The next portage descends nearly 80 feet to Pietro Lake after first climbing over a low rise. The final carry is virtually level.

For the most solitude on Gull Lake, paddle to one of the campsites near the east end of the lake, located well away from the main flow of canoeing traffic. Then cast a line for the walleyes, northern pike and smallmouth bass that dwell in the water around you. The lake has some nice walleyes, in particular.

Day 4 (9 miles): Gull Lake, p. 40 rods, **Gull Creek,** p. 190 rods, **Bald Eagle Lake,** p. 5 rods, **Gabbro Lake, Little Gabbro Lake,** p. 200 rods. At the 190-rod portage, you'll first have to climb a short, but steep hill that borders Gull Creek. The trail then descends most of the way, dropping 125 feet to the shore of Bald Eagle Lake.

The short, swift rapids between Bald Eagle and Gabbro lakes can usually be easily run in your canoe. If you are not comfortable running the rapids, however, you should portage 5 rods across the northwest end of the rocky island around which the rapids pass.

Along the northwest shore of Gabbro Lake and the north shore of Little Gabbro Lake, you may see the charred evidence of a forest fire. During the dry June of 1995, the Gabbro Lake Fire burned nearly 4,000 acres of forest across the region just north of Gabbro Lake and east of the South Kawishiwi River.

Entry Point 84—Snake River

SEASONAL PERMITS: 98

POPULARITY RANK: 45th

DAILY QUOTA: 1

LOCATION: The Snake River enters the Boundary Waters about 17 miles southeast of Ely and about 15 miles northwest of Isabella. To get there from Ely, drive southeast on State Highway 1 for 18¾ miles from its intersection with Highway 169 (Chamber of Commerce building). Turn left onto Forest Route 377. A sign there points to August Lake and Isabella Lake. Continue eastbound on this good gravel road for 6¼ miles to Forest Route 381. Turn left at this intersection and drive north for 1.8 miles to a Y intersection. From the Y drive northwest on the *left* fork for 1.2 miles to the end of the road at a barricade of boulders. The final 3 miles of forest roads north of the Tomahawk Road (F.R. 377) are quite rough and narrow—barely accessible to cars with low clearance. A heavily loaded car may "bottom out" if the driver is not very careful.

DESCRIPTION: A small parking area at the end of the road will accommodate up to six vehicles. The South Kawishiwi River Campground is the closest place to camp the night before your trip (see Entry Point #32 for its location).

From the road's end a 270-rod portage continues along the same old logging road on which you were driving. Just 90 rods down the trail you will pass another barrier of boulders, which marks the place where the portage started before the road washed out in 1994. Beyond that point, you will walk through a couple of large wet areas as you continue to gradually descend another 125 rods to a narrow log bridge that crosses the Snake River at a small set of rapids. After the bridge, the trail climbs for 10 rods to the site of an abandoned 1960's logging camp in a large clearing. At that point large rock cairns mark the trail across the clearing, as the trail veers north, away from the path of the old logging road. The path descends the final 32 rods to the bank of the Snake River.

The habitat along the Snake River is unique, where plants such as blood root, calypso orchids and elm trees are found. The marshy lower part of the river is good habitat for the American bittern, the great blue heron and the common snipe, as well as many other species of birds.

The Snake River provides the quickest access to Bald Eagle Lake, which is a popular destination for anglers in search of the walleyes and northern pike that dwell there. Although this entry point ranks low in popularity relative to other entry points, the limited supply of overnight permits is actually in rather high demand. It ranked 19th among all entry points with quotas filled the greatest number of days in 1997. So, if your heart is set on entering this part of the wilderness, be sure to make your reservation early, especially if you are planning to start your expedition on Friday, Saturday, Sunday or Monday. Motorboats are not permitted. You are not likely to see any day-use visitors on the Snake River either.

For another suggestion for a weekend route, see Route #75-1. That delightful little route could be reversed by starting at the Snake River Entry Point and ending at the Little Isabella River Entry Point. Or, for a longer route suggestion, see Entry Point 34. Route #34-2 (6 days) could just as well begin at the Snake River entry point and end at the Island River bridge.

ROUTE # 84-1: **The Snake and Turtle Loop**

2 Days, 20 Miles, 6 Lakes, 2 Rivers, 1 Creek, 13 Portages

DIFFICULTY: Challenging

FISHER MAPS: F4

INTRODUCTION: This is a fine weekend route for anyone who wants to avoid the crowds found at busier entry points, yet still have quick access to a popular fishing lake on a route with varied scenery. After paddling down the winding Snake River, you will join the Isabella River and continue northbound to and across much of Bald Eagle Lake. Then you'll portage to Gull Creek and proceed north through Gull, Pietro and Camdre lakes to Clearwater Lake. The next morning, you will steer southwest and return to Bald Eagle Lake via Turtle Lake. Finally, you'll backtrack up the Snake River to your origin.

If you are not in the best of shape, you may find this trek a bit too demanding for just two short days. Also, if fishing is a major part of your trip itinerary, consider stretching the route over three full days or longer.

Except for Bald Eagle Lake, the route receives light to moderate use. Only during the busiest part of the summer will you have much competition for campsites on Clearwater Lake. Bald Eagle Lake, however, has long been popular among anglers. Persistence should result in a stringer full of walleyes, northern pike and maybe some pan fish, too. Northern pike are dominant in the other lakes along this route.

Day 1 (10 miles): P. 270 rods, **Snake River,** p. 20 rods, **river, rapids, river,** p. 10 rods, **river, Isabella River, Bald Eagle Lake,** p. 190 rods, **Gull Creek,** p. 40 rods, **Gull Lake,** p. 50 rods, **Pietro Lake,** p. 65 rods, **Camdre Lake,** p. 125 rods, **Clearwater Lake.** Don't be confused by the appearance of the south end of Bald Eagle Lake. Both the Fisher and the McKenzie maps give the impression that Bald Eagle Lake extends all the way to the 190-rod portage on the Isabella River and the 10-rod portage on the Snake River. Wrong. What appears on the map to be the lower part of a lake (about 1 mile long) is actually a grassy bog through which both rivers flow and then merge.

Beware the 190-rod portage out of Bald Eagle Lake. The trail is mostly uphill, climbing to 125 feet above the lake before dropping steeply into the Gull Creek valley. The only other notable uphill trek of the day is on the 65-rod portage from Pietro Lake, where the trail gains about 80 feet elevation before dropping 30 feet to the southwest corner of Camdre Lake. The 125-rod portage, on the other hand, is mostly downhill.

Clearwater Lake is aptly named. You will find several nice campsites along its north shore and a nice, sandy beach at the portage leading to Rock Island Lake. Anglers should find northern pike in the cool, clear water.

Day 2 (10 miles): Clearwater Lake, p. 200 rods, **Turtle Lake,** p. 186 rods, **Bald Eagle Lake, Isabella River, Snake River,** p. 10 rods, **river, rapids, river,** p. 20 rods, **river,** p. 270 rods. Yes, three long portages await you this day, but none is too rough. Your first long portage is nearly level and nothing to worry about, although there is a bog at the end of the trail. Your "reward" for this long hike is a very unattractive scene. The forest along the east shoreline of Turtle Lake sustained considerable damage from a windstorm. The reward for anglers, however, is much more appealing. Turtle Lake is known to harbor big northern pike.

The second portage is more of a challenge. It climbs steeply during the first 30 rods from Turtle Lake but then descends gradually most of the way to Bald Eagle Lake. Of course, you know what awaits you at the south end of Bald Eagle Lake.

ROUTE # 84-2:	**The One Clear Snake Loop**
	4 Days, 38 Miles, 12 Lakes, 4 Rivers, 2 Creeks, 28 Portages
DIFFICULTY:	Challenging
FISHER MAPS:	F3, F-4, F-31 (or McKenzie Map #18)
INTRODUCTION:	This interesting and varied route is a good choice for anyone who wants to experience large and small lakes, a couple of tiny creeks, and a lovely river with many rushing rapids. After paddling down the winding Snake River, you will join the Isabella River and continue northbound to cross much of Bald Eagle Lake. Then you'll portage to Gull Creek and proceed north through a chain of quiet lakes leading to the popular "numbered lakes." From Lake Two, you will proceed northwest across Lake One to the lovely Kawishiwi River. That river's north branch will carry you west until you portage south to Clear Lake. From Clear Lake you'll steer a southeast course on the South Kawishiwi River to Little Gabbro, Gabbro and Bald Eagle lakes. Finally, you'll backtrack up the Snake River to your origin.

Though much of this route receives only light to moderate use, parts of it do attract many visitors. The loop crosses several notable fishing lakes and penetrates a region known for its moose population. Walleyes and northern pike inhabit most of the water along the route, and some pan fish may also be found along the way. Gabbro and Bald Eagle lakes are particularly popular with early summer anglers, when the walleyes are easiest to catch. Lakes One and Two are nearly always popular, attracting both anglers and non-anglers. If you are looking for solitude at night, you should probably avoid camping on any of those lakes. Elsewhere, you will probably encounter relatively few people.

Though most groups of competent paddlers should have no problem completing this loop in just four days, avid anglers and inexperienced paddlers should consider adding a fifth day. Although you will be averaging seven portages per day on this route, 20 of the 28 portages measure less than 100 rods. Most of the trails are well used and well maintained. None is extremely tough, but there are a few steep climbs along the way.

Day 1 (10 miles): P. 270 rods, **Snake River,** p. 20 rods, **river, rapids, river,** p. 10 rods, **river, Isabella River, Bald Eagle Lake,** p. 190 rods, **Gull Creek,** p. 40 rods, **Gull Lake,** p. 50 rods, **Pietro Lake,** p. 65 rods, **Camdre Lake,** p. 125 rods, **Clearwater Lake.** (See comments for Day 1, Route #84-1.)

Day 2 (9 miles): Clearwater Lake, p. 240 rods, **pond,** p. 40 rods, **Rock Island Lake, creek,** p. 40 rods, **creek, Lake Two,** p. 40 rods, **pond,** p. 30 rods, **Lake One,** p. 41 rods, **Confusion Lake,** p. 25 rods, **Kawishiwi River,** p. 20 rods, **river,** p. 40 rods, **river,** p. 8 rods, **river, North Kawishiwi River.** With 10 portages, this might appear to be a rugged day ahead. But it's really not. After reaching Lake Two in particular, the portages are quite easy on well-maintained and well-traveled paths. The 240-rod trail from Clearwater Lake has a rather steep uphill section at the beginning, but it soon levels off and then gradually slopes down to the unnamed pond. There may be some wet and muddy spots on the path.

In the creek connecting Rock Island Lake and Lake Two, if the water level is not extremely low, avoid the temptation to start the portage at the first landing you see. It will add about 20 rods to your carry on a trail that is not well maintained and may be plagued with windfalls. It should be used only when the creek is too low from that point to the start of the 40-rod portage, which also begins on the right side of the creek. If the water level is high enough, in fact, you may be able to eliminate all but the last 5 rods of the 40-rod portage.

You will probably see many canoes on the busy route through lakes One and Two. The Kawishiwi River should be much more peaceful. You'll be paddling on a very pretty part of the river this day. Confusion Lake is also as attractive as it is confusing. The only portage that you might be able to eliminate by walking, lining or running your canoe down the rapids is at the 20-rod trail along the Kawishiwi River (but only if you are absolutely sure that you know what you are doing). Don't ever be tempted to bypass the 40-rod and 8-rod portages by walking or running the corresponding rapids. There is a small waterfall at the shorter portage, and the current is far too swift and the drop is too great at the longer trail. These rapids are not navigable at any time, regardless of the water level.

Plan to camp just beyond the entrance to the North Kawishiwi River. There you will find two very nice campsites with plenty of space for the largest of groups.

Day 3 (9 miles): North Kawishiwi River, p. 210 rods, river, p. 18 rods, river, p. 10 rods, river, p. 160 rods, Clear Lake, p. 70 rods, South Kawishiwi River, rapids, river, p. 122 rods, Little Gabbro Lake. Your first long portage is not nearly as exhausting as it might seem. After a gradual climb near the beginning, most of the trail is downhill, descending nearly 100 feet in elevation over the final 140 rods. It has a good but rocky path with a couple of short boardwalks across boggy ground.

You may be able to avoid the next two short portages by running, lining or walking your canoe through the corresponding rapids (but only if you scout them first and if you know what you are doing in whitewater).

The half-mile portage from the North Kawishiwi River starts out by climbing for 50 rods to 80 feet above the river. It then gradually descends much of the way to Clear Lake. The trail at the other end of Clear Lake is much easier.

You will be paddling upstream on the South Kawishiwi River, and there is no designated portage at the small rapids that you'll soon encounter. The deepest channel is on the west (right) side of the small island that divides the rapids. The shallower east channel might be a better choice if you must step out to walk your canoe through the rapids.

The 122-rod trail gains about 55 feet elevation in as many rods, before leveling off and then descending to the shore of Little Gabbro Lake. It has an excellent path. There is only one good campsite on Little Gabbro Lake, at the end of a peninsula on the north shore of the lake. If that one is occupied, you may want to continue on to Gabbro Lake, where there are many more sites from which to choose.

Note: If you are behind schedule at the end of Day 2, or if you simply want an easier route on Day 3, consider a shortcut to Little Gabbro Lake. From the junction of the north and south branches of the Kawishiwi River, follow the *south* branch instead of the northern route. This alternative is 3 miles shorter and requires only 3 short portages along the river before reaching the 122-rod carry to Little Gabbro Lake.

Day 4 (10 miles): Little Gabbro Lake, Gabbro Lake, p. 5 rods, Bald Eagle Lake, Isabella River, Snake River, p. 10 rods, river, rapids, river, p. 20 rods, river, p. 270 rods. You may have to paddle against some swift current in the narrows between Little Gabbro and Gabbro lakes. It's really not enough drop to label it a set of "rapids" but, depending on the water level, it may require some extra paddling effort. The drop from Bald Eagle Lake to Gabbro Lake (at the 5-rod portage) is far greater. You won't be able to paddle up that set of rapids.

Along the north shore of Little Gabbro Lake and the northwest shore of Gabbro Lake, you may see the charred evidence of a forest fire. During the dry June of 1995, the Gabbro Lake Fire burned nearly 4,000 acres of forest across the region just north of Gabbro Lake and east of the South Kawishiwi River.

Entry Point 75—Little Isabella River

SEASONAL PERMITS: 98

POPULARITY RANK: 45th (tie)

DAILY QUOTA: 1

LOCATION: The Little Isabella River enters the Boundary Waters about 20 miles southeast of Ely and 13 miles northwest of Isabella and flows northeast for 4½ miles to the Isabella River. To get there from Ely, drive southeast on State Highway 1 for 18¾ miles from its intersection with Highway 169 at the Chamber of Commerce building. (From the Isabella Ranger Station, drive 19 miles northwest on Highway 1.) Turn left onto Forest Route 377 (right if coming from Isabella). A sign there points to August Lake and Isabella Lake. Continue eastbound on this good gravel road for 6¼ miles to Forest Route 381. Turn left at this intersection and drive north for 1.8 miles to a Y intersection. From the Y drive northeast on the *right* fork for 1 mile to a dead-end at the Little Isabella River. The final 2.8 miles of forest roads north of the Tomahawk Road (F.R. 377) are quite rough and narrow and parts of the last mile of road after the Y may be under water. A 4-wheel-drive vehicle is not necessary, but high clearance is advisable.

DESCRIPTION: A small parking area at the end of the road will accommodate 3-4 vehicles—sufficient for the few people who use this isolated entry point. The South Kawishiwi River Campground is the closest place to camp the night before your trip (see Entry Point #32 for its location).

A 20-rod portage begins at the road's end and leads north, bypassing a set of rapids, to the bank of the river. The Little Isabella is a slow, narrow, meandering river that is bordered by alder brush, black spruce and jack pine. When the water level is high, the current will be swift in the upper stretches of this little river. During drier periods, the current won't be as swift, but the river's level will never (or very seldom) be too low for canoe navigation. Motors are prohibited. This is a delightful way to enter the Wilderness for anyone in search of immediate solitude and an intimate experience with the natural environment.

In spite of its low ranking in popularity, the limited supply of overnight permits is actually in rather high demand. About ⅔ of the available permits were issued to visitors in 1997. So, if your heart is set on entering this part of the wilderness, be sure to make your reservation early, especially if you are planning to start your expedition on Friday, Saturday, Sunday or Monday. You are not likely to see any day-use visitors on the Little Isabella River.

For an easy 2-day route suggestion, see Entry Point 34. Route #34-1 could just as well start at the Little Isabella River entry point and end at the Island River bridge.

ROUTE # 75-1: The Little Isabella Snake Route

3 Days, 20 Miles, 2 Lakes, 3 Rivers, 11 Portages

DIFFICULTY: Easier

FISHER MAPS: F-4

INTRODUCTION: This river-running route is an excellent choice for anyone who wants to experience the essence of true wilderness—quickly—without having to expend a great deal of energy along the way. The route will first take you northeast, down the tranquil Little Isabella River to its big sister, the Isabella River. You'll then paddle a short distance up the Isabella River to portage into Quadga Lake, where you will spend your first night. The next morning, you will return to the Isabella River and follow it west, this time downstream, to Bald Eagle Lake, where you will sleep the second night. On the final day of this short trip, you will return to the south end of Bald Eagle Lake and then follow the Snake River to end at that entry point, 2¼ miles by road from your origin.

Motorboats are banned from the entire route which, except for Bald Eagle Lake, is very lightly traveled. Only one overnight travel permit per day is issued for both the Little Isabella and Snake River entry points. There is a good chance that you will see nobody else along the route, except on Bald Eagle Lake, which is a popular destination for anglers in search of the walleyes and northern pike. You will also have a good chance to see wildlife in this area, including moose; so keep a watchful eye.

Note: If the quota for the Little Isabella River is booked up on your starting date, you could reverse this route by starting at the Snake River entry point and simply reversing the route described below.

Day 1 (7 miles): P. 20 rods, **Little Isabella River,** p. 13 rods, **river,** p. 27 rods, **river,** p. 15 rods, **river, Isabella River, rapids, river,** p. 65 rods, **Quadga Lake.** All four of the short portages along the Little Isabella River should pose no problems, even to an inexperienced group of paddlers. During mid and late summer, the mouth of the Little Isabella River may be nearly choked with aquatic plants. A narrow passage, however, is found near the east (right) shoreline. Because of the thick reeds, it would be very easy to miss the river's outlet, should you reverse this route.

Soon thereafter, just after pulling through a small set of rapids, you will see a 40-rod portage on the south (right) side of the Isabella River. On the opposite shoreline (left side) is the beginning of the 65-rod portage to Quadga Lake. It's a good trail that passes over a low hill. About half way across the portage you'll come to the junction of another trail on the right that connects Quadga Lake with the Isabella River on the *east* side of the rapids.

Quadga Lake has four campsites from which to choose. Claim yours and then cast your line for the walleyes or northern pike that reside in the lake.

Day 2 (8 miles): Quadga Lake, p. 65 rods, **Isabella River, rapids, river,** p. 33 rods, **river, rapids, river,** p. 190 rods, **river, Bald Eagle Lake.** Don't worry about the 190-rod carry. It is mostly downhill and has a good, dry path. Don't try to avoid the portage by running the adjacent rapids. It's not safe. Help might not pass your way for quite some time, and it's a long walk back to your car.

Don't be confused by the appearance of the south end of Bald Eagle Lake. Both the Fisher and the McKenzie maps give the impression that Bald Eagle Lake extends all the way to the 190-rod portage on the Isabella River and the 10-rod portage on the Snake River. Wrong. What appears on the map to be the lower part of the lake (about 1 mile long) is actually a grassy bog through which both rivers flow and then merge.

The best campsites are located in the north end of Bald Eagle Lake. But then, that's where most of the other people will be too. For an 8-mile day, plan to camp near the middle of this big lake, in the vicinity of the Gull Creek portage. This is one of the best lakes in the area for catching northern pike. Walleyes and black crappies also inhabit the lake.

Day 3 (5 miles): Bald Eagle Lake, Isabella River, Snake River, p. 10 rods, **river, rapids, river,** p. 20 rods, **river,** p. 270 rods. The habitat along the Snake River is unique, where plants such as blood root, calypso orchids and elm trees are found. The marshy lower part of the river is also good habitat for the American bittern, the great blue heron, and the common snipe, as well as many other species of birds.

At the beginning of that long, final portage, you'll climb for 32 rods up from the boggy shore of the Snake River to a large, open clearing where a logging camp once stood. At that point the trail joins the path of an old logging road and drops 10 rods down to cross the Snake River on a log bridge. From the river the trail continues southeast on a good, smooth path leading gradually uphill to the road's end just outside the BWCA Wilderness. You'll encounter a couple of large wet areas along the trail during the gradual ascent from the bridge.

ROUTE # 75-2: **The Little Isabella Confusion Route**

6 Days, 49 Miles, 13 Lakes, 5 Rivers, 2 Creeks, 33 Portages

DIFFICULTY: Challenging

FISHER MAPS: F3, F-4, F-31 (or McKenzie Map #18)

INTRODUCTION: This interesting route is a dandy choice for anyone who likes variety, including large and small lakes, wide rivers and tiny creeks. It will first take you northeast, down the tranquil Little Isabella River to its big sister, the Isabella River. You'll then paddle a short distance up the Isabella River to portage into Quadga Lake, where you will spend your first night. The next morning, you will return to the Isabella River and follow it west to Bald Eagle Lake. From there you will portage to Gull Creek and proceed north through a chain of quiet lakes leading to the popular "numbered lakes." From Lake Two, you will paddle northwest across Lake One to the lovely Kawishiwi River. That river's north branch will carry you farther west until you portage south to Clear Lake. Then you'll steer a southeast course on the South Kawishiwi River to Little Gabbro, Gabbro and

Bald Eagle lakes. Finally, you'll paddle up the tiny Snake River to portage out of the BWCA Wilderness and end your expedition at a parking lot 2¼ miles by road from your origin.

Though much of this route receives only light to moderate use, parts of it do attract many visitors. The loop crosses several notable fishing lakes and penetrates a region known for its moose population. Walleyes and northern pike inhabit most of the water along the route, and some pan fish may also be found along the way. Gabbro and Bald Eagle lakes are particularly popular with early summer anglers, when the walleyes are easiest to catch. Lakes One and Two are nearly always popular, attracting both anglers and non-anglers. If you are looking for solitude at night, you should probably avoid camping on any of those lakes. Elsewhere, you will probably encounter relatively few people. Motorboats are banned from the entire route.

Though most groups of competent paddlers should have no problem completing this loop in six days, avid anglers and inexperienced paddlers should consider extending their journey to seven or eight days. You will be averaging five to six portages per day on this route, but only 10 are greater than 100 rods in length. Most are less than 50 rods. The longest is 270 rods—your final carry of the trip. Most of the trails are well used and well maintained. None is extremely tough, but there are a few steep climbs along the way.

Note: If the quota for the Little Isabella River is booked up on your starting date, you could reverse this route by starting at the Snake River entry point and simply reversing the route described below.

Day 1 (7 miles): P. 20 rods, **Little Isabella River,** p. 13 rods, **river,** p. 27 rods, **river,** p. 15 rods, **river, Isabella River, rapids, river,** p. 65 rods, **Quadga Lake.** (See comments for Day 1, Route #75-1.)

Day 2 (8 miles): Quadga Lake, p. 65 rods, **Isabella River, rapids, river,** p. 33 rods, **river, rapids, river,** p. 190 rods, **river, Bald Eagle Lake.** (See comments for Day 2, Route #75-1.)

Day 3 (6 miles): Bald Eagle Lake, p. 190 rods, **Gull Creek,** p. 40 rods, **Gull Lake,** p. 50 rods, **Pietro Lake,** p. 65 rods, **Camdre Lake,** p. 125 rods, **Clearwater Lake.** (See comments for Day 1, paragraphs 2 and 3, Route #84-1.) This is a short day of travel for one good reason. If you continue onward to the next group of USFS campsites on Lake Two, you will be camping on one of the busier lakes in the Boundary Waters. If you don't claim a campsite there early in the afternoon, you may not find a vacant site. On the other hand, if time permits and you prefer even more solitude than you might find on Clearwater Lake, you might want to continue on to Rock Island Lake. To camp there, however, you must get *prior authorization* from the USFS to spend a night in the Weasel Lake Primitive Management Area (see Chapter 1), which includes Rock Island Lake. The nice, but undeveloped, campsite is located at the southeast end of the lake, away from the main line of traffic. This alternative will add two more portages and 1-2 more miles of paddling to your third day of travel. But it will also reduce the number of portages on your fourth day from 10 to 8. It's something to consider.

Day 4 (9 miles): Clearwater Lake, p. 240 rods, **pond,** p. 40 rods, **Rock Island Lake, creek,** p. 40 rods, **creek, Lake Two,** p. 40 rods, **pond,** p. 30 rods, **Lake One,** p. 41 rods, **Confusion Lake,** p. 25 rods, **Kawishiwi River,** p. 20 rods, **river,** p. 40 rods, **river,** p. 8 rods, **river, North Kawishiwi River.** (See comments for Day 2, Route #84-2.)

Day 5 (9 miles): North Kawishiwi River, p. 210 rods, **river,** p. 18 rods, **river,** p. 10 rods, **river,** p. 160 rods, **Clear Lake,** p. 70 rods, **South Kawishiwi River, rapids, river,** p. 122 rods, **Little Gabbro Lake.** (See comments for Day 3, Route #84-2.)

Day 6 (10 miles): Little Gabbro Lake, Gabbro Lake, p. 5 rods, **Bald Eagle Lake, Isabella River, Snake River,** p. 10 rods, **river, rapids, river,** p. 20 rods, **river,** p. 270 rods. (See comments for Day 4, Route #84-2, and for Day 3, Route #75-1.)

Entry Point 67 — Bog Lake

SEASONAL PERMITS: 49

POPULARITY RANK: 55th

DAILY QUOTA: 2

LOCATION: Bog Lake is located 22 miles by air southeast of Ely and 12 miles north of Isabella. To get there from Ely, drive southeast on Highway 1 for 18¾ miles from its junction with Highway 169 (Chamber of Commerce building) to its junction with Forest Route 377. A sign there points left to August Lake and Isabella Lake. Turn onto 377 and follow that good gravel road east for 13½ miles to a primitive one-lane road on the left. Turn there and proceed north on that rough road for ½ mile to its end. High-clearance vehicles are best suited for this entry point, although most cars should make it if driven slowly and carefully to avoid the rocks and potholes.

DESCRIPTION: A small parking area at the end of the road will accommodate 4-5 vehicles. From there, a 1-mile portage leads northwest to Bog Lake.

If you have waited until the last minute to choose an entry point for a busy weekend or holiday, Bog Lake could be the only choice remaining. These two daily permits are in very low demand. Less than 20% of the available overnight permits are issued to visitors each summer. That ranks *last* among all BWCA Wilderness entry points. Furthermore, very few people visit the lake with day-use permits, perhaps due largely to its remote location and the long portage required to get there.

There are no "routes," per se, from this entry point. Because it is landlocked, Bog Lake is a *destination*, not the beginning of a canoeing route. There are no navigable streams or portages connecting it to a chain of other lakes or rivers. For that reason, there are really only two valid reasons to go there: 1) to fish, or 2) to seek respite from the civilized world, as well as from crowds of other canoeists on busy weekends or holidays.

On the north shore of Bog Lake

Here is what you will find at this entry point. The 1-mile portage starts out on the same old roadbed on which you drove to the parking lot. It stops half a mile north of Forest Route 377 because, north of that point, the road crosses an alder swamp and is often under water. During early summer, either wear waterproof boots or expect wet feet. After ¼ mile, you'll see the former parking lot where the trail rises to higher ground. A good, dry path continues on the former roadbed through a mixed forest of aspens, spruce and fir for another ¼ mile. Then the trail veers off the old roadbed to the right on a path that is somewhat narrower and rougher. After surmounting a small but rather steep hill, the trail follows a ridge that descends most of the way to the southwest end of Bog Lake.

Bog Lake is shaped somewhat like a ping-pong paddle, and you'll be entering it at the "handle." The shoreline is populated with a forest of cedars and spruce, as well as some pines and birch trees. Of the four campsites on the lake three are quite small. The largest and best site is located near the middle of the north shore, in a cedar grove on a rocky point. When the water level is low, you'll find a sandy beach on the east shore of the lake.

Anglers are likely to find many small walleyes in the shallow lake. There are also some northern pike and brook trout.

Entry Point 34—Island River

SEASONAL PERMITS: 267

POPULARITY RANK: 28th

DAILY QUOTA: 3

LOCATION: The Island River enters the south-central part of the Boundary Waters 25 airline miles southeast of Ely and 12 miles north of Isabella. To get there from Ely, drive southeast on Highway 1 for 18¾ miles from its junction with Highway 169 (Chamber of Commerce building) to its junction with Forest Route 377. A sign there points left to August Lake and Isabella Lake. Turn onto F.R. 377 and follow that good gravel road east for 17.1 miles to the Island River bridge.

Or, if you are driving through Isabella from the North Shore, turn right onto Forest Route 172 in "downtown" Isabella. Drive one mile east on F.R. 172 to its intersection with F.R. 369. Turn left there and proceed north on F.R. 369 for 7 miles to a Y intersection with Forest Route 373. Continue northbound (left branch) at the Y on F.R. 373 and follow it another 5½ miles northwest to Forest Route 377. Turn right and proceed 4½ miles on F.R. 377 to the Island River bridge. Regardless of the way you approach this entry point, you will be driving on good gravel roads all the way to the Island River. The final 1½ miles, however, are on a rather narrow road, considered "one lane with turnoffs."

DESCRIPTION: The boat landing is on the east (right) side of the road, just past the bridge. Adjacent to it is a small parking lot. After launching your canoe, paddle under the bridge and then head *west* on the river to enter the BWCA Wilderness.

Several National Forest campgrounds are along State Highway 1, and each provides a good place to spend the night before your trip. While driving down Highway 1 from Ely you will pass the South Kawishiwi River Campground (see Entry Point 32), the McDougal Lake Campground and the Little Isabella River Campground. A camping fee is charged at all three facilities. The closest to this entry point is the

Little Isabella River Campground. It is also the smallest, the least popular and, therefore, the most likely to have a vacant campsite.

Like its neighboring entry point at Isabella Lake, the Island River is a good starting point for paddlers who desire a high-quality river trip. The Island and Isabella river valleys teem with wildlife, including moose and bald eagles. Both are scenic rivers with occasional whitewater and relatively little canoeing traffic. Visitors are well rewarded for the extra driving time it takes to get there.

Because of their close proximity, the Island River and Isabella Lake entry points both provide good access to canoe routes following the Isabella River. Both routes suggested below, therefore, could also begin at Isabella Lake. Likewise, the routes described for Isabella Lake (Entry Point 35) could also begin at the Island River. This is good to remember, in case the entry point you wish to use is "booked up" on the day of your scheduled departure.

If you avoid starting your trip on one of the busiest days of the week, it is usually no problem to get a permit for this quiet entry point. About 40% of its available permits are *not* issued each summer. The quota of three permits per day is normally more than the demand. Also, very few day-use visitors frequent the entry point, perhaps due in part to its remote location. Motorboats are not allowed to enter the wilderness here.

ROUTE # 34-1: **The Three Rivers Route**

2 Days, 15 Miles, 1 Lake, 3 Rivers, 12 Portages

DIFFICULTY: Easier

Fisher Maps: F-4

INTRODUCTION: This is a delightful route for anyone who prefers traveling on rivers rather than lakes. From Forest Route 377 you will paddle for only a couple of miles down the Island River before entering the Isabella River. You'll then follow the Isabella River west, past several rapids, until you reach the portage to Quadga Lake. After a night on that quiet little lake, you will portage back to the Isabella River and continue following it west to the mouth of the Little Isabella River. From that point, you'll paddle up the Little Isabella River, following its southwest course to the edge of the BWCA Wilderness. The route ends at Entry Point 75, about 14 miles by road from your origin.

Except for your night on Quadga Lake, the entire route is on rivers. While 12 portages in two days may seem like a challenge to Boundary Waters neophytes, bear in mind that only three of those trails are longer than 30 rods. And the longest is only ⅓ mile. Furthermore, you'll be paddling downstream on the Island and Isabella rivers, though upstream on the Little Isabella River. Most groups should have no trouble at all completing the route in just two days.

Paddle quietly and watch for moose along the banks of all three rivers. This is a very good region in which to see those magnificent beasts.

Note: If the quota for the Island River entry point is filled on your starting date, you could reverse this route by starting at the Little Isabella River entry point and simply reversing the route described below.

Day 1 (8 miles): Island River, p. 11 rods, **river,** p. 10 rods, **river, Isabella River,** p. 110 rods, **river,** p. 10 rods, **river,** p. 27 rods, **river,** p. 27 rods, **river,** p. 75 rods, **Quadga Lake.** You'll be paddling downstream this day on the two rivers. Though not swift, the current is noticeable. Running, lining or walking your canoe down the corresponding rapids may eliminate two or three of the shorter portages— IF the water level is sufficiently high. Always scout them first. And don't take chances if you are not 100% sure that you can handle the whitewater.

After paddling less than 2 miles down the Island River and hiking across two easy portages, you'll enter the Isabella River. Soon thereafter you'll encounter the longest portage of the route. Don't worry; it has a good path that gradually slopes downhill most of the way. The next portage (10 rods) is not often needed, unless the water level is quite low.

As you approach your final portage of the day, you'll see the landings for two portages—one on each side of the river. A 40-rod portage on the south (left) side of the river is the direct route for those heading on down the river. The 75-rod trail on the right side of the river leads north to Quadga Lake. About half way across the portage you'll merge with another trail that connects Quadga Lake with the river on the *west* side of the rapids. That's the trail that you'll take when you leave Quadga Lake. Both trails pass over a low hill on a good path.

Quadga Lake has four campsites from which to choose. Claim yours and then cast your line for the walleyes or northern pike that reside in the lake.

Day 2 (7 miles): Quadga Lake, p. 65 rods, **Isabella River, rapids, river, Little Isabella River,** p. 15 rods, **river,** p. 27 rods, **river,** p. 13 rods, **river,** p. 20 rods. You will paddle only about a mile on the Isabella River this day. Just prior to reaching a set of rapids (east of a 33-rod portage) watch carefully for the mouth of the Little Isabella River. During mid and late summer, it is very easy to miss the outlet, which may be nearly choked with aquatic plants. A clear narrow passage, however, is found near the east (left) shoreline.

All four of the short portages along the Little Isabella River should pose no problems, even to an inexperienced group of paddlers. Paddling may be a chore at times, however, where the upstream current is noticeable.

ROUTE # 34-2: **The Moose Country Route**

6 Days, 50 Miles, 13 Lakes, 5 Rivers, 2 Creeks, 35 Portages

DIFFICULTY: Challenging

FISHER MAPS: F3, F-4, F-31

INTRODUCTION: This interesting route is a good choice for paddlers who prefer variety in their wilderness experience. It's a good combination of rivers and lakes, with a couple of short creeks thrown in for good measure. From Forest Route 377 you will paddle for only a couple of miles down the Island River before entering the Isabella River. You'll then follow the scenic Isabella River west to Bald Eagle Lake. From there you will portage to Gull Creek and proceed north through a chain of quiet lakes leading to the popular "numbered lakes." From Lake Two, you will paddle northwest across Lake One to the lovely Kawishiwi River. That river's north branch will carry you farther west until you portage south to Clear Lake. Then you'll steer a southeast course on the South Kawishiwi River to Little Gabbro, Gabbro and Bald Eagle lakes. Finally, you'll paddle up the tiny Snake River to portage out of the BWCA Wilderness and end your expedition at a parking lot about 14 miles by road from your origin.

Though much of this route receives only light to moderate use, parts of it do attract many visitors. The loop crosses several notable fishing lakes and penetrates a region known for its moose population. Walleyes and northern pike inhabit most of the water along the route, and some pan fish may also be found along the way. Gabbro and Bald Eagle lakes are particularly popular with early summer anglers, when the walleyes are easiest to catch. Lakes One and Two are nearly always popular, attracting both anglers and non-anglers. If you are looking for solitude at night, you should probably avoid camping on any of those lakes. Elsewhere, you will probably encounter relatively few people. Motorboats are banned from the entire route.

Though most groups of competent paddlers should have no problem completing this loop in six days, avid anglers and inexperienced paddlers should consider extending their journey to seven or eight days. You will be averaging about six portages per day on this route, but only nine are greater than 100 rods in length. Most are less than 40 rods. The longest is 270 rods—your final carry of the trip. Most of the trails are well used and well maintained. None is extremely tough, but there are a few steep climbs along the way.

Note: If the quota for the Island River entry point is booked up on your starting date, you could reverse this route by starting at the Snake River entry point and simply reversing the route described below.

Day 1 (8 miles): Island River, p. 11 rods, **river,** p. 10 rods, **river, Isabella River,** p. 110 rods, **river,** p. 10 rods, **river,** p. 27 rods, **river,** p. 27 rods, **river,** p. 75 rods, **Quadga Lake.** (See comments for Day 1, Route #34-1.)

Day 2 (8 miles): Quadga Lake, p. 65 rods, **Isabella River, rapids, river,** p. 33 rods, **river, rapids, river,** p. 190 rods, **river, Bald Eagle Lake.** (See comments for Day 2, Route #75-1.)

Day 3 (6 miles): Bald Eagle Lake, p. 190 rods, **Gull Creek,** p. 40 rods, **Gull Lake,** p. 50 rods, **Pietro Lake,** p. 65 rods, **Camdre Lake,** p. 125 rods, **Clearwater Lake.** (See comments for Day 1, paragraphs 2 and 3, Route #84-1.) This is a short day of travel for one good reason. If you continue onward to the next group of USFS campsites on Lake Two, you will be camping on one of the busier lakes in the Boundary Waters. If you don't claim a campsite there early in the afternoon, you may not find one. On the other hand, if time permits and you prefer even more solitude than you might find on Clearwater Lake, you might want to continue on to Rock Island Lake. To camp there, however, you must get *prior authorization* from the USFS to spend a night in the Weasel Lake Primitive Management Area (see Chapter 1), which includes Rock Island Lake. The nice, but undeveloped, campsite is located at the southeast end of the lake, away from the main line of traffic. This alternative will add two more portages and 1-2 more miles of paddling to your third day of travel. But it will also reduce the number of portages on your fourth day from 10 to 8. It's something to consider.

Day 4 (9 miles): Clearwater Lake, p. 240 rods, **pond,** p. 40 rods, **Rock Island Lake, creek,** p. 40 rods, **creek, Lake Two,** p. 40 rods, **pond,** p. 30 rods, **Lake One,** p. 41 rods, **Confusion Lake,** p. 25 rods, **Kawishiwi River,** p. 20 rods, **river,** p. 40 rods, **river,** p. 8 rods, **river, North Kawishiwi River.** (See comments for Day 2, Route #84-2.)

Day 5 (9 miles): North Kawishiwi River, p. 210 rods, **river,** p. 18 rods, **river,** p. 10 rods, **river,** p. 160 rods, **Clear Lake,** p. 70 rods, **South Kawishiwi River, rapids, river,** p. 122 rods, **Little Gabbro Lake.** (See comments for Day 3, Route #84-2.)

Day 6 (10 miles): Little Gabbro Lake, Gabbro Lake, p. 5 rods, **Bald Eagle Lake, Isabella River, Snake River,** p. 10 rods, **river, rapids, river,** p. 20 rods, **river,** p. 270 rods. (See comments for Day 4, Route #84-2, and for Day 3, Route #75-1.)

Entry Point 35—Isabella Lake

SEASONAL PERMITS: 326

POPULARITY RANK: 26th

DAILY QUOTA: 3

LOCATION: Isabella Lake is 25 airline miles southeast of Ely and 13 miles north of Isabella. To get there from Ely, drive southeast on Highway 1 for 18¾ miles from its junction with Highway 169 (Chamber of Commerce building) to its junction with Forest Route 377. A sign there points left to August Lake and Isabella Lake. Turn onto F.R. 377 and follow that good gravel road east for 18.1 miles to the road's end at "Forest Center."

Or, if you are driving through Isabella from the North Shore, turn right onto Forest Route 172 in "downtown" Isabella. Drive one mile east on F.R. 172 to its intersection with F.R. 369. Turn left there and proceed north on F.R. 369 for 7 miles to a Y intersection with Forest Route 373. Continue northbound (left branch) at the Y on F.R. 373 and follow it another 5½ miles northwest to Forest Route 377. Turn right and proceed 5½ miles on F.R. 377 to the Isabella Lake parking lot. Regardless of the way you approach this entry point, you will be driving on good gravel roads all the way. The final 2½ miles, however, are on a rather narrow road, considered "one lane with turnoffs."

DESCRIPTION: From the large parking lot a 35-rod portage leads north to the southwest shore of Isabella Lake. The parking lot is shared with hikers using the Pow Wow Trail (Entry Point 86), which penetrates the remote region between Isabella Lake and Lake Three. Most of the vehicles in the lot belong to canoeists headed for Isabella Lake.

The area where the parking lot is located was once part of a large logging camp. From 1949 to 1964, 250 people called Forest Center their home. In addition to a sawmill there were 53 homes, a 2-room schoolhouse, a recreation center and a restaurant. There were also barracks and a mess hall for the lumbermen. Timber was hauled away by railroad. Most of Forest Center is now covered with a young growth of

A moose on the banks of the Isabella River

pine trees, but explorers may still find evidence of the logging era near the parking lot.

Several National Forest campgrounds are located along State Highway 1, and each provides a good place to spend the night before your trip. While driving down Highway 1 from Ely you will pass the South Kawishiwi River Campground (see Entry Point 32), the Mc-Dougal Lake Campground and the Little Isabella River Campground. A camping fee is charged at all three facilities. The closest to this entry point is the Little Isabella River Campground. It is also the smallest, the least popular and, therefore, the most likely to have a vacant campsite.

Like its neighboring entry point at the Island River, Isabella Lake is a good starting point for paddlers who desire a high-quality river trip. The Isabella River valley teems with wildlife, including moose and bald eagles. It is a scenic river with occasional whitewater and relatively little canoeing traffic. Visitors are well rewarded for the extra driving time it takes to get there.

Because they are close together, the Isabella Lake and Island River entry points both provide good access to canoe routes following the Isabella River. Both routes suggested for the Island River (Entry Point

34), therefore, could also begin at Isabella Lake. Likewise, the routes described below could also begin at the Island River. This is good to remember, in case the entry point you wish to use is "booked up" on the day of your scheduled departure. For two more good route ideas, see Entry Point 36 in Volume 2. You can enjoy a wonderful three-day outing by reversing Route #36-1, starting at Isabella Lake and ending at Hog Creek. You can also "plug into" Route #36-2 (an outstanding eight-day loop) by starting and ending at Isabella Lake rather than starting at Hog Creek and ending at Kawishiwi Lake.

If you plan to start your canoe trip on one of the busiest days of the week (Friday through Monday) or on a holiday, a reservation is advisable. About 70% of the available permits for Isabella Lake are issued to visitors each summer. It is usually not a problem to get a permit for mid-week days, however. Motorboats are not allowed to enter the wilderness here.

ROUTE # 35-1: The Isabella Bald Eagle Route

3 Days, 22 Miles, 3 Lakes, 2 Rivers, 14 Portages

DIFFICULTY: Challenging

FISHER MAPS: F-4

INTRODUCTION: This is a delightful route for anyone who prefers traveling on rivers rather than lakes. After paddling across the southwest corner of Isabella Lake, you will follow the Isabella River west, past several rapids, until you reach the portage to Quadga Lake. After a night on that quiet little lake, you will return to the Isabella River and continue following it west to Bald Eagle Lake, where you will sleep the second night. On the final day of this short trip, you will return to the south end of Bald Eagle Lake and then paddle up the Snake River until you run out of water. The route ends at Entry Point 84, about 15 miles by road from your origin.

Except for Isabella Lake and your nights on Quadga and Bald Eagle lakes, the entire route is on rivers. While 14 portages in three days does create a challenge to weak or inexperienced groups, bear in mind that only five of those trails are longer than 35 rods. And, although you'll have eight portages on the first day out, the longest trail is only 110 rods and none is difficult. That leaves only three portages per day for the last two days. The longest is 270 rods, but that will be your final carry, and most of it is on the path of an old (former) logging road. Furthermore, you'll be paddling downstream on the Isabella River during the first two days. Most groups should have no trouble at all completing the route in three days. Strong, experienced groups could surely do it in just two days. They would consider this an "easier" three-day route.

Paddle quietly and watch for moose along the banks of the Isabella River. This is a very good region in which to see those awesome creatures.

Note: If the quota for the Isabella Lake entry point is filled on your starting date, you could reverse this route by starting at the Snake River entry point and simply reversing the route described below. Of course, then you would be paddling upstream on the Isabella River and you wouldn't have opportunities to run some of the smaller rapids.

Day 1 (9 miles): P. 35 rods, **Isabella Lake,** p. 28 rods, **Isabella River,** p. 15 rods, **river,** p. 110 rods, **river,** p. 10 rods, **river,** p. 27 rods, **river,** p. 27 rods, **river,** p. 75 rods, **Quadga Lake.** You'll be paddling downstream this day on the Isabella River. Though not swift, the current is noticeable. Running, lining or walking your canoe down the corresponding rapids may eliminate two or three of the shorter portages—IF the water level is sufficiently high. Always scout them first. Don't take chances if you are not 100% sure that you can handle the whitewater.

The trail from the parking lot descends about 35 feet on an excellent path leading to the shore of Isabella Lake. The rest of the portages also have good paths. At the 28-rod portage, you'll cross the Pow Wow Trail. Soon after paddling past the mouth of the Island River (left), you'll encounter the longest portage of the day. Don't worry; it has a good path that gradually slopes downhill most of the way. The next portage (10 rods) is not often needed, unless the water level is quite low.

As you approach your final portage of the day, you'll see the landings for two portages—one on each side of the river. A 40-rod portage on the south (left) side of the river is the direct route for those heading on down the river. The 75-rod trail on the right side of the river leads north to Quadga Lake. About half way across the portage you'll merge with another trail that connects Quadga Lake with the river on the west side of the rapids. That's the trail that you'll take when you leave Quadga Lake. Both trails pass over a low hill on good paths.

Quadga Lake has four campsites from which to choose. Claim yours and then cast your line for the walleyes or northern pike that reside in the lake.

Day 2 (8 miles): Quadga Lake, p. 65 rods, Isabella River, rapids, river, p. 33 rods, river, rapids, river, p. 190 rods, river, Bald Eagle Lake. (See comments for Day 2, Route #75-1.)

Day 3 (5 miles): Bald Eagle Lake, Isabella River, Snake River, p. 10 rods, river, rapids, river, p. 20 rods, river, p. 270 rods. (See comments for Day 3, Route #75-1.)

ROUTE # 35-2: The Isabella and Kawishiwi Rivers Route

6 Days, 51 Miles, 14 Lakes, 4 Rivers, 2 Creeks, 36 Portages

DIFFICULTY: Challenging

FISHER MAPS: F3, F-4, F-31

INTRODUCTION: This interesting route is a good choice for paddlers who prefer variety in their wilderness experience. It's a good combination of rivers and lakes, with a couple of short creeks thrown in for good measure. After paddling across the southwest corner of Isabella Lake, you will follow the Isabella River west, past several rapids, until you reach the portage to Quadga Lake. After a night on that quiet little lake, you will return to the Isabella River and continue following it west to Bald Eagle Lake. From there you will portage to Gull Creek and proceed north through a chain of quiet lakes leading to the popular "numbered lakes." From Lake Two, you will paddle northwest across Lake One to the lovely Kawishiwi River. That river's north branch will carry you farther west until you portage south to Clear Lake. Then you'll steer a southeast course on the South Kawishiwi River to Little Gabbro, Gabbro and Bald Eagle lakes. Finally, you'll paddle up the tiny Snake River to portage out of the BWCA Wilderness and end your expedition at a parking lot about 15 miles by road from your origin. This is the same route as the Moose Country Route, except it starts at Isabella Lake instead of the Island River (see Introduction, Route #34-2, paragraphs 2 and 3).

Note: If the quota for the Isabella Lake entry point is booked up on your starting date, you could reverse this route by starting at the Snake River entry point and simply reversing the route described below. But then you would be paddling upstream on both the Isabella and Kawishiwi rivers and you wouldn't have opportunities to run some of the smaller rapids.

Day 1 (9 miles): P. 35 rods, **Isabella Lake,** p. 28 rods, **Isabella River,** p. 15 rods, **river,** p. 110 rods, **river,** p. 10 rods, **river,** p. 27 rods, **river,** p. 27 rods, **river,** p. 75 rods, **Quadga Lake.** (See comments for Day 1, Route #35-1.)

Day 2 (8 miles): **Quadga Lake,** p. 65 rods, **Isabella River, rapids, river,** p. 33 rods, **river, rapids, river,** p. 190 rods, **river, Bald Eagle Lake.** (See comments for Day 2, Route #75-1.)

Day 3 (6 miles): **Bald Eagle Lake,** p. 190 rods, **Gull Creek,** p. 40 rods, **Gull Lake,** p. 50 rods, **Pietro Lake,** p. 65 rods, **Camdre Lake,** p. 125 rods, **Clearwater Lake.** (See comments for Day 1, paragraphs 2 and 3, Route #84-1, and for Day 3, Route #34-2.)

Day 4 (9 miles): **Clearwater Lake,** p. 240 rods, **pond,** p. 40 rods, **Rock Island Lake, creek,** p. 40 rods, **creek, Lake Two,** p. 40 rods, **pond,** p. 30 rods, **Lake One,** p. 41 rods, **Confusion Lake,** p. 25 rods, **Kawishiwi River,** p. 20 rods, **river,** p. 40 rods, **river,** p. 8 rods, **river, North Kawishiwi River.** (See comments for Day 2, Route #84-2.)

Day 5 (9 miles): **North Kawishiwi River,** p. 210 rods, **river,** p. 18 rods, **river,** p. 10 rods, **river,** p. 160 rods, **Clear Lake,** p. 70 rods, **South Kawishiwi River, rapids, river,** p. 122 rods, **Little Gabbro Lake.** (See comments for Day 3, Route #84-2.)

Day 6 (10 miles): **Little Gabbro Lake, Gabbro Lake,** p. 5 rods, **Bald Eagle Lake, Isabella River, Snake River,** p. 10 rods, **river, rapids, river,** p. 20 rods, **river,** p. 270 rods. (See comments for Day 4, Route #84-2, and for Day 3, Route #75-1.)

Appendix I

Routes Categorized by Difficulty and Duration

Duration	Rte #	Name of Route	Entry Point Name (and #)
8 Easier Routes:			
2 days	31-1	Kawishiwi River Route	Farm Lake (#31)
2 days	34-1	Three Rivers Route	Island River (#34)
3 days	1-1	Pine Creek Loop	Trout Lake (#1)
3 days	12-1	Two Rivers Route	Little Vermilion Lake (#12)
3 days	24-1	Basswood Lake Route	Fall Lake (#24)
3 days	25-1	Isle of Pines Loop	Moose Lake (#25)
3 days	27-1	Disappointment Loop	Snowbank Lake (#27)
3 days	75-1	Little Isabella Snake Route	Little Isabella River (#75)
36 Challenging Routes:			
2 days	7-1	Big Rice Route	Big Lake (#7)
2 days	8-1	Duck Lake Route	Moose River South (#8)
2 days	9-1	Little Rivers Loop	L. Indian Sioux R. So. (#9)
2 days	16-1	Ramshead Lake Loop	Moose River North (#16)
2 days	26-1	Wood Wind Route	Wood Lake (#26)
2 days	29-1	Kawishiwi Triangle Loop	North Kawishiwi R. (#29)
2 days	33-1	Clear Bruin Loop	Little Gabbro Lake (#33)
2 days	84-1	Snake & Turtle Loop	Snake River (#84)
3 days	14-1	Four Rivers Route	L. Indian Sioux R. No. (#14)
3 days	19-1	Five Rivers Route	Stuart River (#19)
3 days	77-1	Angleworm Fairy Route	South Hegman Lake (#77)
3 days	22-1	Three Falls Loop	Mudro Lake (#22)

Duration	Rte #	Name of Route	Entry Point Name (and #)
3 days	30-1	Clearwater Turtle Loop	Lake One (#30)
3 days	32-1	Split River Route	South Kawishiwi R. (#32)
3 days	35-1	Isabella Bald Eagle Route	Isabella Lake (#35)
4 days	29-2	Bald Eagle Loop	North Kawishiwi R. (#29)
4 days	33-2	Clearwater Gull Loop	Little Gabbro Lake (#33)
4 days	84-2	One Clear Snake Loop	Snake River (#84)
5 days	16-2	Green Rocky Oyster Loop	Moose River North (#16)
5 days	77-2	Pictograph Route	South Hegman Lake (#77)
5 days	24-2	Four Falls Route	Fall Lake (#24)
5 days	26-2	Good Horse Loop	Wood Lake (#26)
5 days	30-2	Adams Boulder Route	Lake One (#30)
5 days	32-2	Clear Confusion Loop	South Kawishiwi R. (#32)
6 days	8-2	Big Moose and Buck Route	Moose River South (#8)
6 days	9-2	Bootleg Buck Route	L. Indian Sioux R. So. (#9)
6 days	14-2	Sioux Hustler Loop	L. Indian Sioux R. No. (#14)
6 days	25-2	Scenic Lakes Loop	Moose Lake (#25)
6 days	75-2	Little Isabella Confusion Rte.	Little Isabella River (#75)
6 days	34-2	The Moose Country Route	Island River (#34)
6 days	35-2	Isabella River & Kawishiwi River Route	Isabella Lake (#35)
7 days	12-2	Lac La Croix Route	Little Vermilion Lake (#12)
7 days	27-2	Lake Trout Loop	Snowbank Lake (#27)
8 days	19-2	Iron Shell Oyster Route	Stuart River (#19)
8 days	22-2	Crooked Border Loop	Mudro Lake (#22)
8 days	31-2	Kawishiwi Knife Route	Farm Lake (#31)

8 Most Rugged Routes:

Duration	Rte #	Name of Route	Entry Point Name (and #)
3 days	4-1	Buck Lake Loop	Crab Lake (#4)
3 days	20-1	Sterling Creek Route	Angleworm Lake (#20)
4 days	6-1	Big Moose Loop	Slim Lake (#6)
5 days	1-2	Cummings Lake Loop	Trout Lake (#1)
6 days	4-2	Little Trout Lake Loop	Crab Lake (#4)
6 days	7-2	Big Trout Route	Big Lake (#7)
7 days	6-2	Giant Portages Loop	Slim Lake (#6)
8 days	20-2	Green Iron Gun Loop	Angleworm Lake (#20)

Appendix II

BWCAW Travel Permit Data* for ALL ENTRY POINTS

EP#	Entry Pt. Name	Daily Quota	Total Permits	Overall Rank	Quota % Full	Summer Day Use	Motor** Usage
1	Trout Lake	14	880	11th	41%	17	894
3	Pine Lake Trail	None	0	69th (T)	n/d	0	No
4	Crab Lake	4	375	21st (T)	61%	56	No
6	Slim Lake	2	150	36th	49%	150	No
7	From Big Lake	2	75	51st	25%	70	No
8	Moose River South	1	74	52nd (T)	48%	29	No
9	Little Indian Sioux River South***	1/2	26	60th (T)	34%	11	No
10	Norway Trail	None	0	69th (T)	n/d	n/d	No
11	Blandin Trail	None	1	68th	n/d	6	No
12	Little Vermillion Lake	14	483	16th	23%	53	150
13	Herriman Lake Trail	None	8	66th	n/d	19	No
14	Little Indian Sioux River North	6	670	14th	73%	84	No
15	Devil's Cascade Trail	None	18	63rd (T)	n/d	29	No
16	Moose & Portage Rivers***	7	856	12th	80%	19	No
19	Stuart River	1	98	45th (T)	61%	26	No

EP#	Entry Pt. Name	Daily Quota	Total Permits	Overall Rank	Quota % Full	Summer Day Use	Motor** Usage
20	Angleworm Lake	2	145	37th	47%	9	No
21	Angleworm Trail	2	60	54th	20%	103	No
23	Mudro Lake (and 22)***	8	984	9th	80%	68	No
24	Fall Lake	14	1,384	5th	65%	233	1653
25	Moose Lake	27	3,060	1st	74%	381	2059
26	Wood Lake	2	204	33rd	67%	69	No
27	Snowbank Lake (and 28)***	9	1,000	8th	73%	135	263
29	North Kawishiwi River***	1	108	40th	71%	63	No
30	Lake One***	18	2168	2nd	79%	617	No
31	From Farm Lake	3	328	25th	71%	175	104
32	South Kawishiwi River***	2	225	30th	74%	92	No
33	Little Gabbro Lake***	2	254	29th	83%	133	No
34	Island River	3	267	28th	58%	39	No
35	Isabella Lake	3	326	26th	71%	71	No
36	Hog Creek	5	422	18th	55%	32	No
37	Kawishiwi Lake	9	959	10th	70%	86	No
38	Sawbill Lake	14	1,717	3rd	80%	453	No
39	Baker Lake	3	350	23rd	76%	109	No
40	Homer Lake	2	208	31st	68%	58	No
41	Brule Lake (with 41A)	10	1,032	7th	67%	122	No
43	Bower Trout Lake***	1	98	45th (T)	64%	27	No
44	Ram Lake***	1	102	43rd	67%	14	No
45	Morgan Lake	1	74	52nd (T)	48%	0	No
47	Lizz, Swamp & Meeds lakes	7	685	13th	64%	80	No
49	Skipper & Portage lakes	2	121	38th	40%	22	No
50	Cross Bay Lake***	3	337	24th	73%	77	No
51	Missing Link Lake	5	429	17th	56%	36	No
52	Brant Lake	4	420	19th	69%	12	No
54	Seagull Lake (with 54A)	13	1311	6th	66%	208	354

EP#	Entry Pt. Name	Daily Quota	Total Permits	Overall Rank	Quota % Full	Summer Day Use	Motor** Usage
55	Saganaga Lake (with 55A)	20	1651	4th	54%	161	1964
56	Kekekabic Trail – East End	2	37	56th	n/d	138	No
57	Magnetic Lake	3	302	27th	66%	108	No
58	South Lake	3	159	35th	35%	32	No
59	Partridge Lake Trail	1	12	65th	8%	1	No
60	Duncan Lake	4	375	21st (T)	61%	314	No
61	Daniels Lake	1	89	49th	58%	76	No
62	Clearwater Lake	4	405	20th	66%	149	56
64	East Bearskin Lake	5	485	15th	63%	122	62
66	Crocodile River	1	34	57th	22%	44	No
67	Bog Lake	2	49	55th	16%	9	No
68	Pine Lake***	1	107	41st	70%	53	No
69	John Lake***	1	109	39th	71%	30	No
70	North Fowl Lake	2	104	42nd	34%	3	No
71	From Canada	3	189	34th	41%	112	No
74	Snowbank Trail & Kekekabic Trail - West	4	100	44th	16%	57	No
75	Little Isabella River	1	98	45th (T)	64%	9	No
76	Big Moose Lake Trail	None	3	67th	n/d	8	No
77	South Hegman Lake***	2	205	32nd	67%	483	No
79	Eagle Mountain Trail	2	28	58th (T)	9%	642	No
80	Larch Creek	1	87	50th	57%	38	No
81	Border Route Trail – West	1	18	63rd (T)	12%	12	No
82	Border Route Trail – Central	2	28	58th (T)	9%	4	No
83	Border Route Trail – East	3	23	62nd	5%	n/d	No
84	Snake River	1	98	45th (T)	64%	12	No
86	Pow Wow Trail	None	26	60th (T)	n/d	12	No

* Based on USFS 1997 Year End Report, the most recent information available at the time this book was written.

Note: Meeds Lake (#48) was not designated as a separate entry point until 1999. Thus there is no data available for 1997.

Total Permits: Total number of overnight permits issued during the quota season (May 1–September 30).

Overall Rank: Based on the total number of overnight permits issued during the quota season for 70 entry points listed above. (T) = tie.

Quota % Full: Based on the total number of overnight permits issued as a percent of the total number of overnight permits available during the quota season (entry point quota per day x 153 days during the quota season).

Summer Day Use: Total number of non-quota permits (day use) from May 1 through September 30, 1996.

Motor Usage: Total number of permits issued for motorized entry, including overnight use & day use.

** Does not include towboat use or exempt permits.

*** Among the top 15 entry points filled the greatest number of days (70% or more days full in 1997). Note: Mudro Lake Entry Points 22 & 23 each exceeded 70%.

Appendix III

Commercial Canoe Trip Outfitters

Canoe trip outfitters provide a valuable service for the first-time visitor to the Boundary Waters Canoe Area Wilderness. For a reasonable fee, an outfitter will provide you with *everything* needed for a wilderness canoe trip. All you must do is show up with your personal items. The outfitter will take care of the rest.

Not all people are "cut out" for wilderness tripping. If you are not sure of yourself, it is foolish to invest hundreds of dollars in your own gear and outdoor clothing. After you have tried it, if it seems likely that you will return to the BWCAW at least once every year, *then* you may want to own your own gear, to save money in the long run.

To obtain current brochures from the outfitters in the Western Region of the BWCAW, contact any (or all) of the agencies listed below for the names, addresses, phone numbers and Internet web sites of the outfitters they serve.

Serving all of the Western Region entry points:
Ely Chamber of Commerce
1600 East Sheridan Street
Ely, MN 55731
(800) 777-7281 or (218) 365-6123
http://www.ely.org

Serving the Northwestern Area entry points:
Crane Lake Visitor & Tourism Bureau
7238 Handberg Road
Crane Lake, MN 55725
(800) 362-7405 or (218) 993-2901
http://www.cranelake.org

Cook Chamber of Commerce
PO Box 59
Cook, MN 55723
(800) 648-5897 or (218) 666-5850

Serving the Trout Lake Entry Point:
Tower-Soudan Chamber of Commerce
Box 776
Tower, MN 55790
(218) 753-2301
http://www.uslink.net/~tower

Appendix IV

Lake Index for **Fishing**

This appendix includes the 185 lakes that lie on the routes described in this book. It does *not* include every lake in the BWCA Wilderness. The appendix supplies useful information of interest to anglers, including the general location, the overall size of the lake, the amount of shallow water in the lake (where most fish are found), the maximum depth, and the fish species that are known to inhabit the lake. When two lakes share the same name, neighboring lakes of each are included in parentheses to identify the one meant. Data for this index was compiled from the Minnesota DNR database (accessible via the Internet at www.dnr.state.mn.us), as well as from personal observations by the author. There may be other fish species in the lakes that were neither found by DNR test netting nor observed by the author.

KEY
W = walleye, **NP** = northern pike, **LT** = lake trout, **SB** = smallmouth bass, **LB** = largemouth bass, **BT** = brook trout, **BG** = bluegill, **CR** = black crappie, **MU** = muskellunge, **n/d** = no DNR data available, **none** = no game fish reported. **Boldface** indicates the predominate species. **(Year)** indicates last known year that the species was stocked by the DNR. **Acres** = lake's total surface area. **Littoral** = acreage of lake less than 15' deep. The littoral zone is where the majority of aquatic plants are found and is a primary area used by young fish. This part of the lake also provides the essential spawning habitat for most warm-water fish (e.g., walleyes, bass, and pan fish). **Depth** = maximum depth.

OTHER FISH SPECIES that could be found in lakes but are not included in this chart as "game fish" include yellow perch, sunfish, rock bass and white sucker.

LAKE NAME	COUNTY	ACRES	LITT	DEPTH	FISH SPECIES
Adams	Lake	448	116	84'	**NP**, W, BG
Adventure	Lake	45	45	10'	**W**, **NP**
Agamok	Lake	n/d	n/d	n/d	n/d
Agnes	St. Louis	984	453	30'	**W**, **NP**, SB
Ahmakose	Lake	38	9	68'	n/d
Ahsub	Lake	58	22	78'	**BT** (97), Splake
Alice	Lake	1,566	438	53'	**NP**, **W**, BG
Amoeber	Lake	386	108	110'	**W**, **SB**, LT
Angleworm	St. Louis	144	144	11'	**W**, NP
Annie	Lake	18	16	16'	**NP**
Ashigan	Lake	189	9	59'	**SB**
Bald Eagle	Lake	1,238	929	36'	**W**, **NP**, **CR**, BG
Basswood	Lake	22,722	7,034	111'	**W**, **SB**, **NP**, CR, BL, LT
Beartrack	St. Louis	169	42	35'	none
Beartrap	St. Louis	n/d	n/d	n/d	n/d
Beaver	Lake	237	95	76'	**NP**, **W**, BG
Big	St. Louis	1,789	1,514	22'	**W** (95), NP
Big Moose	St. Louis	1,032	1,012	23'	**W**, NP, SB
Big Rice	St. Louis	420	420	5'	**NP**
Birch	Lake	711	342	34'	**W** (93), **NP**, **SB**, LB, BG
Bog	Lake	249	232	16'	**W**, NP, BT
Bonnie	Lake	71	71	11'	**NP**
Boot (Ensign)	Lake	209	134	83'	**NP**, **SB**, W
Boot (Fourtown)	St. Louis	313	163	27'	**NP**, W
Bootleg	St. Louis	340	126	26'	**NP**, LB, BG
Boulder	Lake	236	109	54'	**NP**
Bruin	Lake	n/d	n/d	n/d	NP
Buck	St. Louis	228	223	19'	**W**, NP
Burntside	St. Louis	7,139	1,478	126'	**LT & W** (96), **SB**, **N**, BG
Camdre	Lake	51	51	12'	none
Cap	Lake	n/d	n/d	n/d	n/d
Carp	Lake	n/d	n/d	n/d	**LT**, **NP**, **SB**, **W**
Cattyman	Lake	17	17	9'	**NP**, W
Chad	St. Louis	266	239	18'	**NP**, **LB**, BG
Cherry	Lake	147	34	90'	**W**, LT
Chippewa	Lake	n/d	n/d	n/d	n/d

LAKE NAME	COUNTY	ACRES	LITT	DEPTH	FISH SPECIES
Clear	Lake	236	234	17'	**W** (97), **NP, CR, BG**, LB
Clearwater	Lake	641	173	46'	**NP**
Confusion	Lake	n/d	n/d	n/d	n/d
Crab	St. Louis	541	216	57'	**SB, LB, NP**, W
Crane	St. Louis	3,088	618	80'	**W, NP, SB**, CR
Crooked	St. Louis	7,941	1,898	165'	**NP, W**, SB, CR
Cummings	St. Louis	1,121	493	41'	**SB, NP**
Dark	St. Louis	38	38	10'	none
Disappointment	Lake	867	355	54'	**W, NP, SB, LB**
Dix	Lake	n/d	n/d	n/d	n/d
Duck	St. Louis	110	110	5'	none
Eddie	Lake	122	45	95'	**NP**, LB
Elton	Lake	123	84	53'	**NP**
Ensign	Lake	1,408	605	30'	**W, SB**, NP
Ester	Lake	388	155	110'	**LT**
Eugene	St. Louis	166	50	60'	**NP**
Fairy	St. Louis	151	142	19'	**W, NP**, BG, SB
Fall	Lake	2,173	1,178	32'	**W, NP, BL**, SB, CR
Farm	Lake	1,328	459	56'	**W** (97), **NP, BG**, CR, SB
Fee	Lake	n/d	n/d	n/d	n/d
Finger	St. Louis	287	100	60'	**W**, NP, SB
Four	Lake	655	511	25'	**W, NP**, BLG
Fourtown	Lake	1,902	1,084	25'	**NP, W**, BG, SB
Fox	St. Louis	27	27	7'	n/d
Fraser	Lake	811	n/d	n/d	**W**, NP, LT
Gabbro	Lake	896	457	50'	**W, NP**, CR, BG
Gabimichigami	Cook	1,198	149	209'	**LT, NP**
Ge-be-on-e-quet	St. Louis	n/d	n/d	n/d	n/d
Gerund	Lake	98	27	85'	NP
Gibson	Lake	34	24	24'	**W, NP**
Glenmore	St. Louis	n/d	n/d	n/d	n/d
Good	Lake	177	62	51'	**NP**, W, LB, CR, BL
Green	St. Louis	141	75	20'	**NP, BG**
Gull (Pietro)	Lake	503	362	31'	**W, NP**, SB

LAKE NAME	COUNTY	ACRES	LITT	DEPTH	FISH SPECIES
Gull (Home)	St. Louis	169	169	13'	**NP**
Gun	St. Louis	337	101	57'	**W**, **SB**, N, BG
Hanson	Lake	284	43	100'	**LT**, NP
Hatchet	Lake	126	107	40'	**W**, NP
Hoe	Lake	n/d	n/d	n/d	n/d
Home	St. Louis	85	n/d	n/d	**NP**, W
Hook	St. Louis	83	83	13'	**NP**
Horse	Lake	681	325	25'	**W**, **NP**, SB, BG
Hudson	Lake	381	225	35'	**W**, **NP**, **BG**
Hula	Lake	n/d	n/d	n/d	**NP**
Hustler	St. Louis	272	120	60'	**NP**, BG
Ima	Lake	772	208	116'	**LT**, **NP**, W, BL
Insula	Lake	2,957	1,183	63'	**W**, **NP**, BG
Iron	St. Louis	1,851	n/d	n/d	**W**, **NP**, SB, CR
Isabella	Lake	1,516	1,165	19'	**W**, NP
Jenny	Lake	102	53	93'	NP
Jitterbug	Lake	25	25	5'	**NP**, W
Jordan	Lake	136	60	66'	W, NP
Kekekabic	Lake	1,620	97	195'	**LT**
Kiana	Lake	234	89	56'	**NP**
Knife	Lake	5,254	1,037	179'	**W**, **NP**, **LT**, SB
Korb	St. Louis	58	30	27'	NP, SB, BG
Lac La Croix	St. Louis	34,070	8,500	168'	**NP**, **W**, SB, CR, LT
Lamb	St. Louis	80	n/d	n/d	**NP**
Lapond	St. Louis	n/d	n/d	n/d	n/d
Ledge	Lake	n/d	n/d	n/d	n/d
Little Beartrack	St. Louis	53	16	35'	none
Little Crab	St. Louis	61	61	15'	**NP**, SB, LB
Little Gabbro	Lake	154	117	26'	W, NP
Little Loon	St. Louis	n/d	n/d	n/d	n/d
Little Saganaga	Cook	1,575	428	150'	**NP**, LT
Little Shell	St. Louis	n/s	n/d	n/d	W, BG
Little Trout	St. Louis	538	178	37'	**W**, **SB**, **NP**
Little Vermilion	St. Louis	1,331	639	52'	**NP**, **W**, SB, CR, BG

LAKE NAME	COUNTY	ACRES	LITT	DEPTH	FISH SPECIES
Loon	St. Louis	3,101	n/d	n/d	**NP, W**, SB
Lower Pauness	St. Louis	n/s	n/d	n/d	n/d
Lunetta	St. Louis	88	88	14'	**NP**, SB, LB
Lynx	St. Louis	295	15	85'	**W**, NP
Makwa	Lake	143	49	76'	**LT**, NP
Melon	Lake	n/d	n/d	n/d	n/d
Missionary	Lake	n/d	n/d	n/d	n/d
Moose	Lake	1,211	262	65'	**W** (96), **NP, SB, BL, LB**
Moosecamp	Lake	n/d	n/d	n/d	n/d
Mudro	Lake	95	24	76'	**NP**, W
Mueller	Lake	n/d	n/d	n/d	n/d
Newfound	Lake	604	119	45'	**W** (96), **NP, SB**, LB, BL
Newton	Lake	500	358	47'	**W** (94), **NP**, BL, CR, SB
Niki	Lake	n/d	n/d	n/d	n/d
Nina Moose	St. Louis	430	430	6'	**NP, W**, SB
North Hegman	St. Louis	101	60	30'	NP, SB, W
Ogishkemuncie	Lake	701	294	75'	**W**, LT
Ojibway	Lake	371	36	115'	LT (96), NP, BG, SB
One	Lake	876	456	57'	**NP, BG**, W
Otter	St. Louis	78	76	17'	**SB, NP**, BG
Ottertrack	Lake	1,146	251	116'	**W, NP**, LT
Oyster	St. Louis	714	164	130'	NP, LT, SB
Papoose	Lake	n/d	n/d	n/d	n/d
Parent	Lake	326	91	50'	**W** (95), **NP**, SB
Pickle	Lake	n/d	n/d	n/d	n/d
Pietro	Lake	339	78	31'	**NP**
Pine	St. Louis	912	n/d	n/d	**W, NP**
Pocket	St. Louis	226	86	27'	**W, NP**, SB
Quadga	Lake	248	157	35'	**NP**, W
Ramshead	St. Louis	480	480	10'	**NP**
Range	Lake	82	55	19'	**NP, BG, CR**, LB, W
Rattle	Cook	45	28	30'	**NP**

LAKE NAME	COUNTY	ACRES	LITT	DEPTH	FISH SPECIES
Rice (Slim)	St. Louis	110	110	5'	none
Rice (Isabella)	Lake	n/d	n/d	n/d	n/d
River	Lake	n/d	n/d	n/d	n/d
Rock Island	Lake	55	35	21'	NP
Rocky	St. Louis	116	42	40'	**NP**
Roe	Lake	70	70	7'	none
Ruby	St. Louis	n/d	n/d	n/d	n/d
Rush	St. Louis	119	119	10'	**W, SB, NP**
Sagus	Lake	172	107	37'	**W**, NP
Sandpit	Lake	61	18	53'	**NP**, W, SB, LB, BG, CR
Sand Point	St. Louis	8,869	2,847	184'	**W, NP**, CR, BG, SB
Schlamn	St. Louis	n/d	n/d	n/d	n/d
Section 3 Pond	St. Louis	n/d	n/d	n/d	n/d
Seed	Lake	n/d	n/d	n/d	n/d
Shell	St. Louis	n/d	n/d	n/d	n/d
Skoota	Lake	n/d	n/d	n/d	n/d
Slim (E. Loon)	St. Louis	121	73	42'	n/d
Slim (Burntside)	St. Louis	296	86	49'	**W** (96), **NP**
South	St. Louis	35	35	10'	**NP**
South Hegman	St. Louis	110	55	55'	SB, NP
Snowbank	Lake	3,303	879	150'	**LT** (95), **W, SB**, NP, LB
Splash	Lake	97	81	18'	**W, NP**, BL
Spoon	Lake	223	87	85'	NP
Steep	St. Louis	86	34	40'	**NP**
Strup	Lake	n/d	n/d	n/d	n/d
Stuart	St. Louis	752	236	40'	W, NP
Sucker	Lake	382	178	31'	**W** (96), **NP**, SB, LB
Thomas	Lake	1,471	441	110'	**LT**, W, NP, BL
Three	Lake	881	388	37'	**W, NP**, BG
Thunder	St. Louis	n/d	n/d	n/d	n/d
Tin Can Mike	Lake	147	138	29'	**W, SB, NP, BG**
Topaz	Lake	130	29	70'	**LT, SB**
Trader	Lake	54	54	10'	none

LAKE NAME	COUNTY	ACRES	LITT	DEPTH	FISH SPECIES
Trapline	Lake	n/d	n/d	n/d	n/d
Trease	St. Louis	n/d	n/d	n/d	n/d
Triangle	Lake	309	160	43'	**W** (97), **NP**, BG, SB
Trout	St. Louis	7,641	1,613	98'	**W, SB, NP, LT** (97)
Turtle	Lake	337	337	10'	**NP**
Two	Lake	481	158	35'	**NP**, W, BG
Upper Pauness	St. Louis	n/d	n/d	n/d	n/d
Vee	Lake	n/d	n/d	n/d	n/d
Vera	Lake	245	86	55'	**W**, LB
Vermilion	St. Louis	40,557	15,006	76'	**W** (97), **NP** (97), **BG, SB**, CR, LB, MU (96)
Wagosh	St. Louis	n/d	n/d	n/d	n/d
Western	St. Louis	41	41	12'	**W, NP**
White Feather	St. Louis	n/d	n/d	n/d	n/d
Wind	Lake	1,009	686	32'	**NP, LB**, W, BL
Wisini	Lake	n/d	n/d	n/d	n/d
Wood	Lake	643	579	21'	**NP**, W, BL

Appendix V

BWCAW Hiking Trails in the Western Region

In addition to the 27 canoeing entry points detailed in this book, there are also 9 entry points for designated hiking trails in the western part of the Boundary Waters. Although the BWCA Wilderness is renowned for its canoeing opportunities, it also offers some of the most outstanding hiking trails in the Midwest. They include both short trails for day trips and long trails for overnight backpack outings. This appendix briefly summarizes the hiking trails in the western region of the Wilderness. For more details, contact the Superior National Forest headquarters in Duluth or one of the Ranger District offices listed in Chapter 2.

EP #	Trail Name	Length	Loop?	Difficulty
3	Pine Lake Trail	2.5 miles	1-way	Rugged
Highlights	Bear Creek, not all maintained			
10	Norway Trail	2.5 miles	1-way	Moderate
Highlights	Large red pines, Trout Lake			
11	Blandin Trail	2.7 miles	1-way	Moderate
Highlights	Wildlife habitat			
13	Herriman Lakes Trail	13 miles	Loops	Moderate
Highlights	Echo River, scenic overlooks			
15	Sioux-Hustler Trail	29 miles	Loop	Rugged
Highlights	Devil's Cascade, wildlife habitat			

EP #	Trail Name	Length	Loop?	Difficulty
21	Angleworm Trail	14 miles	Loop	Rugged
Highlights Scenic overlooks, mixed forest				
74	Snowbank Trail	40 miles	Loop	Moderate
Highlights Scenic overlooks, old pines				
74	& Kekekabic Trail West	38 miles	1-way	Rugged
Highlights Mueller Falls, wildlife habitat				
76	Big Moose Lake Trail	2 miles	1-way	Easy
Highlights Big Moose Lake, mixed forest				
86	Pow Wow Trail	27 miles	Loop	Rugged
Highlights Solitude, wildlife, variety				

INDEX